Nandanvan & Other Stories

Lakshmi Kannan is a poet, novelist and short story writer. She is also her own translator. A bilingual, she writes both in English and in Tamil. She has published twenty books that include four collections of poems in English, a novel and several collections of short fiction in Tamil, English and Hindi translation. Kannan was Sahitya Akademi Writer in Residence, Charles Wallace Trust Writer in Residence, University of Canterbury at Kent, UK, Fellow of the Indian Institute of Advanced Study, Shimla, and has participated in the International Writing Program at Iowa, USA. She lives in Delhi.

Nandanvan & Other Stories

Translated from the original Tamil by the author

Lakshmi Kannan

Orient BlackSwan

ORIENT BLACKSWAN PRIVATE LIMITED

Registered Office
3-6-752 Himayatnagar, Hyderabad 500 029 (A.P.), India
e-mail: centraloffice@orientblackswan.com

Other Offices
Bangalore, Bhopal, Bhubaneshwar, Chandigarh, Chennai, Ernakulam, Guwahati, Hyderabad, Jaipur, Kolkata, Lucknow, Mumbai, New Delhi, Noida, Patna

First Published 2011

ISBN 978 81 250 4323 2

Typeset by
Le Studio Graphique, Gurgaon 122 001
in Sabon LT Std 10/12

Printed at
B.B. Press
Noida

Published by
Orient Blackswan Private Limited
1/24 Asaf Ali Road
New Delhi 110 002
e-mail: delhi@orientblackswan.com

For

Dr Daisaku Ikeda

Like the lotus softly fragrant
and soul-delighting,
rising clear from scraps of rubbish in
a wayside pond,
The disciple of the Enlightened Buddha shines
in perfect wisdom
Clear above the crowds of ordinary men
who do not see the truth.

"Flowers", *The Dhammapada*, translated from the Pali by P. Lal
New York: Noonday Press, 1967.

Contents

NOVELLA

Acknowledgements

I wish to express my grateful thanks to Sahitya Akademi (the National Academy of Letters), an autonomous body under the Ministry of Culture, Government of India, for offering me a tenure as a Writer-in-Residence attached to the English Department of Jamia Millia Islamia, New Delhi, from July to December 2009, during which period I worked on this translation. I am very grateful in particular, to the Secretary of Sahitya Akademi, Mr Agrahara Krishna Murthy, who was immensely helpful in facilitating all communication between the Akademi and Jamia Millia Islamia in a smooth, swift manner so that I could start my work right away.

This was offered as a part of the Akademi's residency scheme to help me pursue my creative work unhindered for a period of six months. During this period, I could travel to other universities outside Delhi to hold workshops on the short stories, to give keynote addresses on Creativity, on Developing Language Skills and on Translation and to give readings from my works. Equally, I could use the time to concentrate on translating some of my select stories and novellas from Tamil into English towards my next collection of short fiction.

My tenure as a Resident Writer under the Akademi's scheme greatly helped me stay focussed on working towards my collection of short fiction. This kind of focus is invaluable for any writer.

LAKSHMI KANNAN
New Delhi

The Writer and Her Work

Phenomenological Explorations

Introducing Lakshmi Kannan's Short Fiction

C. T. Indra[*]

For the past two decades or more, Lakshmi Kannan has been a presence to reckon with in the field of contemporary Indian literature—both in English and the Bhashas. She has been writing both poetry and fiction, in English and in Tamil (in the latter under the pen name "Kaaveri"). What is more, she has been an excellent translator of her own Tamil works in English. She has achieved wide recognition in the sphere of creative writing and is featured in the Routledge *Encyclopaedia of Post-Colonial Literatures* (ed. Eugene Benson and R. W. Conolly) both in its original edition of 1994 and its revised second edition of 2005. She is well-acquainted with global literary and cultural traditions, has travelled widely and been awarded many prestigious international and national fellowships. She has at once an unmistakably native sensibility (which is accentuated by her being a Tamil from Karnataka, living in Delhi) which blends seamlessly with her transnational, transcultural awareness. In one sense, it may be right to claim that poetry is her forte, for even in her short fiction, it is her vivid poetical imagination, precision and richness of vocabulary that heighten the atmospheric and textual intensity of her stories. But this is not to deny the ideological concerns that have gripped her and the serious manner in which she has engaged with them, be it in poetry or fiction. She is not an aesthete or just a connoisseur of literature.

* Chidambaram Thathachari Indra was Chair, Department of English, University of Madras, from 1995 to 2007.

She is a creative artist, first and last, and no less a conscientious commentator on the world of reality around her.

Her short stories invoke and have developed over the years, some absorbing sites of cogitations on pressing issues in gender, sexuality, filial piety, construction of identity, cultural institutions and interpellation of the self by society. These are forged on the anvil of the staple spheres of human existence such as family, marriage, kinship, academia, public office, and the emergent spheres of interrogation such as discourse and creative writing as an ideological weapon. Lakshmi Kannan fashions men, women, children, and even birds, and situates them in varied locales—be it the home, hospital, a government office, university, the tube in London, public parks and gardens, a temple, a restaurant. Most of the protagonists in the stories are in some existential crisis; some of them ruminate, taking life in their stride. Lakshmi Kannan has created in a couple of striking stories eschatological situations, with characters hovering between life before death and life after death. These are feats of phenomenological explorations leading to a strange epistemology, but no less human, exploring filial ingratitude and conjugal crises. Lakshmi achieves something extraordinary in representing fabulatory encounters in such stories. Thus the spectrum of experiences Lakshmi depicts are absorbing and authentic; none of it is summoned for the sake of fashion or effect.

As a short story writer Lakshmi Kannan is quintessentially lyrical, evocative and probing; she is also discursive, examining issues with an enviable combination of clarity and nuanced perception. We shall explore some of her stories to find out what makes Lakshmi Kannan, a compulsive, urbane, deeply serious and sensitive writer.

Gender and sexuality have a pervasive presence in Lakshmi Kannan's writings. Lakshmi's reflections are embedded in some of her crystalline poems too. In the stories Lakshmi creates objective characters of a different range who experience idiosyncratically their gendered self and offer their own critique.

Family is the institution which gives comfort, security, a sense of balance and we may add, normalcy to an individual. But this is largely a middle class phenomenon and it has its virtue. The woman in the family is the fulcrum, quietly and efficiently managing all the pressures and demands made on her and invariably helping the other members of this institution to tide over crises and find peace and fulfillment. No mean achievement! But what about her self and its inner recesses? Does she store them up with pleasurable secrecy like the golden honey in Lakshmi's brilliant epigrammatic poem 'Autopsy' where the surgeons cut open a woman's brain to find yellow honey stashed away in the honeycomb? Lakshmi does not resort to any such fantasy in her typical story of middle-class milieu, "Ejamaanar". But there are two interesting gender perceptions embedded in it. The title, both in Tamil and Kannada, denotes the respectful way the husband is referred to by the wife and it connotes a man who has absolute mastery in the household. In South Indian middle-class houses, almost up to the 1960s, shall we say, this term had been in vogue and accepted without much fuss. There was nothing monstrous in the figure of the *ejamaanar*; he could turn out to be a kind man too. In this story set in Bangalore, the title is not a literal focus on the husband Srinivasan, who is a quiet gentleman, spending time in the front room, by himself; it asks, in my second reading, who is the *ejamaanar* of your self? The lady of the house Gowri Amma is a model wife, able manager of the land and its produce and the retinue of servants. She is an ideal matriarch, and wise counsellor to the other women in the locality; she is an affectionate grandmother and a shrewd domestic economist. She is a typical example of Indian, Hindu, middle-class womanhood, contented and dutiful. But the surprise of this constructed subjectivity of the middle-aged woman is the private self within her which wishes to immerse itself in the beauty of nature. That self is roused whenever Sambasivam, an elderly relation, comes on a visit and talks to her about his farm in Coorg, the cardamom cultivation, the Jog falls, the rippling rivers, Nilgiri hills, Shimoga and so on. Gowri Amma's person, as noticed by the shrewd granddaughter, is totally transformed, glowing in wonder, enjoyment, and above all, relishing a rare relationship outside of the fold of *ejamaanar*. This extraordinary friendship between an elderly man and a woman, outside the fold of marriage, has nothing salacious or risqué about it. It is far from it. It has a beauty and power to regain one's eternal, youthful and happy being, buried in the *kosa*s, i.e., wrapping of the nine yards saree, not to speak of the other *kosa*s of family duties as the woman of the house. The epiphany of this three fourths run-of-the mill story, comes in the very end, when the granddaughter deliberately switches off the lights in the huge hall and tells her grandmother (comparing her with the other women who visit her, ever whining about their situation), 'I only wanted to say that these women didn't get a Sambasivam Mama in their life, that's all'. The grandmother relishes the girl's intuition and gives an 'unfaltering reply': 'Good night, precious. Some day you too search for a Sambasivam for yourself.' That's Lakshmi Kannan for you—not breaking time-tested institutions, but placing her intelligent women in surprising situations—here, for example, amidst the companionship between man and woman in unorthodox perspective without violating the sanctity of family as an institution.

Lakshmi Kannan's famous story "Muniyakka" treats the issue of gender from an entirely different perspective and is cast in surrealistic mode. Its feminism is the other side of the coin of wifely fidelity. Muniyakka is from a servant class; her life story is one that involves strategies to survive, negotiating difficult situations and yet maintaining her selfhood and independence. Being a shrewd woman, because she is illiterate, she has to exercise her native wisdom. She has no one to turn to—her husband Bairappa wasted his life and hers; her sons are 'shameless bastards'. She has no hesitation in cursing them in her rasping soliloquies, for which she is famous—she is 'The Walkie-Talkie' for the children in the neighbourhood who are amused by the sight. Paradoxically she has a fierce loyalty to her dead husband, for she never fails to perform the rituals on his obsequies day—his *shraddha*—and what is more, punctiliously arrange on the freshly washed banana leaf all the things dear to the departed soul, including a packet of his favourite brand of *beedi* and a bottle of toddy, which she hands to Thimmayya as a ritual offering. She performs the *shraddha* in her hut meticulously. What is odder is that, on that day, she wears a clean saree, flowers on her hair and a bright *kumkum* on the brow, her face glowing as if in youth. The moment the *shraddha* is over, she sweeps the hut clean and delivers a sermon on empty human relationships: 'Husband! Son! What humbug all these relationships are ... huh!' We ask, what is the symbolism? She is delivered of the bondage, of her servile role, she is now a free spirit. Lakshmi Kannan brilliantly exploits the features of the Gothic to underscore this perception. Muniyakka's lonely hut in the corner of Rao's bungalow is iconographic of her fiercely independent spirit. In the 'inky darkness', surrounded by the coconut grove with its eerie atmosphere, the jackfruit tree, the stormy wind howling through the foliage, the incensed figure of

Muniyakka sits, conversing with her favourite 'ghosts' and 'devils', they 'being essentially female in their form'. Her abject poverty and minimal existence, which is a social detail creating awareness of her class situation, is off-set by her undaunted dancing, with the devil. The author succeeds in projecting a supernatural female force out of this famous servant woman Muniyakka, who occupies a prime place in the gallery of female figures Lakshmi has created.

The other aspect of gender critique in the story is Muniyakka's castigation of women's superstitions in propitiating snake idols made of stone in the temple as Fertility gods, feeding them with milk, decorating them with vermillion and flowers. Muniyakka also serves in the shrine and it is her responsibility to clean up the mess of piety created by the worship after the women leave the premises. She curses them heartily and lambastes them for their foolish beliefs. The author surely exposes the ambivalence of such a folk faith, for in ordinary circumstances the snake is feared and distrusted and killed pitilessly, but is revered in stone when women pray for a male child. Throughout the story the hooded cobra is a striking image and contributes much to the Gothic ambience.

If "Muniyakka" is a quintessential Gothic narrative, dealing with the gender issues of woman as wife, woman as mother, woman as a free force, we have, at the other end of the spectrum, a highly discursive, intellectual story, modern and cosmopolitan in its ethos and mode of writing, and yet examining very similar issues, raising the problematic question of 'When is a woman woman?' in "Simone de Beauvoir and the Manes". Where is the rustic (but by no means rusted!) Muniyakka and where is the world-renowned French feminist thinker Simone de Beauvoir? That is where Lakshmi Kannan's keen artistic imagination works discursively. The ostensible story is about a young woman Uma trying to find her inner force as a writer. A male writer Shekar, encourages her to be a Simone de Beauvoir, adding in all good faith, 'Entrust yourself to the care of a suitable companion, like Simone de Beauvoir did'. It is not therefore a flimsy love story, but is about the agonising search for one's writerly self, the *raison d'être* of one's being. Hence Simone de Beauvoir becomes the central symbol and icon of feminist search for a writer's creative source. Her famous relationship with the French Nobel laureate Jean Paul Sartre, with all its ups and downs, has become the stuff of feminist lore. This legendary French woman became an ancestral spirit for feminists, the world over. The protagonist of Lakshmi's story, Uma, is on a painful exploration of the issue of woman artists and their inner roles. Simone de Beauvoir dedicated herself to caring for Jean Paul Sartre, though they were not husband and wife. But hers was a wifely solicitude for him, even during his periods of infidelity to her. Her fidelity to him was shockingly conservative. The modern-day feminists are somewhat disappointed that such a frontal feminist as Simone should be so devoted to a man who set his emotional and creative needs above hers. The story takes us through their chequered relationship, their divergent writing careers, Simone's finding sustenance, although for a brief period, in the American writer Nelson Algren and her tragic turning away from him back to Sartre's obsessive hold on her. Sartre wants her but cannot give space to the writer Simon de Beauvoir. The story muses on this strange legendary literary relationship. The protagonist is curious to know: why this continuing living with Sartre? Was it dependence, or a kind of bondage, or merely a force of habit? Simone was happy as a full, embodied person when she was in the company of Nelson. The being bloomed in the physical body. Going back to Sartre, she withers, but 'nurses him tenderly, like a wife, mother, a sister, or a faithful nurse and maid'. That's it. A woman has to play all these roles in one. Simone de Beauvoir's cogitations on these gender issues found immortal expression in her books such as *The Second Sex*. Her writings paved the way for the feminist movement in the modern era. An Indian feminist raises the ideological question whether a woman is dependent on a male intellectual for her feminism. She wryly remarks, 'A gifted woman does not need a crutch to lean on in order to grow or develop in her art or in her writing.' She is firm in her view. 'If only Simone had decided to stay alone, independent of Sartre, she would've evolved in more strikingly original ways.' Another young feminist deconstructs the Simone-Sartre relationship as a 'mouldy myth' and unveils to a man who believed in it, what cost she had to pay to keep Sartre happy. This revelation is unwelcome to the male because it exposes the faultlines in the myth. New-wave feminism testifies to the paradox of the absent-presence of Simone de Beauvoir, her life becoming a site of interrogation for radicals, who voice their sense of dismay and outrage that she should have submitted herself to Sartre as 'less than a wife and with such a blind devotion'.

It is here that Lakshmi Kannan unexpectedly brings in the ritual of offering rice balls on a smooth banana leaf in Hindu obsequies with the belief that the ancestors would be pleased. Here in the story, men like Shekar who woos Uma, or Mehta who advises her in a seminar in Chandigarh, all counsel her to find a Sartre so that she would become a Simone de Beauvoir. The irony of ironies is that the pioneering French feminist thinker should haunt modern men and return to their consciousness as '*pitrus*'[1] do at the time of *shraddha* ceremonies, as Hindus believe. The radical feminist becomes a sort of ancestral figure invoked by die-hard, patriarchal-minded men to convince women of the sanctity in being dependent on men.

This story examines the dialectics of a woman being a woman, and woman becoming a woman for the sake of men. Its discursive span is quite striking. Thus between "Muniyakka" and "Simone de Beauvoir and the Manes" Lakshmi Kannan has achieved two different realisations of the feminist short story.

Lakshmi Kannan examines some other aspects of treatment of women in patriarchy in two slightly longish stories. "Maria" has several perspectives deftly combined in one. There is the representation of lesbianism through the poet Maria from Philippines, much decorated, but whose poetry comes out of much suffering and deprivation in her childhood. It is problematic even for the protagonist woman writer Lakshmi. Because of her cultural upbringing and her own personal mental make-up, she cannot accept the offer of love from Maria, even though she has deep pity for her. But she cannot, for that reason, endorse the male writers' branding poor Maria and ridiculing her. The story is a sensitive depiction of the pathetic yearning of Maria for Lakshmi's company in intimate terms. Both of them are in the Iowa Creative Writing programme in the United States. Therefore another concern of the story is the source and art of writing. Maria had a horrid childhood, being born in a poor family with a wicked father persecuting her mother. The memories Maria shares with Lakshmi are painful. But what makes her a writer of depth is her harrowing life. She tells Lakshmi, 'So I grew up without even a childhood, Lakshmi.' It is sad that in a creative writing programme, Maria should be shunned and ridiculed for being a lesbian. The very marker of creativity, namely, openness and empathy for varied experiences and people, is what is

[1] 'Pitru' in Sanskrit means ancestral spirits or manes.

lacking among the male writes in the group. Lakshmi is particularly outraged that a male writer like Peter should extol the life of a gay while running down Maria's lesbianism. It is this hypocrisy which impels Lakshmi to express her solidarity with Maria as a woman and castigate the double standards practised by patriarchy. She is also shocked to find out that the male poets in her group are largely anti-feminist. She is humbled by the experiences and predicament of Maria and towards the end of the story acknowledges, through the symbolism of birds and the changing colours of the maple tree, the reality and legitimacy of different forms of sexual relationships. Lakshmi Kannan has written exquisitely about the delicate situation that arises between Lakshmi and Maria when the latter feels a compulsive attraction towards the Indian poetess and is even willing to forego meat and drink to suit her vegetarianism in order to solicit her love. The phenomenology of the heterosexual Lakshmi's sense of outrage is equally brilliantly choreographed.

Yet another interest of the story is the critique of male gaze that Lakshmi Kannan offers. Curiously enough it is the lesbian Maria who sensitises Lakshmi to the male poets' keen appreciation of her physique as a woman. As a married woman and mother of two sons Lakshmi is scandalised. As a stronger person, much exposed to the cruelties and vagaries of life as a South Asian child in a poor agrarian family, Maria's sense of sexuality is grounded on reality. Lakshmi, being brought up in a strict, disciplinarian middle-class, Brahmin milieu, is unable to fathom the motive of either male gaze or female gaze.

On the whole, the story voices resentment at the tendency to treat the female body as an object of consumption and exposes the legitimising apparatus of patriarchy.

The other longish story "Because..." is also marked by a stringent critique of the hegemonic social institutions which 'naturalise' and 'legitimise' asymmetrical sexual relationships under patriarchal dispensations. It is set in a middle-class family milieu and its focus is all on the women and there are many of them. We have a young widow Pattu who has so thoroughly internalised the patriarchal codes that she willingly submits to the dictates of the system though she is by no means happy. Her life of deprivation and self-denials (such as sacrificing playing the *veena*) are what perpetuate the grip of patriarchy over weak women. But her old mother Kalyani is entirely liberal in her outlook and disapproves of the self-imposed restrictions of her daughter. The little girl Kamala in the family cannot comprehend her widow aunt's behaviour. She is also critical of the way princesses and girls are represented in fairy tales (such as *The Grimm's Fairy Tales* or *The Snow White*) as forever dependent on smart young princes for their deliverance. The technique of tale within story is used by the author to articulate her discontent with stereotyped constructions of female subjectivity. A more specific social criticism is offered through the incident of the visiting pontiff of a well-known Hindu monastic order (Sankaracharya) who will not give audience to widows, especially the younger ones who are not tonsured. Pattu accepts this without a demur, but her old mother is quite critical of His Holiness. The cook Vishalam Mami is a run-of-the-mill widow and is therefore filled with reverence for the ascetic pontiff. It is here that Lakshmi Kannan brings in her favourite staple character in many of her stories—Muniyakka—to strike at entrenched establishment thinking. The servant woman dismisses with contempt the practice of avoiding seeing widows, even advocates to the old mother to get her young widowed daughter remarried. The little girl listening to this adult conversation, feels troubled by the treatment of women and widows (for e.g., the sight of cook Vishalam submitting her head to the barber in a corner to have a tonsure every two weeks, the white saree she wraps herself in, covering her head). She has a strange dream which reconstructs the life of the Kaurava Queen in Mahabharata, Gandhari, who famously covered her eyes with a piece of cloth for life before her marriage because her husband King Dhritarashtra was blind by birth. In the child's dream narrative, Gandhari casts off her eye-cover so that she could enjoy the sights of flowers and birds. This apparent anathema is an act of assertion of positive self-construct by a woman who has a cheerful love of life, unlike the forever whining Queen of Mahabharata. In the dream narrative the girl also creates a fusion-epic of sorts by bringing in a female character from the Ramayana to meet Gandhari of Mahabharata. It is Urmila, wife of the loyal brother Lakshmana who chose to accompany his elder brother Rama to the forest, leaving her behind. She is tired of ministering to her mothers-in-law and one day, goes out to another country and encounters Gandhari there. She cannot recognise her because the latter is without her proverbial eye-cover. They decide to sojourn into the forests and have a happy tour with the guidance and services of the devil with his hideous appearance. There is such fun and enjoyment, thanks to the solicitude of the devil that the women really experience a different order of reality. When the girl recalls this strange dream, her traditional mother is aghast. It is Muniyakka in the story who firmly turns her back on the dead wood in tradition and encourages the child to be free. She is the alternative image of women set against the traditional archetypes so that Lakshmi projects her as strong, spirited, independent, and rational. Paradoxically enough she believes in devils, even communes with them, takes direction and protection from the good devil, '*Olle Pichachi*'—against the assault of the wicked devil—'*Kettu Pichachi*'.

Her talk and habits and stories are so captivating to the child that she wants to know, 'Muni ... Muniyakka ... you ... who are you? I mean, are you a woman or a devil?' This innocent doubt of the child can be interpreted as the author's challenge to patriarchy and its cultural practices. Muniyakka's answer at once touches the supernatural and rational levels. She tells the child that she can practise sorcery and out-devil the devil i.e., the wicked one. She explains 'with a broad grin' that 'we should also have some wickedness within us. Otherwise any rogue will devour us. You must realise that, my little one.' Surely it is a lesson in strategy for women to stave off society's attempt to annihilate their self.

This beautifully written, so natural and easy-to-read story, conceals art within art. It has summoned a range of feminist concerns touching upon social and religious sanctions. It creates two different representations of women: a young widow (upper class) who acquiesces to society, and an old widow (lower caste and working class) who is strong, free, confident and so defiant that she can challenge orthodoxy of any kind, the old mother (upper class), enlightened and serene, the old widow cook (lower middle-class) who is part of the patriarchal system. Pitched amongst them is the young girl-child who is open to impressions and who learns to construe the existing reality and construct her vision of life.

Lakshmi Kannan's story "A Political Colour" goes beyond the middle class, goes beyond India and invokes issues of discrimination and subjection in the broader frame of racism. The petty, private concerns of middle-class families in South Indian society, especially the Brahminical milieu, is held to ridicule by the opening up of the wider world for the young protagonist Kalyani, now in the University of London, to pursue research. Her family's obsession with the need for maintaining her 'fair' complexion using traditional methods so that she will be a suitable bride for a smart young man, pales into inanity in the eyes of Kalyani when her insular mind is opened up by her roommate Dulcey, a Trinidadian black. Kalyani is amazed at one level to find that black is beautiful; at the ideological level she finds herself drawn to Dulcey's group which is mobilising support for anti-apartheid and against the racism pervasive in white civilisation. The story thus locates the issue of femininity and construction of beauty in the worldwide ideological forum of ideas inspired by postcolonial thinking. Kalyani, who hitherto, has thought that she has nothing to do with 'Black', comes to realise that she is no less black than an African or a Jamaican. 'Colour', then, takes on a 'political colour', prompting Kalyani to express her solidarity with Robert and Dulcey and their group in organising a public meeting to denounce racism. It is important to note that it is not just blacks who are participants in this event; quite a few enlightened whites too throw in their weight. When Kalyani goes to India for vacation, after two years of stay in England, her people go into ecstasy by looking at her enhanced complexion. She shocks them by declaring, 'I haven't become fair. I am also a Black woman.' Given the fact that Lakshmi Kannan has widely travelled and is conversant with multicultural societies, one is not surprised to find the story launching itself from the individual to the collective, from the personal to the political sphere.

Lakshmi Kannan uses the site of university to unravel the sordid male chauvinism that masquerades as academic leadership in her story "Another Hour, Another Hue". The sharp feminist criticism that stems from depicting the plight of three women teachers exploited by an unconscionable Head of the Department in a Federal University in India, shows that Lakshmi can call a spade a spade when the situation demands it. The ideological thrust of the story is the way a male professor, a senior man at that, can regard his female colleagues as objects of male gaze and gratification. The sinister manoeuvers he makes to keep the young lady research scholar under his thumb and to foment mistrust and hostility between two accomplished women faculty, one strikingly beautiful though past forty, the other newly recruited, but in her thirties, anxious to find a toe-hold in the academia, reveal the unsavoury aspects of patriarchy. How even educated, upcoming women are not free from the threat of male domination, is skillfully dramatised. How difficult it is for women professionals to maintain a balance between their roles as wives and as academics, is graphically delineated through the individual struggles of the accomplished and mature but frustrated Dr Sudharani, the ambitious but unstable Dr Jaya, the unschooled Mala, Akhila, the pathetic PhD scholar working under the Head Dr Verma, with a baby to nurse and a fellowship to utilise. The author represents them as overcoming the obstacles and achieving a solidarity to shame Professor Verma at the end. This positive ending shows that women do not want to be vindictive, but must nevertheless assert their existential freedom and regain their legitimate space in public sphere.

In all these stories, dealing with issues of gender and sexuality, Lakshmi Kannan has sensitively examined forces of enabling and forces of disabling, with regard to women in contemporary society.

Now to the art of crafting the short story painstakingly, with loving attention. Lakshmi Kannan is first and foremost a creative writer, an exquisite one at that and hence ideology seamlessly runs through the warp and woof of her writing. Nuanced representation of any issue is her concern. Hence the texture and mode of her writing deserve attention. She is gifted in creating a fascinating atmosphere which almost renders her short fiction as vividly poetical as her poetry. In some of the stories the atmosphere evoked, pitches the reader between the realm of the living and the realm of the dead. Hence such stories conjure up an eschatological dimension, if we may use the term. "Nandanvan", "A Sky All Around" and "Please, Dear God" can be placed within the category of the Gothic mode and fabulation. In these stories people lie dying, keeping their kith and kin on tenterhooks, or we see how the prelude to their death and the drama that unfolds after death are made absorbing. "Please, Dear God" and "A Sky All Around" are a feat in phenomenological narration and the epistemological processes it engenders. The ICU in hospital is the dominant trope, with its glass partition, rows of beds, motionless bodies, still breathing through ventilators, the magical monitors drawing electronic patterns capturing the tussle between life and death, in bed after bed. The story "Please, Dear God" has a wife who lies in coma, and the husband, who, in sheer desperation, visits her every day in the hope of her revival, but against all odds. The curvature of his mental on-goings marks the soliloquy and internal colloquies that intersperse the narration. Lakshmi Kannan superbly internalises the consciousness of a desperate human mind in fear of death. She specialises in the vocabulary of death—'Die? Expire? Perish?' asks Ramachandran gasping, looking at his comatose wife, who is, for all practical purposes, dead. The most powerful part of the narrative is the way the distraught husband sees across the glass pane of the ICU, the efficient act of the nurse in indicating the thin but decisive line between the living and the dead within that haunted hospital premise. The act of pulling the white sheet tightly over the head and tucking in the sides 'neatly and decisively', is the one symbolic act to distinguish the dead from the living. The act of covering the corpse is bizarre and yet realistic. The husband himself becomes grotesque in the act of pressing his face close to the pane and flattening his nose in the process, to have a glimpse of his wife's face. He is fascinated by that one particular Sister who has achieved absolute mastery in tucking the sheet around the body perfectly. The husband is so exercised and nervous in the way he offers a running commentary on the same that makes us think that he is the one who is dead and it his body that is being wrapped around in that 'blindingly white sheet'. When he sees a young boy and another young woman, being covered thus after they breathe their last, he almost achieves a negative capability as Keats would say. He asks the young mother 'Goodbye, young mother. But who will mother your tiny baby as you snuggle under that cool, clean white sheet?' This is in superb eschatalogical vein. The Sister who fascinates him no end wins from him a curious accolade: 'This Sister in particular, the nurse is someone you can trust with your eyes closed. She will take the sheet around your body perfectly. Just look at her how she enjoys her job as if she was born to it, and it is the prime mission in her life.' The grim irony is almost glossed over by a bizarre admiration for her professional finesse. A very novel perception is articulated when he finds the ICU claustrophobic where death itself seems to need fresh air! So he says, 'God, if you are death in itself, go away; get out. Just leave through the main door and take some fresh air.'

The transferred epithet 'grim' in 'grim register' (for recording Admissions and Deaths), the description of the dead girl's eyes as 'wide open, unblinking, and unseeing' which provokes him to feel 'as if he would turn to stone if her gaze fell upon him' (reminding us of the Greek Medusa whose eyes could petrify an onlooker) are some of the instances which unmistakably tell the reader that the author is a poet and sensitive student of literature. The enervated husband's argument with his comatose wife, urging her to remember her marriage vows and not to desert him, is almost Dantesque. I think Lakshmi simply excelled herself in creating this poignant Gothic tale, making a modern institution like hospital her Dantean purgatory.

"A Sky All Around" is also a story which has a hospital as its locale and we have a man lying there dying. This time the narration is from the point of view of the consciousness of the patient who is in coma. The paradox is that he is able to hear every voice around him and even distinguish its quality as 'silky', as 'coarse', 'female' ('That woman cannot sing. She better not'—look at the cheeky humour), as 'firm' and so on. Indeed it is an eschatological narrative, the ruminating consciousness being that of an elderly man Varadarajan, clinically almost dead, but spirit-wise travelling in uncharted realms, finding the boundary between earth and sky, sky and ocean sliding perpetually. His auditory impressions of the conversations inside the ICU ('This case has turned serious. He has not only been in a coma for several days now, he has this edema now') and his sensitivity to pain when they press the various parts of his body to prove that he is beyond hope ('Ooh that hurts, *Aiyyo amma*, save me from this torture, come, come soon....') are amazingly articulated. When he calls out thus in pain, he makes a voyage in time back to his childhood, and his caring mother, long since dead, responds to his call and comes to console him. By a manipulation of post-modern technique, Lakshmi Kannan creates a fabulation wherein the tense, taut atmosphere of the hospital, is superseded by a relaxed ambience beyond earth and sky with the loving mother reassuring an aggrieved child. Varadarajan is released from the tyranny of time and space, sickness and pain. But paradoxically he yearns to go back to the present, to his family, to the earth (like D. G. Rossetti's 'The Blessed Damozel') and hence his spirit hovers back to his home into his wife's kitchen. The pity of it is, his wife Kanaka could not recognise him. This pathos is intensified when we find him back in the ICU, visited by his children and grandchildren. He is intensely alive to their anxious presence; but they cannot see him except as a comatose patient. Again in another escapade, there is an eschatological encounter when the dying Vardarajan meets his former office colleague Bhaskaran, who is long since dead. But he does not recognise him either. The unreality of this realm of experience saddens

Varadarajan immensely. There is memory, but no reassuring knowledge in his disembodied sojourns between life and death. We are in Yeatsian Byzantine world where spirits float and 'breathless mouths may summon' (to use Yeats's memorable line). His consciousness expands beyond space so much that he loses his identity and hence when his mother calls him affectionately 'Varad, Varad', Varadararajan is beyond any interpellation now. She is young, like Bhishma's mother Ganga and he is old and careworn like Bhishma! He is confused by this incongruity and hence replies: 'There, there, my girl, you're mistaken, I'm very much older than you....' Surely Lakshmi Kannan has created in this story an ethos which is amazing. The ambience of mystery is intensified towards the end with the family resolving to chant the collective Buddhist prayer *daimoku*, from the Lotus Sutra. When the world of medicines gives him up, prayer resurrects him. But in between he has travelled and seen much.

The story "Nandanvan" has nothing eschatological about it, but it too has an old man, who, feeling alienated from his family, communes with birds, while feeding them in the garden. In the tradition of fables in Indian narrative, birds are given the role of observing, commenting, passing moral and ethical judgements on humans. The old man resolves to stay in the garden, abstaining from food, as a silent gesture of protest against his greedy children's scheming to snatch the house and property from him. The birds appreciate his kindness, but not his sons. It is a King Lear-like situation of filial ingratitude. When he dies, something fantastic happens. The sons are more interested in settling scores among themselves while the old man lies dead, waiting to be taken out for the final rites. The priests are outraged by such monstrous behaviour. The birds, which wait and watch this ugly fight for property, decide to act nobly and honour the dead man. By a technical twist, Lakshmi Kannan manipulates a folk-tale turn of events when the grateful birds carry his body out of the yard. The priests and the sons come out only to find the yard empty and the body vanished.

The birds even sing to help them forget the strain of carrying off a heavy human body:

He is not heavy, Ailesa ...
We'd lift him up, Ailesa ...
Let's do it fast, Ailesa ...

When the old man is gone, the birds too are gone from the garden. Lakshmi Kannan creates a fable in this story, providing a profound moral core.

"Savvyasachi Square" is also a story about filial ingratitude, with a grandfather as a protagonist, located in London. But there is no supernatural element in this story. Still, it has a revelation and an experience of epiphany. The treatment meted out to the poor man by his son and daughter-in-law, after insisting that he go over from India to live with them in costly London, can be discerned in the way the couple make him feel as if he is an imposition and a wasteful one at that. To escape the claustrophobic atmosphere in the small apartment, Velayudam daily takes the London tube and goes out. His encounter with a highly skilled performer in St. James's park, comes as a revelation of human spirit. The incredible dexterity with which he manages so many instruments and performing dolls and toys to please the passers by and earn a decent living, astounds the Indian. He calls him 'Savvyasachi' the ambidextrous—a sobriquet of the archer Prince Arjuna in the Mahabharata. It is not only his musical talent and virtuoso performance that stun the old man from India. The reason for the Englishman exhausting himself so completely every day by this road-show, is equally transformative. This multi-talented singer cannot fall back upon his family in his old age; he has to live on his own income and manage London, 'a city of prohibitive prices'. He has to be a Savvyasachi. Velayudam sees in the singer a parallel: both are in the same situation, neglected by their children. But the indomitable spirit of the Englishman has egged him to keep going and not falter. Velayudam learns the value of dignity and inner spirit.

In terms of the technique brilliantly serving the purpose of ideology, we can single out two stories from the corpus of Lakshmi Kannan's short fiction which we are examining here. They are "Just Think About It" and "A Word with you, Father". The psychological pressure under which a husband and a son speak in these two stories, respectively, holds a surprise for the reader. The form of the first one recalls to a student of English literature Robert Browning's dramatic monologues, especially featuring selfish husbands, crooks and such men, bursting out in a crisis, unwinding their psyche. We have in this story of Lakshmi, a husband pleading, bullying, and cajoling his wife to withdraw the divorce suit. After every one of his utterances, there is a dotted line, giving the reader the impression that the wife is absolutely silent and her adamant stand provokes him further and makes him insensate with fury and desperation. The mystification continues for a few more pages until, the waiter intrudes into this imaginary conversation to remind the speaker that he has been talking so long by himself. The locale is a restaurant, a public place, but the male speaker forgets his circumstances and lets off his steam against his wife's alleged female obduracy. The author deals with the ideology of patriarchy which naturalises male chauvinism with admirable dexterity. The absent presence of the wife helps to draw out the unconscious prejudices in the husband: male conception of female freedom, stereotyping of a woman as one who weeps and therefore better than the one who is strong, resentment of the wife's clarity and decisiveness, man's willingness to placate woman by male overtures to make her submit, all brilliantly betrayed through his strategic inferences. We realise that it is after all a monologue and no dialogue. The capacity of the 'new woman' has unnerved him completely. Here the form of a dramatic monologue has been superbly adapted to the exigencies of a short story.

A story with a similar technique of intensifying the mystery by creating an absent character who is more than present, is "A Word with you, Father". It is not exactly the same kind of dramatic monologue. There are more of internal colloquies and mumblings, again as in Browning. However, there is a man who sits on a chair, in a restaurant whom the speaker mistakes to be his father but who does not recognise him. The gothic aspect of the story accentuates the mystery because the father is long since dead and the son knows it. But he accosts him and confronts him as Macbeth does of Banquo's Ghost in the banquet scene in Shakespeare's play. In the process of identifying the father and approaching him from a distance, the son unwinds himself and the family history, the strained relationship between the father and the children, the utter alienation the brother and sister felt when the father died. A King Lear-like situation is relived in memory by the speaker. Is it filial ingratitude that estranged the father from them? Is there some deep guilt betrayed by the son? The story, as it is dramatised, has a hallucinatory quality with the social reality being impinged upon by the extraterrestrial, psychic reality. It is not exactly an encounter with the dead because the stranger who is mistaken for the father, gently tells the speaker that he could not be his father for a simple reason that he is not much older to him; moreover he chose to remain single because he knew 'how children change into problems once they grow up', thus disambiguating some of the myths about filial bonding. Lakshmi uses the short story form to explore the hidden, dark motivation and drives in the recesses of human consciousness and the unconscious.

Lakshmi Kannan's short stories are an important contribution to contemporary Indian literature. Basically she draws her characters and voices from the middle class, with which she is conversant. She also has the necessary power of empathy to construe life lived in other material conditions. She is committed to examining issues in feminist ideology and study the functioning of patriarchy in society. But she is not the one to allegorise human beings into abstract categories, and demonise any particular sex or a system, be it the male or the family. Her writings have always been marked by a certain urbaneness, respect for polyvalence, a genuine concern to resolve problems rather than stand impaled on issues for their own sake. Hence her critiques of institutional structures have invariably been nuanced and multifaceted.

Her art and craft owe much to her sensitivity to language and feelings. Hence she is a mistress of creating a striking atmosphere and ambience. Her word-horde is amazing from which she quarries most appropriate and revealing expressions. They give the texture of poetry to her stories. Her narrative technique and discursive tools are therefore never mechanical. They emerge in consonance with the experiences she wants to depict. The Indian ethos and idiom are superbly captured in her resonant English.

Lakshmi Kannan's Fictional Weltanschauung

An Interview

*Christine Gomez**

CHRISTINE GOMEZ: In the portrait gallery of the memorable women characters featured in your fiction, my favourite are the uneducated working class women like Muniyakka in "Muniyakka"[1] and "Enendral" ("Because..."), and Muniyamma in *Athukku Poganum (Going Home)*[2]. Do these creations have one or more originals from your childhood in South India?

LAKSHMI KANNAN: Yes, these characters have their originals. They're my favourites too. I'm fascinated by their earthy wisdom, their naturalness and their salty, native wit and humour. They're not alienated from their cultural roots, so they continue to be nourished and sustained by their roots and that makes them culturally distinct. They can also handle the tragedies and triumphs of life with their home-spun philosophy.

CHRISTINE GOMEZ: Many of your women characters are brilliant, self-aware intellectuals. Together, are they meant to present a

* Dr Christine Gomez was formerly Associate Professor of English, Holy Cross College (Autonomous) Trichy, Tamil Nadu. This interview was published earlier in Tamil in 'Kaaveri Kathaigal', Chennai: Mithra Arts and Creations Pvt. Ltd., 2007.

[1] Lakshmi Kannan (trans.), "Muniyakka", *India Gate & Other Stories*, New Delhi: Orient BlackSwan, 1993.

[2] Lakshmi Kannan (trans.), *Going Home: A Novel*, Delhi: Orient BlackSwan, 1999.

composite image of the New Indian Woman, your version of Subramania Bharati's[3] 'Pudhumai Penn'?

LAKSHMI KANNAN: The grand senior icon of Tamil literary history and culture critic 'Chitti' (P. G. Sunderarajan) once remarked, half in jest I am sure, if I am the '*Pudumai Penn*' the poet Bharati dreamed of. Even as sanity advises me to keep my head and ignore this as an indulgent comment, at the same time, it shows me in a flash, a male point of view of what a 'New Indian Woman' is.

CHRISTINE GOMEZ: Personally, I would describe you as a balanced feminist who is equally concerned about projecting an androgynous vision. What are your views on Feminism?

LAKSHMI KANNAN: A balanced and an integrated view is what I strive for. It is immature to be partisan and reductive just for the sake of making a point or taking a position, because life is larger than that. It is elusive too. That's one reason why the 'classifying' type of critics find it difficult to 'classify' me. If I am a woman and I'm writing now in contemporary times, I must somehow 'fit in' into their theoretical ideas of what a 'feminist writer' is supposed to be. We seem to be living in prescriptive times! This leaves little room for individuality, or even for the warmth of human nature.

I have reason to believe that every thinking, intelligent, sensitive and sensible woman has inner reserves of strength and understanding that far surpass the circumscribed parameters of theoretical, conventional feminism.

CHRISTINE GOMEZ: Is your use of the image of Shakti in "Shell", "The Coming of Devi" (in *India Gate & Other Stories*) and "Muniyakka", a conscious attempt to place Feminism in the Indian context?

LAKSHMI KANNAN: No, it wasn't a conscious attempt to evoke the Hindu icon of Shakti. In each of the stories it was integral to the mood and came from *within* the protagonist as an expression of a cultural conditioning. In "Muniyakka" the eponymous protagonist comes from a working class/caste background where Shakti is worshipped as 'Mariamma' or 'Mariattha' in a more ferocious form

[3] Subramania Bharati is one of the most intense and distinguished poets in Tamil who worked passionately for the national movement from 1930s onwards until his early, untimely death. He was sincerely supportive of women and evolved an image of the 'New Modern Woman' (*Pudumai Penn*) who will be the face of the emerging free India.

of Devi Durga. Here Shakti is both loved and feared for her power. Muniyakka relates to this and finds it oddly thrilling.

CHRISTINE GOMEZ: Do you see any progress in your stories, from the unobtrusive feminists in the earlier collections to the self-assertive, militant ones in the later ones? Or from balanced feminism to an androgynous vision?

LAKSHMI KANNAN: A balanced, androgynous vision is my ideal but this is a question for my critics to answer.

CHRISTINE GOMEZ: You excel in the presentation of authentic, mature, supportive, nurturing relationships among women as in the novel *Going Home* and in others, which would have gratified Virginia Woolf who had lamented over the rarity of such relationships in literature. Have you done this deliberately as a viable female model to counterpoint the patriarchal model of competition and rivalry?

LAKSHMI KANNAN: Friendship is truly a gift of the gods. Virginia Woolf is right about its not being well-represented in literature but I wish she was around today to see the wonderful change that has actually come about in the relationship among women in India and elsewhere. Some years back I thought that it was difficult, if not impossible for women to develop a sustainable friendship. I noticed that they get defeated somewhere along the way by patriarchal structures of family, relations and the way they prioritise children and so on. These factors claim most of their time and energy. The men however, have always had a comfortable structure within which they invite their favourite friends and expect their wives and the entire family to roll out the red carpet for them. Now I, as well as some of my friends, emulate the same strategy. We make our women friends a part of the family and that ensures a peaceful acceptance!

CHRISTINE GOMEZ: How did Tamil readers react to your vivid, objective portrayal of a lesbian in the short story "Maria"?

LAKSHMI KANNAN: The Tamil readers were surprisingly positive. From metros like Chennai and Madurai to remote small towns, there were readers who amazed me by their empathy and the intensity of the response "Maria" evoked from them. I had sent the story with much trepidation, and did so only after checking with the Editor if he would publish a story with this theme. I was worried if Maria would be ridiculed by the conservative Tamil community although in the story, as in real life, Maria is only 'suspected to be' a lesbian and is more a victim of wild rumours and malicious gossip. Much of it was caused by her strange behaviour, her childhood trauma, and a sense of insecurity as a child who grew up in a broken home. The Tamil readers proved me wrong by their sympathy and ready acceptance of Maria who had a raw deal in life.

CHRISTINE GOMEZ: Is there any difference in the response of Tamil readers to some of your stories, such as "A Fever" (in *India Gate & Other Stories*) for instance?

LAKSHMI KANNAN: Usually, there is always some difference in the response of regional readers and English readers. Still, I get my share of surprises, like with "Maria". The response in English for "A Fever" was objective. The story was taken for what the storyline offered. The readers took keen interest in the unstated, non-verbal but explosive interaction between Girija, a thwarted dancer, and the much older Chandran. Many English readers commented that I had much empathy for the male character Chandran. In Tamil, the response was more guarded.

CHRISTINE GOMEZ: Do you see yourself as a satirist and social reformer, especially on issues relating to women, in stories like "Pain" (in *India Gate & Other Stories*)?

LAKSHMI KANNAN: No, I don't see myself as a social reformer at all, though some satiric element may creep into my lines. I don't have a conscious motive of reforming anyone.

CHRISTINE GOMEZ: In "Zeroing In" and "The Maze" and also in the brilliantly incisive conversation between Gayatri and Rama in the novel *Going Home*, there is a distinctly Marxist flavour in your analysis of the alienation of the worker. How far have you been influenced as a writer by Marxism?

LAKSHMI KANNAN: For many of us Marxism came as a significant movement that was a historical necessity too in social history. For literature and for culture, it gave us a fresh, clear perspective. Marxist criticism had a tremendous impact on literature. In Sukumaran of "Zeroing In" and Rajaraman of "The Maze", I have tried to portray the painful dilemma of men at work. In the novel *Going Home*, Rama Doraiswamy as a professional sociologist, is inevitably steeped in Marxist reality.

CHRISTINE GOMEZ: Your story "Please, Dear God" and others deal with the confronting of the existential truths after a close encounter with death. In the novel *Going Home*, Gayatri's legal alienation from a particular house deepens into a sense of existential alienation from the human predicament. To what extent has Existential philosophy coloured your fictional world view or Weltanschauung? How would you describe the impact of Existential philosophy in your writing?

LAKSHMI KANNAN: I absorbed Existential philosophy as a student of English literature and later, during my years in the faculty of English in various universities. It was intensified further when I worked on the fiction of Saul Bellow for my doctoral dissertation, because Bellow was deeply influenced by European novelists who wrote in the Existential mode. Then there is one's own life touching other lives and you see patterns that you can recognise. The stories you mention are the ones I 'lived through' in the process of writing. As for Gayatri in *Going Home*, you are one of the very few critics who got this point. Ironically, Gayatri outgrows the need of a house at the end. For the very house she longed for is something she finally tries to flee from and leave for some unknown orbit. She has this numbing, incomprehensible sense of alienation even from the people she loves, such as her husband Shankar, her son Arvind, her grandson Siddharth, her dear mother and her close friend Rama. Existential philosophy has coloured many of my later stories as well, particularly those that have elderly people as central characters.

CHRISTINE GOMEZ: You have used a variety of narrative techniques in your stories—first person narrative, the centre of consciousness technique, shifting perspectives, narratives that go circular, spiral or have a zigzag movement, the stream of consciousness method and the flashback. Do you consciously experiment with different techniques?

LAKSHMI KANNAN: Most of the techniques are suggested by the theme, the mood, the tone, and of course, the protagonists of a story. Each story calls for a particular technique that is *inherent* in the story and that will facilitate a development of the theme. I've continued to experiment in my later stories too and have also written in the fantasy mode.

CHRISTINE GOMEZ: Would you consider *Going Home* as a female Bildungsroman tracing the inner evolution of Gayatri's consciousness from childhood to middle age? Did you plan it as one?

LAKSHMI KANNAN: Not really. It just happened to evolve as a Bildungsroman, as it were. Gayatri seemed to come on to the pages with a will and destiny of her own and I just followed her along.

CHRISTINE GOMEZ: Some of your stories like "Writer Proletariat" and *Going Home* have elements of meta-fiction in them, i.e., they are fiction about the writing of fiction. The writer Rama in *Going Home* tells us why she writes. Could you pinpoint the raison d'être of your fiction? *Why* do you write?

LAKSHMI KANNAN: There is this well-known critic (I forget his name) who wrote an interesting book titled *The Story-Shaped World*. He deals with the giant archetypes and tropes in actual life. If you reflect upon life, you can discern a shape, a pattern, a story-like quality that makes one want to write about. The writer Rama in *Going Home* has earned many accolades and is an established name, all of which only makes her husband very jealous of her name and fame. Despite her success, life seems to hold out a threatening void for her and she says she just fills in those "pockets of emptiness" with her writing. As for why *I* write—it is by far the most difficult question you've asked. Perhaps the best answer is silence, if that's permissible within an interview. However, I'll attempt to answer you. I write whenever a luminous something shimmers in front of me—it could be an image, a line, a thought, an experience or a surrogate experience. It could be an epiphany. Even so, I don't immediately set off to write. I wait indefinitely. And when that 'luminous something' persistently presents itself to me, and gets a 'form' or a 'voice', then I write about it so that this fleeting moment endures in my work. There are moments of beauty, glimpses of divinity in people, however 'ordinary' you may take them to be, and then there are moments that are luminescent with such a farewell radiance that they are all the more precious to me for their perishable mortality. That's when I seek to write in order to record them. I still feel it wasn't wise of me to answer this question!

CHRISTINE GOMEZ: You have said that writing for you is like a 'sadhana' calling for concentration and total surrender. Are you conscious of this all the time when you write?

LAKSHMI KANNAN: Whatever I claim to be an inspired piece of writing, has this quality of surrender—to the theme, the protagonists, and if it is poetry, to the mood, the atmosphere and the images that 'take over'.

CHRISTINE GOMEZ: Do you have any favourites among your stories? Why are they your favourites?

LAKSHMI KANNAN: Yes. "Phantoms of Truth" (*India Gate & Other Stories*), "Muniyakka", "Please, Dear God" and "A Sky All Around" are some of the stories I enjoyed writing. I must confess though that the story I most enjoyed writing was "Phantoms of Truth" for I was very drawn to the simplicity and innocence of the tall, slim and swarthy fisherman Saibu who eventually becomes a swimming coach and a lifesaver in the ocean at Puri, Orissa. I met someone like him at the sea coast in Puri and felt that I could learn some profound lessons in joyous living—or dying—from him. The rest of the stories like "Muniyakka" and others mentioned took me out of myself and made the very act of writing a cleansing experience. They restored me to the rhythms of life, of death, of the regenerative processes at work.

CHRISTINE GOMEZ: Do you maintain a journal? If so, how far has it contributed to your writing?

LAKSHMI KANNAN: I maintain a kind of a journal in which I write at irregular intervals. Some of the notes have contributed to my writings while there are many others that I would never publish. They will remain with me and go with me.

CHRISTINE GOMEZ: Do you encounter any difficulty in translating your stories in English?

LAKSHMI KANNAN: There are some stories that lend themselves easily to English, while there are others so deeply ingrained in the Tamil style that one needs to re-invent a language to render them. A bit of the original flavour may get lost in translation but I've been on the scene long enough to realise that it's nothing to despair about. Either one decides to translate a particular text with all the risks involved, or just leaves it alone in the original, in which case, it's pretty much locked within a narrow region.

CHRISTINE GOMEZ: What are your views on translation as a creative writing?

LAKSHMI KANNAN: I don't at all think that translation is a creative kind of writing. The spirit of a translator could be creative in so far as he/she works creatively within the limits of a language or invents new phrases and expressions for a linguistic transfer of a culture, but it would still be a rendering of something that has already been created in the original.

CHRISTINE GOMEZ: What are your views on Indian writers, both the regional ones and those who write in English?

LAKSHMI KANNAN: I am struck by the richness, the authenticity and the strong cultural and social moorings of any good regional writer. He/she always gives me credible people as protagonists, people you can recognise as 'real' within their social/cultural context. If one consolidates the works of regional writers who are available in translation, we will have a solid body of Indian literature, rich in diversity but vivid in being culturally distinct. In English, the scene is so different. A book is preceded by a lot of hype in the media, often with the misplaced emphasis on the huge advance received by the author rather than the book in itself. Much of the media focus is also more on the author than the theme of the book. I mean the author is 'packaged'as much as the book. And yet, there have been some English books that have arrived on a quiet note, and one takes to the author who fights shy of too much media exposure. Alan Sealy, Amitav Ghosh, Arundhati Roy—to name a few—are writers one wants to read. I'm sure there are others but the names escape me right now.

CHRISTINE GOMEZ: You've been to the USA, UK, Canada and The Netherlands for various international conferences and women-related seminars. Could you give us more details about these events?

LAKSHMI KANNAN: It's a very rewarding experience to meet writers, critics, publishers, scholars and students from a diverse geo-political background. I envied some of the writers who came from countries that held literature and writers in high esteem, particularly the ones from Europe. I was also very impressed by the courage and conviction of writers who suffered a lot within their culture because of the political instability in their country and yet soldiered on with their writings. They are strong in facing uncertainties and I wondered where they have the reserves for that. Meeting women writers from across the globe was a humbling experience. Compared to some of them, what we as Indian women go through, seems to be nothing much to lament about. Once again, I was happy to see a warm, healthy bonding amongst the women who reached out to be friends, and who keep it up through e-mails, letters and cards. I hope they build on this sisterhood and strengthen their friendship by linking up with each other.

A Conversation with Lakshmi Kannan

*Sudha Rai**

Unsparing of soul-stultifying social practices and attitudes, especially in their bondage of women, Lakshmi Kannan, novelist, short story writer, poet and translator has established herself as a committed social analyst, centered in her vision of life and impervious to shifting artistic fashions. In English translation, Kannan is the author of a novel *Going Home* (1999), three collections of short story fiction that include novellas, *India Gate and Other Stories* (1993), *Parijata* (1992) and *Rhythms* (1986). She has published four collections of poems in English and *Unquiet Waters* (2005). In Tamil, in her pen-name "Kaaveri", she has written a novel, several novellas and four collections of short stories. Three of her collections of short stories have been published in Hindi translation.

SUDHA RAI: When did you first discover yourself as writer of short stories? How did you hit upon your subject matter?

LAKSHMI KANNAN: As far as I can remember, it was during my teens that I took to writing articles and humorous columns of topical interest. Many of them were styled in a satirical vein. During one such exercise, the 'person' I wanted to attack in my piece revealed that he is quite human in his flaws, that the quality I sought to attack could have been his defense against a harsh world that took advantage of his vulnerability. That is when the satire vanished

* Dr Sudha Rai is Professor in the Department of English and Dean, Faculty of Arts, University of Rajasthan, Jaipur. This interview was originally published in *Journal of Aesthetics and Aesthetics*, vol. 6, nos 1 & 2, January-December 2006, Pattathanam, Quilon, Kerala.

and my article took a story-shaped contour. I returned to revise the piece, and then kept it aside for some time before sending it to a magazine with much hesitation. It got published.

SUDHA RAI: Which magazine published your first short story?

LAKSHMI KANNAN: I think it was *Junior Statesman* that had an entire page for young contributors. This Sunday pullout was edited by the Kolkata office and circulated all over the country.

SUDHA RAI: What kind of readership did you originally write for and has that in any way changed today?

LAKSHMI KANNAN: Initially, I wrote only in English and the readership was largely the English-reading ones, college students, teachers, and other lay readers. It was only later that I started writing in Tamil, naturally with a language-specific, Tamil readership in mind. But whenever my works appeared in English translation, it brought me back to the English readership again. Yes, the readership profile has changed a lot since the last two decades. I am now aware of the fact that readers *per se* have very little time to read, that they are hard-pressed for time, caught as they are by the demands of a profession, family, the social circuit and so on. It is also a readership that is exposed to a visually attractive media, such as the TV, films, magazines and shows.

SUDHA RAI: Your stories were originally written in Tamil and have been translated by you into English. What kind of linguistic and cultural mediations do you negotiate as a bilingual writer?

LAKSHMI KANNAN: The act of translation at once makes me acutely conscious of the target audience in English. One has to leap from a Dravidian source to another language that is spoken and understood the world over. The mediations I negotiate are mostly in the use of language as I am anxious that the translation should read well, that it should be in idiomatic English, that it has to flow without disturbing the laws of English grammar, syntax or the semantic content. To achieve this, certain adjustments have to be made—and I call them adjustments—without distorting the sense of the original. The real challenge is in translating dialogue and grasping the speech rhythms of a people. There are times when one needs to invent an expression to arrive upon a closest approximation to the original.

SUDHA RAI: Your collected poems, *Unquiet Waters* has been published by the Sahitya Akademi. Are the concerns of your fiction diametrically opposite to that of your poetry? Which part of you goes into each genre?

LAKSHMI KANNAN: I would not say the concerns are opposite. It is the theme, the mood, the synergy of various forces that determine a genre. I generally wait for a while before I write. I wait till I can discern a shape, a form, even a nascent development, if you will. For poetry, it begins with an overpowering, compelling image that takes hold of me. It then looms ahead and moves, gathering words on its way to the page and I let it do that with the least interference on my part. I admit though that sometimes, a few of my short stories, or passages in a novel/novella, also take-off on an image, a symbol or a metaphor. I just go along with my instincts and write, never forcing or stretching a poem to be a story, or shrinking a story to fit into a poem.

SUDHA RAI: Where do you locate yourself—as a Tamil writer or a writer in English?

LAKSHMI KANNAN: As simply a writer who loves to write in two languages.

SUDHA RAI: Could you comment on the achievement of the Tamil short story?

LAKSHMI KANNAN: The Tamil short story has drawn a lot of new talent in the past two decades and some writers have dared to experiment with the form, the theme, the presentation and language. A special feature of Tamil Nadu is what we call 'the little magazine' that has become a powerful literary movement in itself. It has been a good platform for the short story and novella to evolve. Tamil has a strong literary tradition of the novella called 'kurunovel'. The 'little magazines' jealously guard their literary values and parameters. They are not populist in taste and do not pander to mass culture or non-culture.

SUDHA RAI: In what way does social protest manifest in your short stories?

LAKSHMI KANNAN: Many of them could be taken as 'protest' writings and they encompass issues that affect women, men, or anyone whose rights as a human being are denied.

SUDHA RAI: Tiruchi, Chennai, Delhi ... the city seems to be so much of a protagonist in your short stories. What do you think?

LAKSHMI KANNAN: Yes, the environs do have a deep impact on the lives of people and the city can be an oppressive 'presence'. In the novel *Going Home*[1], the fast-paced bustle of Delhi makes Gayatri long for the peace and serenity of Mysore as she knew it as a girl-child. But in the story "India Gate", Delhi and its ambience, together with the monument that lends the name to the story, liberates Padmini from the claustrophobic and insular atmosphere of the orthodox Brahmins living within the ghetto of a 'small town' mindset in Tiruchirapalli.

SUDHA RAI: Many of your short stories are a reflection of the ubiquitousness of 'the great Tamil tradition' (your own evocative phrase). What is your own attitude to this tradition?

LAKSHMI KANNAN: There is much mindless tyranny that goes in the name of 'tradition'. It is allowed to fall like a heavy axe particularly on women. Many of these so-called 'traditions' are anachronistic for the contemporary times we live in. While men move ahead lightly, it is the women who are expected to be the custodians of this 'great Tamil tradition' that is only a veiled control over their space and time. If one must learn about traditions, I would rather take an interest in literary traditions, traditions in music, dance, in customs that have a symbolic meaning or beauty.

SUDHA RAI: Several of your stories relate to individuals helplessly trapped by disease and acute illness in wards and ICU's. In "Pain"[2] you explore cancer, in "A Sky All Around" renal failure and in "Rhythms"[3] paralysis. Any reason why you are drawn to these subjects?

LAKSHMI KANNAN: There is one more story set in an ICU. It is "Please, Dear God". These experiences take man and woman to the very brink of existence. While some people crumble and get crushed under this kind of adversity, a few others are amazingly resilient and courageous. The existential struggle with the uncertainty of life brings out the best in them. I am drawn to the two seemingly contrary traits—an indomitable human spirit on the one hand and a graceful acceptance of destiny or mortality on the other.

[1] Lakshmi Kannan (trans.), *Going Home: A Novel by Lakshmi Kannan*, Delhi: Orient BlackSwan, 1999.

[2] Lakshmi Kannan (trans.), "Pain", in *India Gate & Other Stories*, trans. Lakshmi Kannan, Delhi: Orient BlackSwan, 1993.

[3] See "Rhythms", in *India Gate & Other Stories*.

Sudha Rai: I find your stories propel the reader towards a point of 'illumination'. Could you comment vis à vis your own craft of the short story?

Lakshmi Kannan: Thanks so much for asking me a very sensitive question that rarely occurs to many. You are very right about the element of 'illumination'; only I would call it epiphany. I love the form of the short story—and the poem—for its very brevity. It adds to the intensity of a composition and is an excellent medium to accommodate a sudden experience of epiphany that comes upon you like a revelation. I like to receive this moment within the silences of a story, without a comment, without a single word that may explain it away.

Sudha Rai: Would you say that in a short story, the distinction between a 'major' character and a 'minor' character is invalid? What about Kamala and Muniyakka in your story "Because...", or Padma in the story "Pain"?

Lakshmi Kannan: Even within the small confines of a short story, the distinctions between 'minor' and 'major' characters may blur or dissolve according to the way a protagonist makes the story 'move' or illumine a certain point of view. In a story titled "The Phantoms of Truth", a humble fisherman who teaches people to swim in an ocean in Puri (Orissa) eclipses the two other educated protagonists by the sheer force of his character. He becomes 'major' on his own. In "Pain", although the central protagonist is Padma, it is the elder daughter who gives a sharp perspective about womanhood and the utilitarian way it is taken by a crass community. Her own emerging womanhood makes her sense the pain most sharply. She could well be taken as the 'major' character in the story. In the case of "Because...", both Kamala and Muniyakka seem to have met their match in each other. They keep challenging each other in a way that eventually makes for a bonding between the two. Kamala is the kind of child who relentlessly asks questions that adults find unsettling, and Muniyakka is the one adult in the family who does not shy away from any of her disconcerting queries. Though small, Kamala sets the story moving, so she is 'major' in so far as she unravels the obsolete customs of a culture.

Sudha Rai: Are you committed to the idea of closure in your short stories?

LAKSHMI KANNAN: By 'closure' do you mean a conclusive end? If so, then I do not think many of my stories end on that note. Actually, it is the characters who take you that far and no further, and I largely go by them. You may even say that I am 'led on' by them, instead of me leading them on to where I want them to go. Therefore, some of my stories are 'open-ended'.

SUDHA RAI: Do you privilege writers as characters in your stories?

LAKSHMI KANNAN: No, I do not. In fact, if you read the story "Writer Proletariat", I show the writer here as any other person, quite selfish in the way he sets about achieving what he wants. He even runs away from a responsibility in order to catch up with an important appointment with a publisher.

SUDHA RAI: Several of your stories are distinctly cerebral. Is that a conscious decision?

LAKSHMI KANNAN: It is not. But I would like to reflect on this.

SUDHA RAI: Would you regard yourself as an experimental short story writer at the level of form and technique?

LAKSHMI KANNAN: The form of the short story, or for that matter, even a novel, lends itself to many experiments. Every composition is an experiment in fleshing out a theme. My collection of short stories in Tamil titled *Engum Vaanam* (2000) has quite a few stories that handle subjective time, shifts in time and space, and an alternate reality.

SUDHA RAI: Your stories are framed by images, motifs and symbols, traversing dimensions from the mythical to the real. Is it for the reader to make the connections?

LAKSHMI KANNAN: A few other critics have also made this observation. I often wonder if my love for poetry spills over a bit when I write fiction. It is a happy thing for a writer if a reader can make the connections. At any rate, I am not very conscious of the fact that images, motifs and symbols get into the texture of my short story. If they do, it is on their own volition.

SUDHA RAI: Your stories have already dealt with an astonishing range of issues from diverse points of view such as the gendering of the girl child ("Nagapushpam"), neglect of the elderly ("Nandanvan"), complexity of the self ("Muniyakka") to deconstructions of feminism ("Simone de Beauvoir and the Manes"). Is there a new dimension to your vision? And is it about how we can transcend cultural boundaries? I'm thinking of stories like "Savvyasachi Square".

LAKSHMI KANNAN: Yes. Just look at the multiplicity of cultures around us and the way we easily absorb and understand literatures from other cultures. This in itself, is an antidote to insularity or parochialism, two factors that are best left to our politicians. The scene is multivalent and one needs to widen the screen in order to capture even a fraction of it. While culture can give one a sharp identity, it should not keep us in fetters. In "Savvyasachi Square", Velayudam from Tamil Nadu relates so very well to the Briton in London that he even senses a certain kinship with him.

SUDHA RAI: How do you create a personal space for your women persona within the traditional edifice of religion?

LAKSHMI KANNAN: The women constantly contest and challenge certain elements in religion that they perceive as sexist. The culture, to be sure, is frankly patriarchal. Muniyakka does the *shraddha* for her dead husband and curses him the next moment. You could not read my story "The Coming of Devi". It became controversial in Tamil because Kausalya, the protagonist, has a dream about Devi Rajarajeswari, whose image has to be installed in a temple with Kumbabhishekam. The event is inevitably postponed as two factions are caught in a wrangle about the installation—the temple trustees on the one hand and the *Shankar mutt* of Shankaracharya on the other. Kausalya's dream is somewhat humorous, but the people who objected to this story seemed to be utterly humourless. When they said, 'Not only is Kausalya a feminist, the Devi in her dream is also a feminist!' I had to laugh, though I laughed alone, sitting in Delhi. They were hostile to Kausalya because she is an intellectual and a brilliant mathematician who questioned the politicisation of a temple. All that she had was this harmless (or so I thought) vivid dream that got her and me (her author) into much trouble.

SUDHA RAI: Your story "A Fever" suggests that the rational realignment of human relationships, delivered from sin and guilt, fear and silence, is your nucleus of change. Is such a formulation of your position acceptable?

LAKSHMI KANNAN: It is hard to comment on this story as even I do not quite understand it totally, with my mind. The three people are within a charmed circle, as it were. They took me along and I just followed them. All three of them are friends because they were destined to be, in this lifetime. When published, it turned out to be the one story that gave me the most surprise in terms of reader-response. Actually, the story comes through as more intense and sensuous in the original Tamil and the title is different. In Tamil, it is *Kall Veri Kolludhadi* which is a phrase about 'intoxication' from the poet Subramania Bharati, who wrote the most passionate love poetry. Therefore, when some Tamilians (critics, writers, scholars and lay people) whom I had always thought of as rather staid or diehard conservative, said they could relate a lot to the story, specially to Chandran for whom they had this empathy, I was very surprised! Others averred they would not like to see any change in the way the events unfold in the story. Your observation about a rational realignment makes me think again, though what I see is a strange bonding and affection between the men, Chandran and Ramesh, although Girija is a very disquieting factor for Chandran. Within the small physical scope of a *short* story, an unexpected episode accidentally bursts upon Chandran, transforming something in him. Will things ever be the same for them? To know that, I need to follow him in another story!

SUDHA RAI: Your symbols draw on figures in traditional Hindu mythology as well as more generalised symbols of the 'pitcher', 'river', 'ferryman' and 'ocean'. Do you re-inscribe these symbols to make them permeable?

LAKSHMI KANNAN: I am not aware of doing that. The Hindu myths are there in the background as perhaps an inevitable part of my conditioning. The generalised symbols you mention are all a part of the larger scheme of water imagery that this collection is steeped in. Hence the title *Unquiet Waters*.

SUDHA RAI: I find images of water more pronounced in your poems just as spatial and architectural metaphors are in your fiction. Can you say why? Is there a personal symbolism evolving?

LAKSHMI KANNAN: What an accurate observation. Like I said, most of the poems in this collection are moistened by water in all its ramifications. Fiction gives me more room to go spatial and architectural. As for symbols, I think they are at once personal and general.

SUDHA RAI: Interrogation and dialogue are intrinsic to your poems and to your short stories. How far is the 'personal' the 'political' for you?

LAKSHMI KANNAN: Yes. The two are very essential for the dialectics in life. The more I see a culture of silence for women in India, the less inclined are my women protagonists to be passive or acquiescent. They have a dynamic equation with their experiences. And of course, the personal IS political at this point in time. Yet, by a curious paradox, I happen to be a very private person, and would fiercely protect and respect the privacy of others too. There is a fine line that divides the personal from the private.

Short Stories

Nandanvan*

Strange, the way the façade of the house has such a dry, bare look, thought the sparrow. An utterly arid look that could not be even remotely associated with words like 'garden' or 'park'. The parched look of this portion does not even permit such words to touch the rim of the mind. It is a frontage that seems to allow no place for trees, plants, flowers, grass or creepers. But what a stark contrast over here, wondered the sparrow, amazed at the sight as it flew on, circling the rear part of the house.

Great God, what a different sight! It is a difference that instantly and sharply registers on the mind, thought the sparrow. It is so green in here, green as green can be! The sparrow thought it was like a paradise. Here, at the back of the same house is a garden so lush and luxuriously grown with a rich profusion of plants, shrubs and climbers exuding a pervasive freshness that wraps itself around the heart. The sparrow looked around. In a place like this, surely one can find some water to drink, it wondered, circling around as it peered down, searching for a comfortable and safe place to land.

Goodness, just look! There are so many sparrows around, already. Now I know why I heard the voices of other sparrows as I flew along the side of the house. And yet, for a moment, when I saw the drought-stricken look in the façade of the house, I wondered what one can ever find in a place like this. It was so misleading. Why, there's a whole army of sparrows in here. I can even recognise some of them for I have seen them in other parts of the city. But first, I must get some water to drink.

* *Nandanvan* means a celestial garden. Translated from the original Tamil "Nilam Nandavanamaanapin" by the author, published in *Kanavu*, Thiruppur, Tamil Nadu. This translation first published as "Nandanvan", *The Little Magazine: 'The Wall'*, vol. II, no. 4, New Delhi, 2001.

There it is, in that corner. How the water shines in the small trough. Some sparrows, two crows, two woodpeckers and other birds were also dipping their bills in and out of the water. All right, why don't I fly down and take a chance?

Briskly, the sparrow flew down and perched itself on the rim of the trough. Some sparrows moved aside to make room for the newcomer. The sparrow cautiously edged away when it saw a few crows. As if they noted its apprehension, the crows hurried up with their drinking and flew off.

'How did you find this place?' asked a sparrow.

'I was flying past and I felt thirsty. One look at the façade of the house and I thought, O God, it's so dry, there is not even a blade of grass! What can anyone hope to get here? So I flew on but stopped when I saw this amazingly beautiful garden at the back,' replied the new sparrow.

'Yes, it's really amazing, isn't it?' said the other sparrow. 'Even I was confused at first, when I had seen the front portion of the house. Perhaps that is everybody's first impression but now it has become a favourite haunt for all of us. We come here everyday to drink water, to hunt for food, to make love, to frolic, play around and enjoy ourselves. Come, let's feed on the grains with the others,' invited the friendly sparrow.

'My God! There is such a lot of grain scattered around,' said the new sparrow. Eagerly, it picked the grains with its beak. The friendly sparrow said, 'you call this a lot?' it chuckled. 'You've come very late today. Come early in the morning tomorrow and see for yourself how generously Thatha[1] takes fistful of grains every morning and scatters them for all of us. Come, come and see how he feeds us.'

'Which Thatha?' asked the new sparrow.

'Look, that man over there, can you see him? The one who is calmly reading a book, sitting on the easy chair? See there in the garden, under the tree? That's Thatha.'

It was a human form and the new sparrow felt a bit scared. It drew away a little, tilted its head this way and that, and then cautiously watched Grandpa. The friendly sparrow laughed aloud. 'Silly fellow, why are you afraid? It's only because of Thatha that all of us have been coming here for so many years. We come and eat our fill of grain, we find plenty of worms too in this garden, and

[1] Thatha: Grandfather

we drink clean, cool water from that trough, then take a bunch of soft grass in our beak and fly back to our nest. We caper, scamper and gambol about in these trees, in the cool shade of the plants. We also rest here. The one who created this beautiful garden is none other than this Thatha. He is always to be seen outdoors. He goes into the house may be only to sleep, in the afternoon, and at night,' explained the friendly sparrow.

The new sparrow tilted its head to one side and looked at Thatha from the corner of its eye. Then gradually, it inched its way towards the man in short, hopping flights. It gave him an appraising glance, taking in the figure that was reading quietly. His hair had turned completely grey. He looked calm and on that peaceful face, a pensive sadness had spread out like a thin film. Is this the man who works so hard on the garden? Surprising, thought the sparrow, turning to look at the garden again.

Dense, luxuriant trees, healthy plants and so many varieties of flowers! Roses, petunias, pansies, jasmines, balsam, salvia with honeybees buzzing about. Dahlias as big as a human face, hibiscus and many, many more. He is a Grandpa with green thumbs. Then why has he neglected the front of his house and let it go so bone-dry, wondered the new sparrow.

Suddenly, the back door of the house burst open with much noise. A fat woman came out. Instantly, the sparrow took wing and joined the others that were at some distance. They sat frozen as it were, watching the woman who had come out of the house.

'What's this Appa, how many times must I ask you to come in and have lunch? You just sit here and ... ,' she said to Thatha who cut her midway.

'I don't want any lunch,' he replied.

'What! For three days now you've been saying that you don't want to eat anything. You say no to lunch, dinner, and tiffin and refuse even the dilute buttermilk we make for you. Why are you so obstinate?' asked the woman. 'You son has touched your feet and begged you to eat something. And here I am, standing here and entreating you like this, neglecting all my house work.'

He did not reply.

'What are you so angry about? Have we done something wrong?' she asked. 'Look at me, your elder daughter-in-law, standing here like this, imploring you to come and eat, please come and eat. Serves me right too. All right then, let me send Mangai. She talks very sweetly, doesn't she? You might come and eat if she asks you to. Mangai, *Aiye* Mangai!' she hollered and went back into the house.

The sparrows hopped and edged closer to Grandpa. He continued to read his book quietly.

'Thatha,' said an agitated female sparrow in a shrill voice. 'How long will you starve like this? Let them be. It is rightly said that the human mind can be filthy. All they want is your house, your property and the harvest from your lands. But they don't want you. That's why they haven't even given a decent room to you in the house. Just let them be. But why must you torture yourself like this? God has given you this body, look after it well. Eat well and sleep well,' said the female sparrow.

Grandpa looked at the sparrow and smiled in reply before turning to the book that lay on his lap.

'She is absolutely right,' agreed a male sparrow. 'You should take care of your health, Thatha, shouldn't you? After all, this house, the garden, everything belongs to you; you are the Master, the King. Then live like a King! Eat well and rest Thatha, please,' pleaded the sparrow.

'Please, please! Eat something for our sake,' shrieked all the sparrows in chorus. He lifted his eyes from the book, looked at them and sighed. Hush! he warned, bringing his index finger to his lips. But the sparrows continued to shriek in protest.

'*Aiyyo*, what'll happen to Thatha if he keeps refusing food and water like this?' asked another sparrow. 'True, your sons, all three of them, are merciless opportunists. They're useless men too. Your three daughters-in-law have no decency or propriety whatsoever. Still, why should you ruin your health, hmm?' asked another sparrow.

'Why ruin your health?' clamoured the rest of the birds.

'God has given you every kind of wealth. For your *puja*, the plants shower you with a rain of jasmines, oleander and hibiscus. Then there is the flowerbed with *marukkozhundu*[2], the southern wood that spread a heady, divine perfume. You have this soft, silky spread of grass. What an enthralling garden! If anything happens

[2] These are small green leaves that have a strong fragrance. They are used along with flowers in garlands and strings of flowers and are very special to Tamil Nadu.

to you Thatha, the whole garden will die, it will perish! Won't it?' said a bird.

'Not only the garden, we'll perish too, all of us,' said a baby canary. 'Yes! If you're not around to scatter the grains for us early in the morning, Thatha, what will I do,' it cried. 'Then my mother would have to fly far afield in search of my food.'

'It was here that I found the courage to fly for the first time,' said a baby sparrow.

'And it was here that I learnt to pick at grain with my beak,' said another.

'Where will we all go?'

'Where will we all go?'

'What do you mean, where will *we*,' said an assertive voice. It was the woodpecker. It briskly flew down with another woodpecker. 'Why are you leaving us out,' it asked the sparrows and the other birds.

'Thatha is our Grandpa too,' it said.

'He is everybody's Grandpa,' said the cuckoo and the robins with their red breast as they flew in from all sides. *Caw*, *caw*, crowed the black birds in agreement, flying down from the trees. 'Please go in and have lunch Grandpa, please,' they said, hopping around him.

'Just what we needed!' said Mangai, as she came out of the house, her arms flailing about to drive the crows away.

Here is Mangai. Guests are coming for you from another city, crowed the crows. They're coming to eat, they crowed.[3]

'What are you saying, you *shanians*?[4] Are you announcing that guests are coming from another city, go get lost, out!' she said, driving them off furiously.

Along with the crows, the sparrows, robins, woodpeckers and canaries fluttered their wings in great agitation and flew off in four directions.

'Appa,' Mangai called out softly. 'Please come in for lunch. It has been three days since you ate Appa,' she pleaded.

[3] 'Guests are coming': A popular superstition in Tamil Nadu that when crows caw persistently in front of a house, they announce the arrival of unexpected guests coming for lunch or dinner.

[4] *Shanian*: *Shani* is Saturn, a planet believed to have malefic powers. It is often used as a swear word.

'Oh! Just listen to her voice, it's sooo soft and sweet,' said a sparrow perched on the compound wall. 'Indeed. But then she has always been a gifted actress, isn't it,' said the crow, sitting on a branch above the sparrow.

'She can speak very nicely, in a low, well-bred tone,' said the woodpecker. 'She is well-versed in the art of fooling people. But behind Thatha's back, she is up to so many scheming plans with her husband.'

'Yes,' said the crow. At night, along with her husband—that's Grandpa's second son—she hatches her game plans, standing beside this window here. I've often heard her from the branch of the tree, shaking myself out of half-sleep. Once I hear her, I lose my sleep completely,' said the crow.

'Why, what do they talk about, the husband and wife?' asked the new sparrow, sitting on the gate.

'Ah, what do you know about their atrocities,' said the crow. 'You're new around here. It's such a very big house with large rooms, a hallway, an open courtyard, a front portion, a rear portion, this garden here,' continued the crow. 'Besides all these, Grandpa has cultivable fields out there. "Just calculate the worth of this property," Mangai would say. "Take in all the assets and ask your father to divide it into three equal measures for all three of us" she would insist, but all in a soft voice,' informed the crow.

'Really? What happened then?' asked the cuckoo.

'Once her husband said, however much I try, my eldest brother refuses to agree. "I'm the eldest, so I have a right to get the largest share of the property," he argues.' The crow then explained how the eldest son wanted the front portion of the house, the hallway, all the bedrooms on one side of the house and this garden. He had a long list!

'*Aiyyo Morakattai*, the garden indeed!' said the woodpecker, striking its sharp beak against itself. 'Wants the garden, does he? Humph! Has he ever touched the soil of this earth even once with his hands? Has he ever watered the garden?' it fumed.

'Has he ever fed us grain?' said the baby sparrow, its voice ringing out loud and clear.

'You've said it,' said the crow appreciatively.

'And then? What happened next?' asked the birds.

'Then there was a big fight around midnight,' said the crow. 'It woke up all the baby crows in my nest.'

'What happened, tell, tell,' said the birds.

'The youngest of the three sons and his wife quarrelled with this woman Mangai and her husband. "What a stupid way of dividing the house," they said. "Give one room in the front portion to one son, and another room on the side to another son? Sheer foolishness. We warn you! My wife and I are educated people. You can't fool us. Let the whole house be sold, and then each of us will take a third of the money." "Our Anna[5] will not agree to that," said the second blighter. "I'll see how he refuses," challenged the youngest son, hotly. At the point, the lights were switched off in the room. But long after that, I could still hear them whispering among themselves. I could not hear clearly though, so I don't know exactly what they were saying,' explained the crow.

'How very atrocious,' the sparrows chorused together. 'Look at the way they've driven Thatha out of his own house, the vultures!'

'The vultures!'

'The vultures!'

All the birds shrieked aloud together but the voice of the new sparrow resonated clearly.

'Hell! What's going on here?' said Madhavi, the third and the youngest daughter-in-law, who now came out of the house. She tried to drive the birds away.

'Daddy, please come and have lunch. It's getting so late. Come Daddy, please,' she pleaded with Thatha.

'You go ahead with lunch,' said Thatha, without raising his head.

'How can that be? Impossible! We won't eat without you. I'm so hungry, come Daddy, please,' said Madhavi.

'I'm not hungry,' said Thatha.

'Oh please don't say so Daddy. Think of your health. Pease come in,' begged Madhavi, her voice soft.

'Ah, just look at the way she is fawning on him, please come Daddy, please,' mimicked the cuckoo, musically.

'I'm not hungry,' repeated Thatha.

'But you haven't eaten anything for three days!' protested Mangai. 'Please forgive us Daddy, if we've done anything wrong,' she added.

Please forgive, ha, ha, caw, caw, said the crows.

[5] Anna: Elder brother

Please forgive, ha, ha.

Caw, caw, caw.

'Hey, shut up all of you!' shouted Madhavi, waving her handkerchief in the direction of the crows. '*Che*! What a perfect nuisance they are,' she said, waving her arms to drive them off. The crows and the birds scattered in all directions, only to return again to perch on the compound wall, on the gate, and on the branches of the trees. Some sat on the grass, at a little distance, and some others sat around the trough of water. They carried on their conversation.

'Look here Daddy, the way you're sitting here and throwing a tantrum like a child, it's not nice. Not nice at all,' said Madhavi. 'Now please hurry up and come for lunch. We've to go out somewhere.'

'It's all of you who drove Thatha out of the house,' said the rose, with a sigh.

'It's all of you who didn't even give him a decent room of his own to rest in peace. You didn't give him as much as a corner,' said the birds.

'Yes,' agreed the phlox, 'it's you who drove him out, you!'

'You drove him out!'

'You drove him out!' said the jasmines, the hibiscus, salvia and the lilies, swinging and swaying in the breeze.

'Hereafter, this garden will be Thatha's home. The earth is his floor and the sky above, his roof,' said the dahlia. 'He won't go into the house any more, not ever.'

'He won't go in.'

'He won't go in,' cried the birds in chorus.

Madhavi glared at Thatha, shrugged her shoulders and went into the house. Mangai followed her. Thatha lifted his head from the book and watched them retreating. Then he turned towards the birds, the honeybees, the plants and the trees and winked at them secretly, with a laugh.

The birds left their perches and hopped up to Thatha. *Keech, keech*, they talked amongst themselves.

The back door opened again. Now Karthikeyan, Thatha's second son and Madhivelan, his youngest son, came out of the house.

'What's all this Appa?' asked Madhivelan.

'I should be asking you,' smiled Thatha. 'All I said was that I'm not hungry and don't want lunch. Why are you all making such a fuss about it?' he asked.

'What else can we do? Did you think that we would just carry on with our lives?' said Karthikeyan.

'Perhaps Anna would be able to do that, but we can't,' said Madhivelan. 'Madhavi, Mangai *Aanni*[6] and elder *Aanni* came here to plead with you. They begged you to come. But you're so stubborn. If you stay outdoors all day, what'll happen to your health? Please come indoors, Appa,' said Madhivelan.

'*This* is his house, the garden is his house. This is *Nandanvan*. Thatha will stay here, he'll stay here,' cried the birds in a rich chorus.

'Hey, quiet, I say quiet! What an utter nuisance they are,' exclaimed Karthikeyan, taking up the small towel that he had flung over his shoulder. He waved it in the air to drive away the birds. Only a few birds moved away. Many of them stayed on and shouted. Many of them stayed on and shouted, 'He is our Thatha, this is where he'll stay. This is where he'll stay.'

'*Che*! Just look at them! Such a brazen lot, they don't even move,' said Madhivelan, picking up a cane. He swung it around.

'It's all because of Appa, he has spoilt them silly,' said Karthikeyan. 'He brings sack after sack of grain from the house and feeds them generously every morning. He doesn't seem to have anything else to do.'

'No wonder then, a whole army of birds invade us here and now they behave as if the place belongs to them, *shanians*!' cursed Madhivelan.

Thatha got up from the easy chair.

'Rest awhile Thatha,' said the delicate, dulcet-voiced cuckoo.

'See you tomorrow,' said the honeybee.

'See you tomorrow,' joined in the other honeybees, whirling round and round.

'Come Appa,' said the two sons. '*Appada*,' they said, heaving a sigh of relief. Thatha walked slowly behind them. He turned back once to look at the birds.

'Don't take it to heart,' said Thatha. 'Don't take to heart the way the two of them talked. Let them be. Tomorrow morning, I'll give you plenty of grain, much more than usual. All of you come and eat your fill, all right?' The birds jumped about merrily and cried with joy.

Madhivelan jerked around to look.

[6] *Aanni*: Sister-in-law; elder brother's wife.

'What did you say Appa?' he asked.

'Nothing,' said Thatha.

'But I heard you say something now,' he said.

'Who, me?' said Thatha, shaking his head with a smile. Seeing the mischief gleaming in his father's eyes, the son stood still for a moment, confused.

The next moment, a burst of laughter rippled up from the birds. Madhivelan looked even more bewildered than before. Thatha winked at the birds, nodded and smiled once more and went into the house.

When the ten sparrows reached the house, the new sparrow was already sitting on the gate. It was hopping around and shrieking loudly, looking very agitated.

'Ah, you've come much before any of us today, haven't you,' said one female sparrow in a friendly banter. 'Want to grab a lot of grain? Is that why you're here before us, you the proverbial early bird?' The other sparrows also joined in. 'Come, come, what's the use of sitting in front of the house? Grandpa will give us grains only in the rear portion of the house,' said another sparrow.

'No, no!' The new sparrow screamed. 'Thatha hasn't come out today.'

'What! He hasn't come out yet? That can never be. There's not a single day when he ... ' the sparrow was about to continue when it noticed something.

'What has happened? Why is there such a big crowd in front of the house,' asked a sparrow.

'Who are these people? They look like relations and friends. But all of them look so dispirited. Why?' asked another sparrow.

'Come, let's fly over to the back of the house and ask the crows that live on the trees,' suggested the female sparrow. 'Only they get to know the news of the house,' she added.

In the back garden there were already a few sparrows, crows and other birds that were screaming and shrieking amongst themselves. The backdoor was firmly shut.

All the birds gathered together and flew again towards the façade of the house. They sat down in different places and watched the crowd milling about. There were two old women amongst them.

One of them wailed, '*Aiyyo*, your father has let you all down, *hai, hai.*'

'Oh God, is Thatha dea ... ?' The birds flapped their wings and flew up in great alarm. They circled round and round and flew down again to take their positions in different places in front of the house. A few people from the crowd shooed them off. 'Oosh, oosh!' they said, trying to drive them away. The birds flew up for a moment but returned resolutely, each to his/her perch.

From the open front door, four people came out bearing Thatha's body. They laid him on a bier on the ground. He looked as if he was sleeping. Around his neck were garlands of flowers. A few people wrapped some more heavy garlands around his neck. They also placed flowers around him.

'Oh God, Thatha has gone! He has left us orphaned,' cried the cuckoo.

'He has left us orphaned.'

'He has left us orphaned,' cried the birds.

'I had a hunch all along,' said the female sparrow. 'Especially when I saw the way Thatha gave up food and water ... '

The birds lines up in the front portion of the house. They watched with dismay the still form of Thatha that seemed to be sleeping serenely. They turned their heads this way and that, helpless and completely at a loss. The old woman stood weeping. The other old woman looked at Thatha and cried out, '*Enda*[7], why didn't you take me with you?'

Some loud noises could be heard from within the house. A priest stood near the door.

'*Thambi*[8], I've been asking you to come out. It's getting late. We'll have to start the obsequies. Come along now,' he urged.

'No, I won't' came the refusal from within, loudly.

'*Che, che*! You are the eldest son, how can you talk like this?' asked the priest.

'Oh, I'm the eldest son when it comes to the obsequies. But when my younger brothers fight with me over the property without any respect for my status as the eldest, is it a nice thing then?' he retorted.

[7] This expression is similar to the one in Hindi, 'kyon re?'—an expression used for someone younger or someone inferior in status.

[8] *Thambi*: Younger brother; an informal way of addressing a younger man.

'It's you who blew it up into a fight, yes!' hissed Madhivelan. 'Why didn't you agree to an equal share of the property with grace and dignity?'

'What! Getting audacious, are you?' said the eldest brother, raising his hand. Two people firmly held him back.

'For God's sake, this is not the time to talk about such things. It's very ugly. Begin the obsequies with *bhakti* and devotion. Give a send-off to your father with respect,' pleaded the relations and friends who had assembled there.

But the fight got more violent. Some people from the crowd took the side of the eldest son while others argued on behalf of the younger sons.

The old woman who had wailed some time back flew at the brothers angrily: 'This is disgusting. Aren't you all ashamed of yourselves? You're grown men but you're not even fit to do the last rites for your father. *Karmam, karmam*![9] Come on, hurry. It's your duty and you *have to do* the rites for your father. Let his soul rest in peace.'

'It's good that the elderly man passed away without having to see all this fight,' remarked a friend. The priest was furious with the three brothers. He lashed out at them: 'Are you coming now or shall I complete the obsequies along with the other priests here?' he demanded. 'What else can one do if there are arrogant, useless sons like you? Beware of one thing, the *Veda*s permit us, the priests, to perform the rites on our own. We can very well do without you!' he roared.

Now all the three brothers attacked the priest. Another fight erupted. The five priests who had come to perform the obsequies hotly argued with the brothers inside the house while the relations struggled to handle the chaos.

On the front porch, right at the centre lay Thatha as though he was asleep. No one seemed to pay attention to him. One by one, the birds, the sparrows, crows, woodpeckers, cuckoos and canaries came down from their perch and surrounded the man's body.

'Can we do it?' asked the cuckoo.

'Why ever not,' replied the crow. 'If all of us set our mind to it, we can surely do it.'

'Suppose these men see us when we lift him?' asked the sparrow.

[9] Said in exasperation, 'the result of some bad karma'.

'We'll simply stab them with our beaks, won't we,' challenged the woodpecker.

'We'll peck them with our beaks and wound them till we draw blood,' said another woodpecker, sharpening its beak.

'Don't worry about that,' said the sparrow. 'We'll simply flutter our wings over everybody and frighten them. That'll surely drive them off. All right then, come on everybody!'

'Come Thatha, let's fly. Come Sir!'

The birds surrounded his body.

'Uh ... uh ... it's heavy, the body.'

'Naturally.'

'Let's all sing together and lift him. Then we'll get the strength and the courage for our work. Come on everybody, sing!'

'He is not heavy, *Ailesa*![10]

'We'll lift him up, *Ailesa*!'

'Let's do it fast, *Ailesa*!'

'Let's go up, *Ailesa*!'

'Come on Thatha, *Ailesa*!'

'Let's go flying, *Ailesa*!'

'Just go to hell, all of you! There is no respect whatever for tradition and obsequies in this wretched house,' said the Head priest to his fellow priests. 'Anyway, let's do our duty. Why should *we* commit the sin of not performing the rites properly?' he said angrily, coming out of the front door along with the other priests.

'Hey, who is there?' he shouted as the servants came running to answer him.

'*Chami*?'[11]

'I say, what is this farce going on here? Who moved away the body of the elderly person without my permission?' roared the priest. 'What a place! Even the servants in this household are atrocious.'

[10] *Ailesa*: A folk song sung by workers and labourers whenever they have to manually lift inhumanly heavy loads. They join together to sing songs, with each line ending in '*ailesa*' and they do so with the strong belief that the song, sung collectively, gives them extraordinary strength. Invariably, the workers do manage to finish their work with the help of this song on their lips.

[11] *Chami*: A servant's respectful form of addressing a master.

'I don't know *Chami*,' said the servant.

'What do you mean you don't know? Where's the body of the elder man? You were here all the time, weren't you?'

'I don't know *Chami*.'

'Don't talk so stupidly. And don't just stand there. Go on, both of you and carry the body back to this place' ordered the priest.

'It's not there, Sir,' said the other servant.

'What do you mean, it's not there?'

'The body of the elderly ma ... '

'You lunatic, what are you blabbering? Where can a dead body go?'

They searched for Thatha's body. They looked for him everywhere as they scurried around but Thatha was nowhere to be found. Totally flustered, they went inside the house and checked, then they came out and went into the garden and searched for him all around the house. Frightened beyond belief, they kept searching.

But Thatha was not there. Nor was there a single sparrow or bird.

Ejamaanar*

'Nine, ten, eleven, twelve ... ah ... that's it, Amma. That's about all. There are altogether twelve coconuts,' said Muniyandi, filling them into a sack.

'Okay. Here, take this,' Gowri gave him ten rupees and reclined on a chaise longue.

'Next Sunday I'll pick up all the coconuts from the other tree, over there.'

'Yes, do that,' said Gowri.

'Look how the jackfruit and coconuts grow abundantly in our house, Amma! Please ask the gardener to sprinkle rock salt around the coconut trees generously. Only then will the coconuts will ripen nicely, oozing with a lot of sweet coconut water within,' said Muniyandi. Gowri noticed how even as he spoke about coconut water, he seemed to salivate hungrily. She burst out laughing.

'All right Amma, let me go now,' said Muniyandi. He shook out the cloth he wound around his head a couple of times but continued standing there.

'Amma, can you give me a couple of coconuts? My wife is pregnant. She has morning sickness. Doesn't eat her food properly, but she craves for coconuts,' Muniyandi grinned.

'That's why you've taken care to stash away two coconuts beforehand,' replied Gowri calmly.

* Translated from the original Tamil "Ejamaanar" by the author, published in *Kanavu*, Thiruppur, Tamil Nadu. This translation first published as 'The Husband', *The Little Magazine: 'In Other Words'*, vol. v, nos 2 & 3, New Delhi, 2004. *Ejamaanar* means 'manager' or boss in Kannada and implies husbandry in the sense of management of resources. The same word is also used to refer to a husband.

'*Aiyyo!* Why do you suspect me like that, Amma? Am I not your faithful servant?' he faltered. Bending down, he took the two coconuts and said, 'They just rolled in like that on their own, Amma, Heh, heh ... '

'Indeed they did. Because the coconuts know, don't they, how to roll on one side obediently and hide themselves?' said Gowri.

'Let me go Amma,' said Muniyandi. As he was about to put the two coconuts inside the sack, Gowri said, 'No, take them with you. Break the nuts and give them to your wife. What did you think Muniyandi, that if you ask me I won't give you coconuts?' said Gowri.

'No, no Amma. You'll never do that. Only I felt shy about asking. Okay Amma. Let me go now.'

'Where are you going? Finish your work before you go. Keep the sack of coconuts in the store room. Wait. I'll ask Iyer to open the door for you,' said Gowri.

'Iyer! Iyerei!' she called out. She took out a key from the bunch that was dangling from her waist and went inside the house.

All along, Rajiv and Sheila were watching with much amusement the exchange between their Gowri Patti[1] and Muniyandi. Now they followed their grandmother inside the house.

'Grandma, you're great! Nobody can fool you,' said Rajiv. Gowri winked at him in reply and went in search of Iyer, the cook.

Iyer unlocked the door of the store room. Muniyandi went in and kept the sack of coconuts in a corner. It was a large store room. All the three walls were covered by wide shelves within doors that were fitted with fine wire netting. Stored on one side was rice, black gram, varieties of pulses and grain. On the shelves of the other two walls were stored all the things required for the daily cooking, along with the various snacks that were prepared at home. There were fruits as well, such as banana, mangoes and jackfruit. Rajiv and Sheila breathed in the wholesome, collective smell of the things. They loved the ambience of the store room which was the size of a large bed room and they loved its distinctive smell. Whenever the room was unlocked, they would rush in with their grandmother

[1] Patti: Grandmother

and come out with *murukku*[2], or *mysore pak*[3] or some other snack in their hands. All the things harvested from the farms owned by the family were also stored in this room. Thimmappa Gowda, the farmer who looked after the family's farm in Mysore, would come all the way down to Bangalore after harvest time with two of his men.

They would weigh the rice, paddy and grain on a large balance in front of Gowri and stack them up in the store room. Thimmappa Gowda always personally supervised this work for Gowri.

The meals for Gowda and his men would be arranged for by Gowri. Millet flour thickened into a kind of pudding, to be eaten with eggplant in a spicy gravy, then rice, lentil, coconut chutney, a vegetable dish made with sponge gourd, *appalam* (a thin dried crispy thing prepared with black gram), then buttermilk and a sweet. Gowri would give them a complete meal without a single item missing in the menu. Thimmappa Gowda would wolf it down with great pleasure and satisfaction.

Actually, Gowda was here a while ago. He left for Mysore only two days back. With folded hands, he invited Gowri with utmost respect to visit her farm once and see for herself how everything was flourishing under his supervision.

'*Ammauvre*, you and your Ejamaanar, your husband, haven't visited your farm for a very long time now. Please drive up in your car and come at least once. You can then see for yourself, how fresh and abundant your farm is. I'm a poor man, of course. But I request you to visit me too in my humble little hut,' he said, all humility.

'Poor!' Gowri silently laughed within herself. 'Our Thimmappa Gowda has done very well for himself. He has built a nice, comfortable two-storied house with a lovely red shingled roofing that looks so stylish! He has a good lifestyle too. He always cleverly takes away one-fourth of our harvest for himself, then reports to me with a straight face as if nothing has happened. Like butter wouldn't melt in his mouth!'

[2] *Murukku*: A salty, fried snack prepared with rice dough.

[3] *Mysore pak*: A sweet prepared with the flour of Bengal gram, sugar and clarified butter or *ghee*.

'We'll certainly come, Gowdare,' she said aloud, smiling.

'All right Madam. Allow me to take leave of you now. If there is anything else that is worthy of being done by this poor man, do tell me. I'll be only too happy to serve you. Shall I take leave of my *ejamaanar* too?' he asked.

'Rajiv,' Gowri called out to her grandson. 'Ask Thatha[4] if we can bring Gowda over to his room.'

Rajiv went to his grandfather's room. He returned and said, 'Come, come this way,' and led Thimmappa Gowda towards his grandfather's room.

'Hey Bhora, Bhasava, come on. Come quickly,' Thimmappa called out to his two men. 'Let's pay our respects to the *ejamaanar* and then leave for our village,' said Gowda.

Bhora came over and stood beside Gowda.

'Where's Bhasava?' asked Gowda.

'I'll bring him right away,' said Bhora and rushed to the garden. He found Bhasava squatting, smoking a *beedi*[5]. 'Hey Bhasava, come on in, we have to pay our respects to the *ejamaanar*,' shouted Bhora.

'What's this sudden 'paying of respects'? We've slogged for our *ejamaanar* the whole day and he broke our backs taking work out of us,' said Bhasava and continued smoking.

'Stupid fellow, I don't mean *our ejamaanar*, Thimmappa Gowda. I mean the *ejamaanar* of this house, the boss of our boss. We've to pay respects to him and then leave for our village. Come, hurry up, you've an appropriate name. When you sit down, you become as immovable as a Bhasava. I say get up!' urged Bhora.

'Oh,' said Bhasava, extinguishing his *beedi* by rubbing the stub on the mud. He got up and the two of them went inside the house to join Thimmappa Gowda. Ever the complaisant 'worker' for his boss, Gowda said to Gowri with extreme comity: 'Amma, please allow us to see your *ejamaanar*. We'll receive his blessings and head for our village.' Gowri ushered them to her husband's room.

'By all means, Gowdare. Come in. He is in his room,' said Gowri.

[4] Thatha: Grandfather

[5] *Beedi*: Tobacco rolled up in leaf for smoking. An inexpensive 'cigarette'.

Gowri was amused about the whole thing. She got married when she was very young. She left Madurai of Tamil Nadu and moved over to the state of Karnataka with her husband. With that, the Tamil term '*Ahatthukkarar*' which meant husband, changed to '*Ejamaanar*', and that meant husband in Kannada. It also meant boss. She would often laugh at the layered semantics.

'How're you doing Gowda? Is everybody fine at home? What about your wife and children?' enquired Srinivasan, as he reclined on a chaise longue.

'Everybody is fine with your blessings, *ejamaanare*,' said Gowda. Turning to his men, he said, 'Hey you boys, come and pay your obeisance,' he commanded.

Bhasava bent low as he muttered, 'My respects to you, *ejamaanare*.'

Bhora followed with a deep bow, 'My respects to you, *ejamaanare*'.

'Hmm. How did the harvest turn out this time?' enquired Srinivasan.

'Splendidly, Sir. You can ask Madam about it. I got everything weighed properly in the balance and have stacked them up inside,' replied Gowda.

'All right.'

'So, by your leave *ejamaanare*, shall we return to our village? We have to catch a bus,' said Gowda.

'Oh yes. You get going. Wish you all a safe journey,' said Srinivasan.

After sending them off, Gowri went to the central hall, a large room that was so spacious that it was like four bedrooms put together. On one corner dangled a swing with a wide and smooth teak wood plank. Beyond that was a settee. She stretched herself on this settee and closed her eyes. She did not sleep though. She was lying down, quietly listening to all the sounds around her. Her daughter Maitreyi (the mother of Sheila and Rajiv) along with her cousin Kamala and her husband had gone out to visit relatives.

The house had fallen silent without them. Sheila and Rajiv went round and round the hallway on their roller skates. With the wheeled skates firmly strapped on to their feet, they would run to and fro, agile on their rounds.

On the ceiling above the hallway was a very large skylight, like an octagonal window. Sunlight filtered through the pale blue tinted glass panes of the 'window', bathing them with a cool effulgence. Some of the panes were open and a few doves were perched over the wire netting, making clucking sounds. Sheila glanced up at them and resumed her roller skating. Rajiv loved the ambience of this hall, with his grandmother resting in a corner. Gowri tossed around in the settee a couple of times and then sat up. Instantly Iyer, the cook, made some coffee for her and served it in a tumbler within a *davara*[6]. Sipping her coffee, Gowri enjoyed the scene of her grandson and granddaughter going round and round on their roller skates.

'Bravo! Bravo!' she cheered as they skated up and down the hall.

'You too join us, Grandma. I'll teach you,' said Rajiv, ripping ahead.

'In that case, ask your elder sister to buy me a pair of jeans just like the one she is wearing,' smiled Gowri.

'Very good, Grandma. I'll buy you jeans, come on,' said Sheila as she whizzed past on her rounds.

'Oh no, Patti! Not jeans,' objected Rajiv. 'You look so good in this nine yard saree, it looks like a Bharatanatyam costume on you,' he added, now encircling his grandmother on his rounds, like a *parikrama*.[7]

Maitreyi returned from her visits. 'Hey, what's all this? Is this hall a place for roller skating?' she scolded her children. Kamala and Venkatesh followed her and settled down to narrate all the news from the family of their relations. All three of them were served coffee by Iyer.

'Amma.'

The voice came from the door opening into the backyard. Gowri turned around to look. It was Govindaraju Reddi.

'Reddi? What's the matter?' enquired Gowri. Reddi usually showed up only in the early morning hours. He removed the cloth

[6] In a traditional household in Tamil Nadu or elsewhere, coffee is served in a steel tumbler. Since it would be hot to touch, the tumbler is placed in a small steel container called *davara*. It was a normal practice to serve coffee in cups and saucers mainly to people considered as 'outsiders' and that includes people who belong to other castes.

[7] *Parikrama* is 'circumambulation', i.e., walking or going around an object of worship in reverence, like the devotees do *parikrama* around the Golden Temple in Amritsar and all the temples in the South.

that was wound around his head, gathered it in his hand and quietly smiled at Gowri.

'Yes Reddi, what's the matter?' she asked again.

'Uh ... uh ... our Vishalakshi gave birth to a calf this morning, Amma,' he said with a wide grin.

'Aha! And you were hesitating so much to give me this good news?' said Gowri, getting up.

'Ah a calf, a calf!' said Sheila and Rajiv excitedly. Gowri went past them to reach an inner room and returned with Rs 15 in her hand. She gave it to Reddi.

'Here you are Reddi. Take this and buy some fresh green grass and sugar cane for Vishalakshi. Keep vermillion on the brow of the little calf,' said Gowri.

'I'll definitely do so Amma, for it's a female,' said Reddi.

'Is that so? My greetings to the calf.'

Reddi received the money from her and stood lingering.

'Amma,' he drawled.

'Tell me, Reddi. Is there some problem?'

'Nothing of the sort Amma.'

'Then what are you fighting shy of?'

'Uh ... that is ... uh ... the new calf looks beautiful.'

'All by the grace and compassion of the Goddess,' said Gowri.

'We want to give it a good name,' said Reddi.

'Fine. Let's name it then,' said Gowri.

'That's why ... uh ... that is, if you don't take it amiss ... at home, they sent me to ask you if we can keep your name for the calf,' said Reddi, his head bent, eyes on the ground.

'What nonsense!' The daughter Maitreyi was about to pounce on him.

'*Che!* How do you have the audacity to ask something like that?' said Venkatesh, his face all red. 'How very brazen, I must say!'

Taking aback the commotion that he caused, Reddi turned to go, fear and embarrassment writ large on his face.

'Yes indeed, how brazen you must be to ask our mother if you can keep *her* name for the calf of a cow,' shouted Kamala.

'Sshh! Quiet everybody,' said Gowri. 'Reddi, by all means you can keep my name for the new calf. Do it on a good, auspicious day,' she said and sent him off.

'How crazy! One can understand an illiterate man like him, making a preposterous request like that. He doesn't know any better, but Amma, why do *you* have to agree?' said a furious Maitreyi.

'I say keep quiet, all of you. It's the calf of our very own Vishalakshi. Let it frolic about and run around carrying my name, what's wrong with that? How eagerly Reddi asked,' said Gowri, settling down on the swing.

Sheila always found her grandmother amazing. She would share her impressions with her friends in college. Sheila's mother, her aunt Chitthi, that is her mother's younger sister, and the various visiting women relations—everybody would gather around her grandmother Gowri in that central hall and whisper about their everyday grievances—family politics, complaints about a husband and so on. How come grandmother Gowri could handle the entire responsibility of running this big extended family, work tirelessly round the clock and still remain cheerful with a smile on her fresh face? Gowri's husband Srinivasan does not even converse with her much and generally does not seem to put two words together. Sarada, the Kannadiga woman next door, often joined in these 'whispered meetings'. 'My *ejamaanar* suddenly stopped talking to me. It has been years now,' she wailed one day. Sheila happened to overhear her and was quick to point out, 'But Aunty, I saw Uncle talk to you only yesterday, in your garden?' Everybody including Gowri burst out laughing.

'Sheila, what are you doing here amongst elderly people?' scolded her mother Maitreyi.

The following day in college, Sheila recounted the incident to the girls. Only then did she come to know of the implication behind the expression of 'not talking' when it referred to a husband and wife. It was a euphemistic way of saying that a husband and wife 'don't sleep with each other any more.'

'Is *that* the real meaning?' asked Sheila, very surprised. 'Even so, what's the big deal if they don't sleep together? For instance, my grandmother and grandfather sleep in their separate rooms. And if one must mention talking in the usual sense, they don't seem to talk to each other much. Still, my grandmother ...'

'Oh go on,' interrupted her friend. 'Not everybody can be like your grandmother, can they? Your grand Mom is like a *Rani*, the Queen of Mysore.' Sheila felt proud of her grandmother. Yes indeed, grandmother is such a well-groomed person. Her body glows like a burnished bronze sculpture washed with the juice of tamarind. Twice a week Chelli, the maid, massages grandmother's arms and legs, snapping her toes and fingers, then she massages her body and helps her with her bath. Once the bath is over, Gowri has her lunch and lies down on the wide swing with her eyes closed, all lost in a deep slumber. How she sleeps, like a baby. On waking up, Gowri again swings into action briskly, attending to all the work at home. Come evening, she would sit on the swing and rock gently to and fro, listening to the women who whined as usual. She heard them out, each one of the women in the 'whispering session'. There was Shanta too, Maitreyi's sister-in-law, that is, the wife of her brother-in-law. There was Shanta's younger sister Bhavani and many others who congregated to pour their heart out—'my son isn't doing well in his studies', 'my daughter is getting old but we're unable to find a proper boy for her marriage', 'my husband is a short tempered dipsomaniac who dissolves all the money in drinks', etc. Gowri would hear them out patiently though her face would occasionally betray her boredom with the whole lot of them. Still, she would offer her counsel according to how she felt about the issues. One day, she told a woman, 'Look, you're not smart enough to be frugal with whatever money you get for household expenses. Save money but learn to be clever and hide the money somewhere, for your own use.' To the other, she said, 'If your husband returns home drunk, just don't open the door for him. Let him stay out.'

'My *ejamaanar* goes to Thumkur very often on the pretext of some 'work' and stays back for days on end. Some people ask me if he has a woman there,' Sarada the Kannadiga woman, said one day, holding back her tears.

'If that's true Sarada,' replied Gowri in fluent Kannada, 'say good riddance to your *ejamaanar* and then you take over your family as the '*ejamaanar*', the manager of your household. Why do you need an *ejamaanar*?' Although she was addressing each of them on a one-on-one basis, beyond all that she said, a certain remoteness would steal into her eyes. Aloof and away from it all, her eyes took on an unapproachable distance as if Gowri was there and yet not there. Gently moving to and fro on the swing, Gowri herself became the swing or the swing became Gowri.

Members of the family seldom sat on the swing, even the senior ones. But one of the few rare elders who actually claimed his place on the swing is Sambasivan. To Sheila and Rajiv he was 'Sambasivan Mama', a distant relation of the family but a close friend. He had a farm in Coorg on which he cultivated cardamom, cashew nuts and various things, but he had his house in Shimoga. He visited Gowri whenever he came to Bangalore. He would first talk to her husband Srinivasan in his room at the front portion of the house, and then move over to the central hall to talk to Gowri. Settling himself comfortably on the swing, sipping the steaming tumbler of coffee served by Iyer, Sambasivan would move on the swing slowly as he described the Nilgiri hills, the waterfall in Jog cascading down and so on. He always talked about rivers, waterfalls and rain. How they rippled through his words when he spoke. He could hold forth on Thalaikaaveri, the source of the river Kaaveri with Gowri as a rapt listener, reclining on a settee at some distance. Sheila never failed to notice how during these moments, her grandmother Gowri's face glowed with an extraordinary radiance. For one whose body was steeled and hardened by her day-long work, supervising a retinue of domestic helps and farm hands for that large household, Sheila noticed how Gowri could now unwind completely on the settee, her body totally relaxed. Along with Rajiv, Sheila would also join in the conversation with Sambasivan. Hearing him speak was always interesting, peppered as it was with details about horses, tigers, lions and other wild life in the forest, and they absorbed all the information that came their way about game sanctuaries and hunting trips. So engrossed were Sheila and Rajiv in the descriptions he narrated that they often lost count of the hours ticking. The four of them—Sambasivan, Gowri, Sheila and Rajiv—seemed to be within such a charmed, inviolable circle that nobody in the family ever ventured to disturb them.

A volume of Bhagavad *Gita*[8] was spread out on the bed with the pages open. Gowri sat on the bed reciting some lines from the *Gita* in a low voice. Sheila went to her room and took in the scene. How

[8] Bhagavad *Gita*: The philosophic discourse of Lord Krishna to Arjun in the battlefield of Kurukshetra.

very clean—squeaky clean—my grandmother is, she thought. How does she maintain herself like this? Just look at her hands, nails, her feet, her skin, hair and the saree that she wears in the style of a nine yards *madisaru*.[9] Sheila sat down quietly beside Gowri on the bed. The recitation stopped.

'What's the matter my dear? Not feeling sleepy?' enquired Gowri.

'I'm feeling very, very sleepy Patti. That's why I thought I would walk around a bit. Tomorrow is the final day of my exams,' declared Sheila.

'I know, I know. Go and study then. After the exam tomorrow you can have a blast. You can go to Lal Bagh, Cubbon Park, you can see films too, right?'

'Yes Patti, my friends and I've drawn out a long list of things to do. By the way Patti ... ah ... how do you maintain and preserve yourself so well?' asked Sheila.

'Ah ... nothing to it, really.'

'For my Amma, Chitthi, my aunt and our next door neighbour, it's problems, problems all the time. They've already lost a lot of hair, their faces are all wrinkled and they look so tired even after attending to some small work. God! They've become so ... ' Sheila sighed.

'Oh let them be, my child,' said Gowri. 'At least you be intelligent and smart. You've seen how many times I have told them not to waste their time whining and lamenting about the knotty situations in life? They're wasting an entire lifetime, and they go on and on as if this character called 'husband' or '*ejamaanar*' or whatever is almost like an eclipse that can darken the very face of the sun! Imagine. They allow themselves to talk like this endlessly and now it has become a full time occupation, like it's almost a career! That there is a world beyond this very imperfect character called an '*ejamaanar*' is something they don't realise, or don't want to realise. What can I do?'

'Patti?'

[9] Senior Brahmin women wear a saree of 9 yards (as against the standard 6 yards worn by women); it is also draped in a different style, with the *pallav* coming over the right shoulder. Slim and tall women could carry this style well, so Gowri's grandson remarks that she looks like a dancer.

'Tell me, child,' said Gowri as Sheila kept looking at her grandmother under the glow of the one solitary light in the room, in the quiet of the night.

'Shall I tell you something? Will you get angry, Patti?'

'Of course not. What is it? Just speak out whatever you want to say, my child.'

Sheila got up.

'Patti, are you going to continue reciting the *Gita*? It's eleven. It's time to get some sleep. Good night. Shall I switch off the light, Patti?' asked Sheila, moving over to the doorway of the bedroom.

'You can switch it off. But you gave me a big preamble about wanting to say something?' asked Gowri.

'Oh, it's nothing very important, Patti. I just wanted to say that for my Amma, Chitthi my aunt and the likes of our neighbour Sarada ... ' said Sheila and switched off the light. The room was plunged in darkness.

'Yes, what about them ... ?' asked Gowri, peering at the figure of her granddaughter silhouetted on the doorway by the light outside the room.

'I only wanted to say that these women didn't get a Sambasivan Mama in their life, that's all,' said Sheila.

'Why, you naughty girl!' said Gowri from the bed.

'Good night Patti.'

'Good night, precious. Someday you too search for a Sambasivan for yourself.'

The unfaltering reply of her grandmother reached Sheila's ears clearly, through the darkness.

Please, Dear God*

It was not just his aching feet that bothered him. When he stood in the same spot for some time, his ankles too invariably began to itch. They started itching now, furiously. One ankle after the other. He was forced to scratch the right ankle with his left toe, then shift his feet to scratch the left ankle with the help of his right toe. He blamed it all on the dust and dirt on the floor. That is what sets off this itching, he mused, shuffling his feet restlessly. He continued standing there in stoic silence, staring through the glass pane of the large, single panel of the window at the motionless figure under the sheets.

She is so still, is she dea ... ? he wondered, biting his lip. His ankles began to itch annoyingly. He felt hunger gnawing at his insides. How long can I ignore my hunger, my fatigue and discomfort and keep standing here, staring stupidly through the glass pane of this window? You're not going to get up from that bed and fix a nice dinner for the five of us, are you? No, you're not going to set the table and serve me some freshly cooked food. Not you. Chandra, can you imagine how difficult it is for me to stand like this day in and day out as you lie there, luxuriating in your coma? What am I supposed to do? Wait hopelessly for the day when you might pull out of that coma, or perhaps wait patiently for you to die? If you must die, you're taking your own sweet time about it, while here I am, shifting from one aching foot to the other, from left to right, right to left, all the while staring at you through this glass pane like a dumb fool, as if something is going to happen very soon. But

* Translated from the original Tamil "Thottathum Vittadhum" by the author, published in *Kanaiyazhi*, Madras. This translation first published in *Parijata and Other Stories*, Delhi: National Publishing House, Delhi, 1992.

nothing ever happens. Nothing whatsoever. Everything is so still and ominous in this ICU. Even when they allow relatives to visit you briefly in the evenings, things are so maddeningly unchanging!

As for you, you don't as much as turn a hair for all the trouble that I take for you. Every day I report here dutifully, put on that stale, smelly hospital gown they hand me to get into this ICU, kick off my shoes and tiptoe inside this 'holy' Intensive Care Unit. I eagerly touch your face, your brow, your hair, hoping you might flicker an eyelid in response. But no, Madam disdainfully keeps her eyes shut. Where have you slipped off to, Chandra? What kind of dreams do you have within those heavily curtained eyelids? I cannot dream at all these days, for I have this reality to face day and night. The reality of waking up only to realise that I will have to make my own cup of coffee, send Asha to school with a packed lunch, then cook and feed your old parents who always nag me with their repetitive questions—how is our Chandra? Will our daughter live? Does she have a chance? Sometimes they accompany me to this wretched place, and those days are even worse. Your mother takes to wailing ... God! Can't you hear her wailing? Can't you hear anything, anything at all? You lie there still, like a drowned pebble. D-r-o-w-n-e-d ... have you really drowned Chandra?

There were some signs of activity at the far end of the ICU now. A senior doctor rushed in and joined the four people who had gathered around the bed in the corner on the extreme right. Are they shifting the patient to a ward? Has he come to? Some of the nurses were scurrying across the narrow passage. One of them walked back to the bed briskly, a white bundle tucked under her arm. Oh no, not again! Ramachandran left the window and walked hurriedly towards the last of the large panes on the right hand corner. He had great difficulty squeezing through the small crowd that had collected near the window.

'Excuse me,' he almost said, but bit his lips when he saw a woman sobbing uncontrollably. Another woman held her by the shoulders. A man stood by her, stroking her hair from which her *pallu*, the loose end of the sari, had slipped down to her neck. Two others muffled their cries.

Ramachandran stood at the edge of the crowd and craned his neck to look through the glass pane. He peered past the heads and necks and ears silhouetted against the pane and saw the senior doctor talking to another doctor by the patient's bed. The nurse was busy tucking the white sheet neatly around the figure on the bed. She tucked in the ends expertly, as if this was the single great calling in her life. One could see the contours of the motionless figure after the nurse has tucked it in, with the white cloth. One could clearly make out the rounded shape of the head and the face, with just a hint of a nose jutting out, the torso, the length of the legs, and the upturned feet sharply pointing towards the sky. Like they were about to take off. No, he (or she) had actually taken off. It was all over. And now, there was all the time in the world to settle down and have a good cry ... like the one this grieving crowd was indulging in.

Ramachandran wormed his way out of the small crowd and hurried back to the window from where he could see Chandra lying as motionless as before. His tongue had gone dry, and was now stuck to his palate. Chandra, are you also dea ... ? Chandra, please hang on ... don't let go yet ... I'm sorry for my ungracious thoughts, I'm really ashamed. I'll look after Asha and your parents, I'll cook and run the house, I'll do anything but don't leave me, don't leave us. 'Please, dear God, save my Chandra, save her....' he muttered softly, checking quickly to see if anyone had heard. In a sweep, his eyes took in the row of motionless figures in the ICU. 'God,' he said, 'save everyone here, save Chandra and that one, and that one there, and that ... don't let them die, yet.'

Die? Expire? Perish? Ramachandran's breath came out in short gasps as he narrowed his eyes and brought his face close to the pane, flattening his nose to stare hard at Chandra. Her face was slightly tilted to the left and her dark hair clung to her brow, lank without a wash. How her hair would bounce softly after a rinse!

He could see the white sheet on her chest gently rise and fall. Oh yes, see, the sheet rose ever so slightly and then fell, up, and then down, in tune with her breathing. Chandra was breathing, but on her own. Wasn't that something in this accursed place? Thank God. If she were to stop breathing, it would take them less than ten minutes to get organised. The sheet that was now loosely gathered around her neck would be swiftly pulled over her head. That is all the ritual involved in the drama of life and death, mutely played over again and again in this ICU. Once the struggle was over, they just pulled the white sheet tightly over the head and tucked in the sides neatly, decisively. The doctors would cover the face instantly as if, if they didn't, some terrible change would have come over the features all of a sudden. And as if they were all in a great hurry to distinguish the dead from the living by this one symbolic act that was carried out with such solemnity.

Ramachandran recalled how shocked and dismayed he had been when he saw the sight for the first time. It was someone on the third bed from the left. They had covered the young man—a mere boy of twenty-four—from top to toe in a white sheet, and the same nurses had tucked in the ends deftly, with an assured air as if there was no doubt whatsoever that any life lingered in the young body beneath the sheet. The finality of the act had hit him hard and he had come out in a cold sweat.

'A fatal case of brain fever,' someone had whispered. 'He's not even twenty-four, the first son of his parents. Look at them, they're shattered.'

That day he had rushed back to the window near Chandra's bed. The scene had brought him down on his knees, begging. Please, dear God, spare my Chandra. She is young. Yes, she is thirty-two and this boy was only twenty-four, but I call her young.

Thoroughly demoralised, Ramachandran's lips moved incessantly as he muttered fragments of prayers. None of them were whole or complete—he had never made an effort to learn any prayers. Isn't this much too narrow to be effective, he thought. How will my prayers be answered if I address only one God, of only one religion? There are some evil forces playing havoc with the lives of the people in this ICU. Can one really ward them off by limiting one's prayers to one language and one faith?

But now, he found himself mouthing half-remembered *sloka*s[1] in Sanskrit. He said them along with the bits he recalled from the Holy Bible. He wished he could beat a large brass disk with a resounding gong and pray like a Buddhist, his face serene. He wanted to kneel down on the ground and raise his face and hands towards the sky like a Muslim doing *namaz*. He would do anything, even tie a white cloth around his mouth in silence like a devout Jain and pray the way God wanted him to.

[1] *Sloka*s: Prayers in Sanskrit.

His face had lost all its calm. It looked shameful as he prayed fervently for Chandra, with the other patients dying every hour all around her. They perished like mere flies while he hastily muttered his prayers, appalled at his own single-minded selfishness. 'Save Chandra, she is special.' It seemed as if he was swearing at God, his truncated prayers coming forth like clipped curses, the short rasping sounds edged with an anger he did not know how to quell or handle.

'You must concentrate, Ramu,' his friend Venu had advised. 'Just zero in on the object of your interest and concentrate, if it has to work at all. A prayer has infinite powers. It can even lift things off the ground. It can move mountains.'

Ramachandran had given him a sardonic smile. May be you have a point there Venu, a quasi-scientific point. Here, let's see how one applies it, he thought, as he began to mumble to himself, his eyes focused steadily on Chandra's prostrate figure. Training his eyes over her head, he took in the dark, limp hair, the pale, moist brow and the face with the eyes resolutely closed. He mumbled continuously, unconcerned about his incomplete prayers. Snippets in Sanskrit, in Tamil, bits in English from the New Testament, the Buddhist incantation of Tibetan monks, the indescribable sounds from the lips of faces wearing caps in a synagogue—anything, just anything would do.

Only, dearest Chandra, hang on to life for my sake, for the sake of our child, for the sake of your distraught parents. People are dying every moment, to your left, to your right. Get out of this haunted place, fast ... he muttered in a secret tongue, his words gathering in a dense cluster around Chandra's head as he tried to move that still face. Feverishly, he concentrated on his work, sending fervent messages to that sleeping head, his words piercing through her skin. Clenching his clammy fists, he said aloud: 'No, not those white sheets for my Chandra, please. Spare her. Drape a sari around her, help her to her feet and help her into my waiting car outside.'

Ramachandran recalled the way his parents-in-law prayed with appropriate rituals, meticulous about every little detail, as if they would otherwise be faulted by God. His little daughter Asha joined them, arms folded, eyes closed, making her request simple and direct: 'God, let my mother live. God, let her come back home quick and play with me.' He now pushed aside an uncomfortable feeling of envy that he could never quite surrender himself as easily, by becoming limp and suppliant like them.

That day his mind had knotted itself up in rigid arguments. If we are lucky to get Chandra back, then it will finally be a triumph of medicine, his mind had argued wordlessly. It will be a conquest of science that has been monitoring her condition so closely till now, and the wonders of bio-engineering that will enable her doctors to pull her out of this insentient state. Medical science it will be, not this mumbo-jumbo her parents indulge in.

The doctors had been forthright in their comments. 'There is no room for any illusion,' they had said flatly. 'It is most unfortunate and unexpected that your wife should've slipped into a coma at all, in the first place, after what seemed to be a routine surgery for a burst appendix. But from now on, we'll have to monitor her comatose condition and treat it on general terms, like the few others here. The chances of survival are fifty-fifty.'

Ramachandran had appreciated their straightforward talk. Now it was up to the expertise of the doctors, together with the miracle of modern medicine to pull her out of this. 'God,' he whispered, 'let medical science take over. Please don't come between medical science and my Chandra.'

His feet ached and his ankles continued to itch infuriatingly. Hunger gnawed at his insides. He was forever thirsty, but nothing could quench his thirst. Neither juices, nor soft drinks, chilled beer, tea, coffee, or buttermilk, nothing would do. He downed litres of water but they vanished without a trace.

Everyday he had to go through the motions of living briskly—getting ready for the hospital, then the long wait for the doctor and the worrisome queries that elicited staccato, non-committal replies from the doctors. He would then take up his position near the window and continue staring with what he felt was a stupid expectation. It is ironic how when difficult situations overwhelm you, drown you and make you struggle for breath, you stand frozen, stultified and rooted to the ground.

A doctor was bending over the patient on the bed next to Chandra's. The occupant was a young woman. Ramachandran heard that it was again a case of an unexpected complication after an apparently successful Caesarian operation. That young woman had delivered a healthy baby after which she was suddenly overcome by violent convulsions that had laid her back stiff and motionless. Now she breathed only with the help of a ventilator. Tick-tock, tick-tock ... her body functioned like a clock. Like a clock without its hands, but one that continued to tick meaninglessly and mechanically. Her respirator seemed to go tick-tock in answer to some terrible command from somewhere. What a strange face she had. Every time Ramachandran went past this young woman to Chandra's bed in the ICU, he was frightened. The girl's eyes were always wide open, unblinking, and unseeing and that somehow made Ramachandran feel as if he would turn to stone if her gaze fell upon him.

Now the doctor was bending over her and trying to shut her eyes. The nurses were rushing in and out and sure enough, sure enough, there was that white sheet, that familiar goddamned white sheet! There seemed to be no dearth of white cloth in this hospital. Oh no! The tick-tock has stopped, has it? Those eyes that were fixed in a stony stare, they are perhaps in some faraway place now. She was gone then.

Goodbye, young mother. But who will mother your tiny baby as you snuggle under that cool, clean white sheet? This Sister in particular, the nurse is someone you can trust with your eyes closed. She will tuck the sheet around your body perfectly. Just look at her, how she enjoys her job, as if she was born to it and it is the prime mission in her life.

Ramachandran roused himself and stole a look from out of the corner of his eyes at Chandra who was on the bed next to that young woman. Chandra was so quiet and still. Was anything wrong? God, will they pull out another white shroud? He rushed to the door of the ICU and accosted the doctor.

'How is she today, Doctor? Have you taken a look at her?' he asked.

'At whom?'

'At my wife there, on that bed,' he pointed.

'No, I haven't examined her yet. Have a heart. You can see how we've been scuttling around without even pausing for breath. Did you witness our latest loss? There, that young girl. Poor thing, she didn't even see the face of her newborn baby. And here you are, asking ...'

Brusquely, the doctor turned to the nurse with a cryptic command. She brought him a long, heavy book that said 'ADMISSIONS AND DEATH REGISTER.'

'When you make a note next time Sister, please be accurate about the time of death,' said the doctor.

'Yes doctor, Sir.'

'Be precise to the exact second. I'll have no bungling here any more.'

'Yes Sir.'

'Can't you even read the time?'

The doctor left the ICU after ticking her off. The nurse opened the grim register and turned the pages.

Ramachandran could feel his trousers sticking to his thighs and legs. A secret stream of sweat ran down his legs. His palms felt damp. Please God, don't let Chandra be the next victim merely because she is on the bed next to that corpse. God, if you are death in itself, go away. Get out. Just leave through the main door and take in some fresh air. Have an ice cream or something nice. Don't touch Chandra with your cold, trembling fingers.

Oh, please don't pull that white sheet over her head, I implore you. I have to get her out of this deathly place. They bring in people here only to watch them die. And when death arrives, they just drape a white shroud around the body, silently. In fact, they are doing that very ritual right now, in front of my eyes. Not only to the young girl there, but to that young man as well, there in that corner. He was wheeled in only thirty minutes ago. Was he perhaps dead when he was brought in? Who can I ask?

There is nobody near that boy's window. Nobody to weep for his end. No one has come yet to claim the body. People at the ICU seemed to be paying their last respects to this anonymous death. The sheet they spread over him is blindingly white. And so clean it sparkles.

More and more people die. The ghosts from the bodies that have just lost their lives are stricken by loneliness as they haunt this ICU. Spirits yearning for company, they probably long to grab other victims. There are the dead on one side and the dying on the other. A difference of only shade or colour. Tomorrow, a few more may die. Chandra, you cannot be selfish and leave me so easily, do you hear? You have a contract with me, do you remember? A promise you made that you would abide by me and live with me, come rain or shine. Have you forgotten how I held your right foot and placed it on the *ammikkal*[2] and helped you take those seven steps, my shy bride? Now don't turn your back on our marriage vows. Hold on tightly to your life. I'm going home now. I'll be back early tomorrow morning, as usual. Till then Chandra, don't let me down, please don't let me down ...

Ramachandran walked through the corridor and stepped out of the building. He breathed in the wholesome air outside eagerly. It was so innocent and undefiled.

The next morning he came early to the hospital. He hoped he would not have trouble with his itchy ankles. He had carefully applied cream all over his ankles and heels to protect his skin from dust and grime.

'Oh hello Mr Ramachandran,' said the doctor, coming from behind. He placed his arm on Ramachandran's shoulder. 'You're fortunate,' said the doctor. 'Your wife opened her eyes last night.'

'What!'

'I just told you,' smiled the doctor.

'Oh God, this is unbelievable! Oh God!'

Ramachandran sank on his knees without even glancing at Chandra through the window.

'Well then, for God's sake get up, will you?' said the doctor. 'You've my permission to go in for a short while, but quietly. It is not visiting time.'

'Yes Doctor. Sure, I'll be very quiet. Thanks. Oh, many thanks. Thanks for all your efforts, thanks for everything, Doctor. You're ... '

Ramachandran found her fast asleep. Yes, he could now use this innocuous word. Chandra was sleeping.

'Ssh!' whispered the nurse, smiling. He nodded as he smiled back at her. He stood beside the bed and looked at Chandra. 'God, how can I thank you,' he mumbled. He muttered something and

[2] *Ammikkal*: A rectangular slab of stone with a stone roller used for grinding spices. The right foot of the bride is placed on the *ammikkal* by the groom as a part of the wedding ceremonies.

peeled off from his lips sheet after sheet of white cloth. And he flung them away. The shrouds lay in a white heap. Beneath them were figures whose contours were clear, but they were figures without features like eyes, ears, nose, a mouth—they were without a face. Uncoiling from his lips were reams and reams of cloth that had a blindingly cruel whiteness. In the middle of the absolutely white sheets was a naked, defenseless face of a *bhikshu*, a mendicant, who begged uncaringly, praying with a single-minded concentration.

The shrouds floated up like clouds carrying their destinies to an unreachable distance. They whispered secret messages in Ramachandran's ears. He sat with his head bowed in the middle of it all, exulting for a moment in his triumph. He felt totally humbled and subdued by this triumph.

Muniyakka*

Muniyakka had mastered the art of soliloquy. She would keep muttering to herself fluently as she walked, without any hesitation. The most meaningful conversations she had were the ones she had with herself. Everyone was used to the way this old woman freely held forth with herself.

Carrying herself on thin, spindly legs that looked more like a pair of drumsticks, Muniyakka was surprisingly mobile as she went about her work, shivering in the cold winter of Bangalore. She would wash vessels and clothes, sweep and clean the courtyards in front of the houses and decorate them with *kolam*, a *rangoli* patterned skillfully with finely powdered rice. As she went about doing all the work, she would tirelessly and continuously talk to herself, 'argue' with her relations and her enemies, and supply herself with suitable answers from them. Children playing on the sides of the street would laugh at her and cry out, 'Look, there goes Muniyakka, the walkie-talkie!' Adults who chanced upon her, noticed her in passing, mildly amused. Meanwhile, Muniyakka went about nonchalant, perpetuating a habit that seemed to sustain her even as she worked. Washing utensils in Anjaneyulu's house brought her twenty rupees. She received another thirty-five for sweeping, mopping the floor and washing the clothes at Vasudev Chetty's. Having worked for a long time at Rama Rao's, she now received a kind of gratuity from them and they had allowed her to build a small hut for herself in a corner of their garden. It was convenient. There was a tap near the hut and a raised stone platform over a cemented surface in which she washed her own clothes as well as those of the Rao household. She put out her rags to dry on a short washing line tied to a *neem* tree and a coconut tree.

* Translated from the original by the author. Originally published in *Kanaiyazhi*, ed. Kasturi Rangan, Chennai. This translation first published in *Truth-Tales*, New Delhi: Kali for Women, 1988.

Upon finishing her work, Muniyakka would return to the Rao bungalow. Mrs Ratna Rao had a genial temperament and she treated Muniyakka as an old member of the family. No festivities would take place in the house without the participation of Muniyakka. Ratna Rao shared some of her free moments with the old woman, chatting about various things at times in an almost serious vein. Only Ratna could truly relate to Muniyakka's strange ways. She found the old woman's queer sense of humour very enjoyable.

Every day, Muniyakka concluded her day's work with her duties in the temple closeby. This fetched her fifteen rupees apart from a sense of fulfillment. At the end of the day, she cleaned and washed the floor of the temple, after which she took refuge in her hut. Then she would heave a sigh of relief and call it a day. Lighting an earthen oil lamp and guided by the dim glow, she got a log-fire crackling in a rather functional oven and got a pot to boil her broth. After preparing the broth, she cooked the flour of *ragi*, a kind of millet that she cooked real soft and tender and made some curry to go with it. Then she sat down to eat.

Alone in the hut she wolfed down large helpings of food. Sweeping up food with her palm, she swallowed mounds of *ragi*, all the while freely scolding her dead husband and her absent sons. Eventually, it shook off the feeling that she was alone in the hut. Her appetite whetted by her anger, Muniyakka ate ravenously till she was pleasantly suffused with the satisfaction of eating the food that she had earned in exchange for her hard labour.

After finishing the meal, she cleaned up the hut, took a piece of jaggery in her hand and came out of the hut to sit for some time. Sitting down, she nibbled lingeringly on the jaggery. After swallowing the last little morsel, she sat back and chewed lazily on an areca nut, her eyes fixed on some distant point in the darkness. In that still moment, she felt evacuated, her mind swept clean like the interior of the hut, purged of all disturbing thoughts and stilled to a mute point. Not a fibre of her being moved. And yet, this sense of peace never lasted for long....

With the failing vision of her old eyes, she peered into the inky darkness around her. The Rao bungalow was surrounded by a large garden. Segregated on one side was a group of coconut trees. Beyond the coconut grove, sprawled a large jackfruit tree. Nestling under its shade was Muniyakka's hut. The gardens and groves in Bangalore invariably howled in the strong breeze at night. To Muniyakka's eyes, the coconut trees seemed to sway around with their 'hair' flying loose in the breeze, dancing the dance of the devil in the darkness of the night. Kokkina Halli, Muniyakka's village, was a few miles away from Bangalore. The people of that village always described ghosts and devils in this way, as being essentially female in their form. The devil was personified as a wild, mad woman, with the incisors in her row of teeth curving over her lips, revealing a hideous smile as her voice cackled and echoed resoundingly in the cloud capped night sky. Hair swaying in the breeze and over the face, the devil danced in a trance to a mad rhythm.

Outside the house and above the wall that enclosed the garden, a big *peepul* tree stood under the dim glow of the moon. The oily gloss of the *peepul* leaves shimmered in the night light. It was a garden pampered by the care and attention of the Raos. With a dense variety of plants and many flower and fruit bearing trees, the garden looked a picture of health, exuding a great sense of luxurious well-being so characteristic of any well-maintained garden in Bangalore. Looking at it, one might forget for a moment that things like abject poverty, squalor or disease existed elsewhere. Collectively, the trees and plants looked like children who had been brought up with care and affection. Muniyakka was very fond of the garden and lavished her affection on it. In the afternoons, she would try to compete with the gardener and pour buckets of water for the plants, covering the entire garden even if the exercise threatened to break her back. For a while, the flowers and fruits would take on a golden hue under the Midas touch of the setting sun. Taking in the sight, Muniyakka would feel infinitely enriched, as if she had somehow inherited a vast, great wealth. And yet, when the sky darkened....

She was back in her retreat again, squatting outside her hut in the darkness and looking at the same swaying plants and trees in the menacing form of the devil's dance. Her heart quickened as it learned to keep pace with the devil's beat outside. In the turbulence of the breeze, the swish of the branches sounded like a number of snakes furiously hissing; Muniyakka could completely identify herself with this. Her mind danced, pulsating with the rhythm of the *dhvamsha*[1] of Goddess Kali.

[1] *Dhvamsha*: The dance of destruction expressing the indignation of Goddess Kali at the wrong things happening in the world.

One could hear windows being slammed and bolted. The servants of the Rao household and their eldest daughter were securing the windows against the storm. Through the glass windows, the light of the house spread a quiet glow in the middle of the dark garden. There was peace inside but storm outside; Bangalore was being lashed by cold gusts of wind like whiplashes. The night was pitch-dark. Each of the leaves of the trees, fanning out like the enlarged hood of a snake, sighed 'hoos', 'hoos' as they collectively surrounded the solitary Muniyakka like a thousand snakes.

Snakes, snakes and more snakes ... everywhere there is a snake hissing. If it slithers in green or brown colours in front of us, or if we find it curling down from the eaves of the ceiling, then we take a sturdy pole of bamboo and bring it down hard on the snake, beat it instantly! Beat till it quivers in agony and is smashed into a pulp. But if the same genus of serpent comes crowned with the title of 'cobra' and we see the proud tilt of its hood and feel the heat of its hissing breath, then instantly we reach for some milk and offer it to the cobra humbly. Then we kneel down and do our obeisance. And if the same cobra does not slide or slither, but is frozen as a stone in a corner of a temple, or under a black berry tree, then there is no limit to our worship and fertility rites. We apply *kumkum* or vermillion on the stone snake, dash our foreheads on the curved stone as we entreat favours and dreams that need to be fulfilled. We offer flowers to the stone snake, break coconuts and let the tender coconut-water bathe the stone as we repeat our prayers, shivering and damp from our holy ablutions, our stomachs caved in from a devout fast. The women who come to the temple, muttering their prayers, go round and round the stone snakes and the black berry tree, round and round dizzily like fervent dervishes. Ripe berries drop from the tree on the stone snakes below, smashing their rich pulp against the stone, dyeing it in vivid spots of blue and purple. The dumb mouths of the snakes carry the sweets smeared by the women. Armies of large, black ants file in orderly rows towards the sweets. Stones scarred with crazy lines of *kumkum*, *haldi*, sandalwood paste and the smudgy sprinkling of withered flowers.

It was Muniyakka's responsibility to wash the stones clean of all these stains. She doused the stones with buckets of water and then with a rough coir brush in her hand, she fiercely scrubbed the stains away. With the broomstick held firmly in her hand, she swept away the stones of the half-eaten berries dropped by the squirrels. She cursed the women who came to worship and made such a mess at the temple. 'Foolish women ... banging their brows on stone begging for favours—give me a son, Lord of Snakes, great Nagaraj! Please give me a son.... idiots! I was like you when I was a young woman, bruising my brow on this stone and praying for sons. The result? Today I have three useless sons in whom I once had a deep, implicit faith. I visited their homes so eagerly, but not one of them would give me even a single, tepid bowl of broth. Each of them a worthless son, lusting for his wife. They don't need a mother any more. Shameless bastards! But naturally! After all, they were fathered by an equally worthless man, Bairappa. That husband of mine, dying after leading a life of waste—smoking, drinking, gambling, squandering my hard-earned money ... Bairappa be damned!', she spoke to herself.

'So, what news *Ajji*[2]? Finished your work for the day?' asked Thimmayya, the temple gardener, emerging from the bushes.

'Yes Thimmayya, I've finished my work. But I will have to get up early tomorrow. It is the death anniversary of that worthless man I had married. I will do my duty and perform a small *shraddha*[3] in my hut. Come over tomorrow and have a special lunch. Will you come?' she asked.

'Of course, *Ajji*. I'll certainly come,' said Thimmayya, with a big grin. Then he asked, '*Ajji*, have you bought all the necessary things for the *shraddha* or has anything been left out? You always take care not to leave anything wanting in Bairappa's banana leaf—it must be complete with his favourite brand of *beedi*, sweet buns made with jaggery, then spiced rice ... even the toddy ... Mmm ... ,' Thimmayya licked his lips in candid anticipation of an appetising meal.

Muniyakka laughed aloud. 'All right then, come tomorrow. You can have everything from the wretch Bairappa's banana leaf,' she smiled. Then, picking up her bucket and the broom, she went out of the temple.

Bairappa's *shraddha*. It was done just the way it had been all these years in the past. Muniyakka performed the rites that

[2] *Ajji*: 'Grandmother' in Kannada

[3] *Shraddha*: A Hindu ritual performed for a dead relative.

should rightfully have been performed by her sons. Her three sons ignored the day. She kept all her husband's favourite dishes on a clean banana leaf. This was meant to appease his departed soul. The gleaming banana leaf carried fish curry, tenderly cooked cabbage, sweet buns made with jaggery, spiced rice, a small bottle of toddy and a packet of his favourite brand of *beedi*s. On this day, Muniyakka had a youthful glow on her face. This day, she also felt emboldened to have a large, round *kumkum* on her brow. She wore flowers on her hair. A clean cotton saree was wrapped around her old, withered body. Briskly, she attended to all the rites and rituals of the *shraddha*, never however ceasing to curse her dead husband. Ratna Rao saw the items on the banana leaf and had a good laugh. She teased Muniyakka pleasantly in Kannada, her voice ringing lightly like silver bells. Muniyakka blushed at the teasing but joined Ratna Rao in her light-hearted banter.

When she got through with all her work, Muniyakka began to sweep and clean the hut. That is when her face registered a subtle transformation, 'Husband! Son! What humbug all these relationships are ... huh!' she thought. She came out of the hut as usual and squatted outside, her back resting on the wall, eyes peering into the darkness. The tree began to dance in the darkness. Muniyakka enjoyed the devil's dance once more, with a vicarious pleasure. In that lonely hour, she experienced her own sense of isolation with a private thrill. Felt the damp air caressing her hollow cheeks. The pleasant smell of earth dampened by the prelude of a drizzle. Even the language of Kannada seemed to have mingled with the damp earth and now it reached her nostrils delicately. Muniyakka smelt everything around her and heard the distant thunder. I don't have to water the garden tomorrow, she thought. There will be a heavy downpour. Thunder will crack the sky and there will be rain, pouring down on the trees, on the plants and on this hut, here. On the temple, on the stone snakes—everything will be washed clean.

In the strong breeze, the branches waved wildly. Muniyakka sat in the darkness, a small speck, peering, watching, thinking. 'Who's a devil and who's not a devil? Who am I? And you? Who the devil are you? Where are we going? How far ... and for what?'

Nagapushpam*

Ratna selected a nice, wide branch of the *champaka* tree and settled on it comfortably. Hmm ... it was cool in here, for the tree was thickly covered over with leaves. They almost hid her inside. She raised her face and smiled at the birds chirping on the branches above. Then she rose, adjusted her skirt and climbed over branches that were higher with a dense cluster of leaves. She selected a broad branch once again and lay back on it. Now it wouldn't be easy for anyone to find out where she was. It wouldn't be easy at all.

Reclining on the branch, Ratna tried to close her eyes, but they remained open under her eyelids. From her lowered eyelids, she could see them. Rows and rows of an army of big black ants that were going past her in an orderly file, carrying something to eat in their 'hands'. Only recently had Ratna got over her fear of being bitten by the big ants, and the pain it could cause. She could now handle the ants easily enough. She would just play possum. If they happened to move past at a close range, she simply remained motionless, as if dead. That helped. That way the ants did not get startled on their way to some mission. They just filed past, minding their own business.

* *Nagapushpam* in Tamil is *Thaazhampu*, *kewra* in Hindi, and flowers of screw pine in English. Their strong heady fragrance is believed to attract snakes. They are small dioecious flowers with sword-shaped leaves in the plant that belong to the genus of *pandanaceae,* a family of tropical woody plants native to India and Malaysia but naturalised over a wide tropical area. This story has been translated from the original Tamil "Poonagam" by the author; published in the special issue of the Women's Day, *Dinamani*, Chennai. This translation first published in *The Little Magazine: 'Rite Stuff'*, vol. I, no. 4, New Delhi, 2000.

Aha ... if one takes refuge in this *sampangi*[1] tree, one can be transported into another world altogether. Even so, Ratna could not fight down the annoyance in her mind. She struggled to get rid of the irritation that fumed within her. *Chee!* Look at the people at home who consider themselves to be the 'elders'. What sort of people are they, actually? They don't speak about anything clearly or in a straightforward manner. They seem to be confused and finally end up confusing us too. They tell me all the time: Don't interrupt us while we talk, don't talk out of turn, don't bother us by asking so many questions, don't argue endlessly, don't do this, and don't do that and so on. If I ask a question, they want to avoid the point, so they just wriggle out evasively and escape. Neither can they explain nor give me a straight answer. Hell!

All that I said—or rather pleaded for—was *nagapushpam*, the flowers of the screw pine. 'Please don't do my *jadai alankaram*[2] with jasmines this time,' I had said. 'Decorate my braided hair with *nagapushpam* instead,' I had begged. But no way!

Ratna closed her eyes and thought about the festivals and the *jadai alankaram* done during those special days such as Sankranti,[3] Deeepavali,[4] Dussehra and Navaratri[5]. All the little girls of the extended family would be dressed in sparkling silk *pavadais*, long pleated skirts reaching the ankles, with blouses to match. The elderly women of the household that is the grandmothers, grand aunts, along with the mothers would adorn the girls with pieces of ancestral family jewellery and then stand back to fondly admire the beauty of their efforts. In addition, they would also do an elaborate *jadai alankaram*. Brushing the girls' hair till it shone, they braided

[1] *Sampangi*: A deep yellow flower with a strong scent that grows on large trees, commonly found in Bangalore, Mysore and parts of Karnataka.

[2] *Jadai alankaram*: Working out decorative designs and patterns with various kinds of flowers on the braided hair of young girls and women on festive days.

[3] Sankranti: Usually falls on the 14th of January. A harvest festival celebrated with sugar cane and pongal, a sweet dish made of rice, green gram and jaggery.

[4] Deepavali: Diwali, the festival of lights celebrated all over India

[5] Dussehra and Navaratri : A festival for the three goddesses, Durga, Lakshmi and Saraswati celebrated for nine days. Dussehra is a festival of ten days in which goddess Durga is worshipped.

it, and then decorated it in myriad ways with a variety of flowers—different kinds of jasmine, kanakambaram[6] and of course, the odorous green southernwood, the *marukkozhundu*. Occasionally, they would also include *nagapushpam* and work lovely patterns on it with other flowers. Using a needle and thread, they stitched the flowers over the sword-shaped petals of *nagapushpam*. The strong odour of *nagapushpam* would easily dominate over the rest of the flowers and penetrate the nostrils. It never failed to attract attention. Ratna remembered the last time her hair was decorated with *nagapushpam*. How proudly she had strutted around that day, the cynosure of all eyes. Wherever she went, people turned to look at her and her braided hair. She had felt very important indeed on that day, but ...

All that is over. The family does not allow *nagapushpam* to even enter the house any more. Not since two years. And if Ratna asks why, nobody answers her. Eventually she got to know the reason for it when she eavesdropped on the elders one day as they whispered amongst themselves. It seems a friend of the family had bought a lot of *nagapushpam*, strips and strips of them, because it was the favourite flower of that household. Then sure enough, a snake had got into their house. It bit the little girl who had a *jadai alankaram* with *nagapushpam* in her hair. She had died instantly. After that tragic incident the family wouldn't so much as touch a nagapushpam if they chanced upon it at a florist's. They wouldn't even talk about it. They only exchanged frightened looks with one another.

Ratna loved the fragrance of *nagapushpam* very much. Now, for this year's Navaratri, she had begged and pleaded with the elders in her family for a *jadai alankaram* with *nagapushpam*. But everybody, just about everybody including her gentle mother Ahalya, had refused to comply with her request. Let them suffer now. I'll make it real hard for them to find me. Let them run around all over the place in search for me. I must torment them. Then they will come begging. I'm not going to get down from this tree. I'm not going to eat. And I'm definitely not going to talk to anyone. Yes!

Ratna reclined on the branch and closed her eyes. She felt something crawling on her ankle. It was a big, black ant. *Hey you!*

[6] *Kanakambaram*: Small sunset-hued, odourless flowers with light petals that are often mixed with other flowers for garlands or for strings of flowers that women buy to adorn their hair.

Just go your way, will you? Get on with your work and don't you bite me, OK ... ? She sent the thought out to the ant. The black ant went past her ankle and moved over to the trunk of the tree. The garden below was soaking in the evening hour, a time when some of the buds slowly folded up their petals. It was laden with the pleasant fragrance of the many odorous flowers in the garden—*parijata*, jasmine, roses, tuberoses, mistress of the night and *marukkozhundu*. The collective redolence rose up from the flowerbeds and bushes and reached her nostrils.

'Ratna, hey Ratna! Don't keep nagapushpam in your hair, because if you do, it'll approach you. Then it'll bite you.'

'What'll bite me, Amma?'

'I told you the other day, don't you remember? Come on, you remember only too well, so don't pretend. Just understand one thing, my child. You shouldn't even utter its name in the evenings.'

The more they warned her about it, the more curious she grew. If the dreaded thing is a snake, then which of the snakes will approach her? The rattlesnake that is called *changili karuppan* in Tamil? Or the viper with black linear markings? Will it be the green whip snake by any chance, or the king cobra himself? Ratna had learnt the names in her zoology class. Once, her Mama, her mother's brother took her along with the children of the family to the Snake Park in Chennai. She had seen a wide variety of snakes. It was very interesting. The sluggish boa constrictor, for instance. It looked so hopelessly harmless, the way it was lying around sleepily. The children got totally engrossed in the sight of the snakes that crawled and curved around sinuously, wiggling and meandering in front of their eyes. Some of the snakes slithered along gracefully, catching the rays of the sun on their jewelled bodies that shone dazzlingly, their eyes glinting like bright gems. Ratna remembered how the cobra had put out its tongue delicately between its poison fangs every other minute, and was hissing away. How quietly, and how very calmly the snakes crawled along tortuously, unmindful of the awestruck, admiring crowd milling around them.... And yet, it was a somewhat pathetic sight, thought Ratna, to see the snakes cluttered around like that in a pit that was shaped like a well, or to see them coiled around the stumps of dead branches that were painted in bright, artificial colours. Why don't they release the snakes to roam free in the open?

Ratna would often approach anthills to find out what was happening in there. 'Shh! Ratna, don't get too close. Anthills are the homes of snakes!' her mother would warn her. But Ratna would continue to stand near the anthills for hours on end till her legs ached. Once, she went to the extent of breaking up the sandy towers of an anthill in the hope that snakes would tumble out of their collapsed homes. It fell back in a sandy heap out of which a few red ants came scurrying. That was about all. It had been a very hot day. People say snakes come out if they find the heat unbearable, but not a single snake had come out.

'Ratna, Ratna?'

Ah ... that's mother looking for me. Even if I hide myself in one of the tallest branches of the *sampangi* tree, mother can find me out.

Ahalya, Ratna's mother, stood below the tree, peering into the branches.

'There you are,' she said. 'Caught you! I knew you'd be here. Come my child, come down. It's getting late.'

'No, I won't.'

'Why ever not?'

'I just won't.'

'What!'

'I like it here. I want to stay here.'

'The sun will set anytime now. Then all kinds of insects and worms will creep out in the open. It's very dangerous. Come down, there's a darling.'

'There's no danger whatsoever over here. There are just a few black ants and some squirrels, that's about all,' said Ratna from her perch on the branch.

'That's what you think. But once it gets dark, all kinds of insects and sna ... ' Ahalya bit her lip and stopped midway in her sentence. Her face was suffused with fear as she looked up at Ratna.

'What did you say, Amma?' asked Ratna, from the top of the branch.

'Nothing, nothing at all. You just come down, quickly. Aren't you my very own little Ratna, my little gem, my golden girl?'

'Amma, did you say snake just now?'

'Shh! I said nothing of the sort! I was about to say insects. All right, come down quickly. How long should I stand here? I've work to do.'

'I'll come down on one condition,' said Ratna.

'What condition?'

'I want a *jadai alankaram* with *nagapushpam*.'

'Oh god! With *nagapushpam*? We've told you so many times that we can't. It's for your own good. That flower has such a strong, intoxicating smell that it'll give a headache to small girls like you. Do you know, sometimes it can even make you bleed through the nose, because the smell is too strong. Besides, you know very well don't you, that the fragrance of *nagapushpam* attracts sna ... ,' Ahalya stopped dead again. She didn't want to complete the sentence because she dreaded even uttering the word 'snake'.

'Were you about to say snakes?'

'Ratna! How many times have I asked you not to utter that word after dark? This has become some kind of a joke or what? Now come down soon like a good girl, come.'

'What about *nagapushpam* then?'

'We'll talk about it later. You come along now.'

Ahalya looked very tired. Ratna was sorry that she was harassing her dear mother. With an agile leap, she alighted from the tree and wrapped her arms around her mother's waist the minute she touched the ground.

'My darling girl, my very own little gem, my frisky baby gazelle.... You're the *Nagaratna*[7] of the house,' Ahalya whispered the last line as she stroked her daughter's cheeks and hair.

Only very occasionally would Ahalya call her girl by her formal name 'Nagaratna'. And only if no one happened to be around. 'Nagaratna, Nagaratna,' she would call out softly, whispering into Ratna's ears as though it was a big secret. In the beginning, Ratna had kicked in protest against the name. It sounded so very old-fashioned. There were plenty of Nagaratnas in Mysore—teachers, family cooks and other grandmotherly types. Some of them added an 'Amma' to their names in deference to their age and carried their names heavily as 'Nagaratnamma.'

'I don't want a name like *that*,' Ratna had resented. 'All the boys and girls in my school tease me. They laugh at me.'

[7] 'Naga' is King Cobra, 'Ratna' means gem.

She had her way. Her parents and other elders of the family agreed to shorten her name to just 'Ratna' in the school records.

Ratna. The literal meaning of the word is 'a gem'. 'A gem of a girl,' they said fondly, pampering her on days of festivals. They dressed her in fine silk *pavadai*s and blouse, her hair smoothly brushed, braided and adorned with fresh flowers. Sometimes a length of *kanakambaram* would be coiled around her hair. They would fix that beautiful *jadabillai*.[8] It was a jewel that was the pride of the family. Exquisitely crafted in the shape of a large cobra, it had a broad hood spread out with two large rubies on either side for 'eyes' that glowed lustrously, like hot live coals. Rich in colour, the superior rubies dripped blood. It was a rare classic piece of jewellery so stunningly regal that whenever they took it out of the velvet box in which it nestled and fixed it on Ratna's hair, her whole body tingled and flushed with pride. She felt honoured.

The first time Ratna came to know that the name 'Naga' (for cobra) was entwined with her formal name, Nagaratna, she had been very surprised. She would often wonder about it. The elders in the family who didn't allow her to utter the very word 'snake' and hushed her up instantly, the elders who exchanged frightened whispers about snakes, were the same elders who had merged the name of the fearful cobra with hers. But why? Why did they name me 'Nagaratna'? One day she was to find the answer.

That was the day of Nagapanchami.[9] For the *puja* that was a part of the ritual, Ratna had accompanied her mother and her Athai, her father's sister, to the temple. Once inside the temple, her mother Ahalya had joined the other women who had gathered for the ritual. All of them recited their prayers to the large, sculpted stone snakes in the temple. Ratna looked around. Good God, there are such very large stone Nagas, the cobras, all around. Some of them had a wide hood spread out, while some others had several heads. They were frozen in stone. The women garlanded them with soft, fragrant flowers. Many of them adorned the stone snakes with *nagapushpam*. One of the women placed two large strips of *nagapushpam* on either side of the Naga, prayed and

[8] *Jadabillai*: A round ornament encrusted with gems and with a screw-shaped coil on the reverse to fix on the hair.

[9] Nagapanchami: A celebration of fertility on the fifth day of the lunar month in *shravan*, the season of monsoon.

did her obeisance. Some women 'fed' the Nagas by placing sweets in their mouths. They also poured milk into their mouths. Then they went around circumambulating in a *parikrama*. Ratna's eyes were riveted on her mother as she came round along with the other women, her bead bent over her two hands that were pressed together in prayer. Ahalya whispered her prayers as she went around, a simple, soft, much-washed cotton saree clinging to her slim figure.

Ahalya often fasted on *Shashti*, the sixth lunar day and on *Ekadasi*, the eleventh day from new moon and also full moon, and on many other special days. It showed on her worn out, wasted body, which was now silhouetted by her simple handloom saree. She had given up eating snake-gourd as a part of a vow, a vegetable she liked very much.

But this is strange, thought Ratna. When they're so frightened of the very sight of a snake, why do they worship the same snake so fervently if it stands sculpted in stone? How many times will these women go round and round in circumambulation? My poor mother, her legs will ache, she thought.

One of the women, the one in a purple saree was talking to Ahalya, 'Why do you whisper your prayers like that Ahalya?' she mocked. 'Say them loudly so that at least this time around the Lord Nagaraja, the king of the cobras, can hear them right and grant you a male child!'

'O, be quiet,' the woman in the green saree chipped in with a laugh. 'Poor Ahalya, she is shy about saying her prayers aloud because Nagaraja disappointed her last time. Instead of giving her a Naganna, a male child, he gave her a Nagaratna, a girl child. *Tch, tch*!'

'Yes,' said the woman in the purple saree. 'There she stands, the little girl.' She pointed at Ratna as the woman in the green saree laughed.

Is that how I got my name, wondered Ratna. Was it the snake that gave me to Amma? Do snakes make babies? And if by mistake the baby is born female, do they still have to fuse the name of 'Naga' along with the girl's name? Is that done out of fear? Do we worship what we fear? Or do we fear whatever we worship? Perhaps women are afraid of living without a male child. Because a woman's mother-in-law, father-in-law, husband and relations taunt her. Is that what women are really scared of?

Ratna had often heard her grandmother, that is her father's mother, tell Ahalya in her presence: 'Look here, if you fail to have a male child, then your entire life is an unfulfilled one, bereft of any value. A womb that doesn't swell with a male child is but a vacuum. After all, if we don't give a male child to our family, there's really no point in our living, is there?'

Whenever grandmother talked like that, Ahalya would go red in the face, she would shrink back and tremble all over. Was it out of a sense of shame or sadness or bitterness or was it because she was very angry? Ratna could never say for sure. Ahalya would instantly rush to her own room and if Ratna happened to follow her, she would pull the child towards herself, bury the little girl's face in her bosom and plant frenzied kisses on her brow, on her cheeks, and cry out, 'My very own little Ratna, Nagaratna my little gem, my golden girl ... ,' and burst into tears.

Ratna's search for deadly snakes in gardens and anthills ended many, many years later, after she got married and moved into a house on Rash Behari Avenue in Kolkata with her husband and her little daughter. Her search ended because there were plenty of snakes in the nearby districts, plenty that roamed freely in the open, just as they did in parts of the southern district of Salem and up north in Rajasthan. These were not snakes that stood at a distance, sculpted and frozen in stone. They would not accept offerings of flowers, sweets and milk from desperate women who worshipped them. They were venomous snakes in green and brown that crawled craftily about, taking on the colours of their surrounding, blending into situations without ever giving away their own true colours. In the neighbouring state of Bihar, in places like Katihar, Fasia Tola, Teja Tola and Budhuchak, and in some districts of Rajasthan, these poisonous snakes got into bushes and grass and houses. They even got into large, wealthy houses and they got in without the help of *nagapushpam*. The snakes entered the *saurighar* that was the room reserved exclusively for childbirth in a house, and hid themselves inside. In the various *saurighar*s all over the districts of Bihar, Rajasthan and Salem, in fact wherever mothers gave birth to tiny little Nagaratnas of the world, one could find these snakes promptly swinging into brisk action.

The snakes functioned by taking on different forms and shapes. They got into the delicate spinal cord of the newborn Nagaratnas, bent it backward and snapped it, helping the midwife in killing the female baby. The snakes transformed themselves into ropes, twined around the neck of the tender, young female infant and strangled her. Or they turned into a large, black rock salt, blocked the mouth of a baby till she struggled for breath and choked to death. They even metamorphosed into fertilisers and finished their mission by poisoning the baby. They changed into various forms. They became the rope-like dough coiled around the lid of the large earthen pitcher so as to seal off all air. The female infant stuffed inside the pitcher struggled for breath. Slowly, very slowly indeed, they granted freedom to the female soul that was trapped inside the pitcher and helped the midwife again in snuffing out the young life.

Next, the snakes also entered the bodies of husbands whose wives protested against the killing of their baby daughters and who sobbed and screamed. The snakes made the husbands hiss in fury and spread out their hood. They slithered into the strong, muscular arms of these fathers of tiny daughters, helped them fling their own infants against the walls of the *saurighar* till the tender young brains spilled out. Snakes and more snakes. Venomous snakes, wherever you looked.

But what happened to the Ahalyas? Where have the Ahalyas of the world disappeared, Ahalyas, whose bodies were wasted by fasting and praying for a male child, Ahalyas who were nevertheless all gentleness with their little girls, their Nagaratnas? Ahalyas who wrap a simple cotton saree around their thin figures and exude the smell of mother in their very skin and hair? The mother's smell. A distinct smell. A pleasant blend of the scent of flowers, camphor, turmeric, of affection, milk, talcum powder, the scent of love, *kumkum*[10] or kindness ... it's difficult to describe. Where are the Ahalyas for all those babies in the country who are born by mistake, as little Nagaratnas?

[10] *Kumkum*: Vermillion powder.

It has been a long time since Ahalya passed on. Nagaratna was told by her family that it was not proper to keep on mourning and brooding for her mother, because after all, Ahalya had died well, hadn't she? She had died a *sumangali*.[11] That was so auspicious. Ahalya can therefore be allowed to vanish from their lives without a murmur. She faded like a lovely, remembered perfume.

But Ratna tried to recapture the redolence of her mother Ahalya to an extent, with an old yellow trunk that had once belonged to her mother. It was Ratna's treasure-trove now. She would not let anyone touch it. It was packed with her mother's things. The beautiful, classy silk sarees that she never wore, the exquisite jewellery that she never wore, not even once, the familiar soft, much-washed simple cotton sarees that she always wore, the sandalwood figurines wrapped in silk to preserve the aroma, the table linen and the cover for the radio that she had personally hand-embroidered in floral patterns, her old diary, old sepia photographs in black and brown tints, and many other personal belongings. Occasionally, whenever Ratna opened this old yellow trunk, it would hit her strongly, the smell of her mother. It would wrap around her overpoweringly till she would drown in it.

Mother's smell. One can always recognise it anywhere unfailingly. It is a mix that touches the aroma of other things even as it fades. Dried petals, clove, camphor, sandalwood, frankincense and all other loved scents. All except *nagapushpam*.

[11] *Sumangali*: A married woman with a husband who's alive.

Zeroing In*

I must complete writing this article tonight, I simply must, or else there would be no time to even think about Chola sculptures in the following week, thought Sukumaran. Because next week, the 'Examination Cell' of this office UPSC, that is Union Public Service Commission, would be totally roused from its long beauty sleep and swing into action briskly. All the work that will slide down the slimy back of the top brass in UPSC will engulf the likes of me and take us drifting down the mucky stream. So I better finish writing this article now or it'll never be done.

Ah, the peace of the night. It is as quiet as a graveyard in here. In the room next to mine, my wife Vatsala is sleeping with our baby girl Uma Shankari. Now let me continue with my writing ...

If the Pallava art in stone sculpture has an austere, ethereal beauty that goes far beyond the senses, the Chola sculptures reach us with a full-bodied, happy abandon that bursts out of the stones, as if it celebrates the very life in this world as a great opportunity granted. A fine example of this is the temple of Nageswara in Kumbakonam. On the southern walls one sees the voluptuous figures of the Apsaras[1] *sculpted with an exuberance that leaps out of their face, their shoulders, arms, legs, thighs, breasts, in fact their whole 'being'. Together, they make a statement in ultimate sensuousness that you cannot miss.*

Sukumaran felt sleepy but he forced himself to get on with his writing.

* Translated from the original Tamil "Thiruvaaleswara Natarajan Muruvalitthar", published in *Nikazh*, Coimbatore. This translation first published in *Parijata and Other Stories*, New Delhi: National Publishing House, 1992.

[1] *Apsaras*: Beautiful celestial nymphs

The pride of Kodumbalur, approximately twenty-seven miles from Pudukkottai, is the triad, the Moovar temple. Built by Bhuti Vikramakesari during the time of King Sundara Chola Parantaka II, the temple is roughly attributed to the time 956–973 A.D.

The three shrines in this temple form a unique blend of the flowing elegance of the Pallava style and the tangible beauty of the Chola period. Each of the three shrines rests on a base that is shaped like a double lotus, with the petals curving out in full bloom. Friezes of yalis[2] *border the column above the petals. The sheer dynamism of the art speaks through the figurines.*

Inside the temple, on two of the niches are Kalari and Gaja-Samhara Murthi. How they look, as if they would burst out of the stone. They articulate two different expressions of Shiva. The lines of the sculptures have an amazing spontaneity in the way they depict the live poise of a dance frozen for a moment in stone. All of these are rare treasures of beauty that have endured till date as our heritage of art. They are also sculptures that are believed to have been guarding over our cities and civilisations for over hundreds of years now.

Sukumaran's eyelids were heavy with sleep. His shoulders ached and his hands went limp with exhaustion. There were just two more pages to go for this article, let me complete it, he told himself. If I let it go midway, then God knows what may happen in the next few days. I can't even be sure that the day may 'dawn' for me or if something may take shape as a 'day', for that matter. Come to think of it, it is very doubtful if this person I know as 'I' is going to be 'me' or if I may just dissolve in the flow of time.

Am I really tangible? This lingering doubt has since swollen into huge proportions. It is a doubt that always haunts me and engulfs me, however much I try to dispel it. The doubt is slowly eating into me, and slowly unmanning me. Yet, everyday the dawn breaks as usual and I go through the motions of brushing my teeth, drinking my coffee, gulping down some food after which I throw some clothes over me and set off for this thing called 'office'.

I work the whole day in this office without being visible to anybody and then I go home. At home, even the tables and the

[2] *Yalis*: Sculpted figures of a mythical animal that has the face of a lion and the trunk and tusks of an elephant. *Yalis* are an integral part of temple sculpture and architecture.

chairs seem to be more solid than I am. And what about office? I'm lost there among the old, discarded pieces of furniture, the termite-eaten tables, chairs and shelves. I'm one of the termites that occasionally puts out its head to peer from the gaps and crevices of the furniture. There are others like me, my colleagues Bajaj, Chandran and Pantulu though I'm not sure if they too think along the same lines as me. Only my thoughts seem to be coiling around me like pale ghosts that haunt me down wherever I go.

I'm fading off. My office and the society I live in are out to prove that I am 'non-existent'. Still, even as I am fading away like this and I am just about to vanish, how do my thoughts acquire such a solid, indestructible shape, by contrast? My link with life is already tenuous. Even that is weakening by the second, then how come my thoughts are gaining a rounded, well-defined articulation? From where do they gather the diabolical force and the power to chase me down relentlessly, like this? This person called 'I' is getting blurred in my own eyes because I'm rapidly becoming unreal to myself. How then do my doubts and disbelief gain in proportion, as it were, their firmness and tenacity? By what obstinate logic? It is amazing! In a few days from now, I'm going to disappear completely. I'm just going to melt into thin air—for my office, for my society, and for my family. Only my thoughts may remain with a lasting permanence.

Sukumaran looked at the blank sheet of paper. All right then, let me finish this piece and I'll then call it a day, he thought, picking up the pen.

What is life? And what is death or 'extinction'? One has to delve deep into an ocean of knowledge to find a clue. Drinking from the fathomless depths of the ocean, Nataraja, the dancing Shiva in the temple of Vaaleeswara at Thiruvaleeswaram near Tirunelveli, has a face that fascinates. It is deeply mysterious and at the same time, it exudes a consummate wisdom.

This temple was built before Rajaraja Chola ascended the throne in 985 A.D. The sculpture of Nataraja in this temple has a smile on his face that communicates with us till date. With Rishabarudra and the Devi on one side, Nataraja's smile expresses the very enigma of life. If one concentrates and focuses one's eyes on that face, one can see how it magically flashes a variety of emotions, now exciting, now mystifying, calm one moment and enigmatic the next, all with a smile that hovers on the lips so capriciously. Holding our eyes riveted as if under a spell, one could go on looking at the smile on the face of Nataraja for hours on end.

As one drives away from Ambasamudram ...

At last the article was done. Sukumaran wrote the concluding portion. Satisfied that he could complete the job, he went to bed. Call it sheer exhaustion, or the fulfillment of completing the article, or the cultural richness of the Chola period, Sukumaran perhaps owed it to all three the blissful, dreamless sleep that he slipped into, that night.

The following morning, he reached his office only after he mailed his article, taking care to have it weighed properly at the post office. When he entered his room in the UPSC office, it was already 10:45 in the morning, but who cares? The UPSC was functioning as usual, as if to say it was all right with the office if Sukumaran reported late for work or just decided to die on the way to office. It was all the same. The UPSC that conducted important qualifying examinations nationwide for bureaucratic positions went on as usual. I'm caught somewhere between the many folders and files of this office, or perhaps I've been totally flattened out between the folders and files, he thought.

The 'room' he occupied in the office was an indefinite-looking hall. When Sukumaran went in, he found his colleague Pantulu sharpening a pencil. The other colleague Bajaj's seat was vacant. A gossip floated around in the office that Bajaj was engaged in some small business enterprise that often kept him away from his office work. True to the gossip, Bajaj would suddenly disappear from the office and then return as suddenly, with a smooth smile. If anybody questioned him, he would retort without hesitation: 'This office doesn't need me, so I went out. But I need the chicken-feed salary I get from this office to cover my house rent, so I came back.' Once he was back in office, Bajaj set about finishing all his work briskly. How clever he was in converting his spare time into money! And here I am, squandering all my time scribbling on art history, sculpture, archaeology and so on, emptying my wallet for postage, thought Sukumaran.

His desk was dusty. Sukumaran wiped it off with a piece of old paper and sat down. He opened a file. In a short while, the office peon brought him the morning cup of tea. But for some heat, the liquid had no taste to speak of. A creature of habit, Sukumaran swallowed it and then got up to answer a call he got from his boss Luthra, the Joint Secretary. He went over to Luthra's room.

'Good morning, Sir,' he said.

'Morning, Sukumaran. Please come in and be seated,' smiled Luthra. Instantly, he got a call on his phone. He talked for a while over the phone, then hung up and said: 'Ah then Sukumaran ...' when the second phone on his desk started ringing.

'O damn!' he cursed, lifting the receiver. But his tone changed and he started speaking chirpily to whoever was at the other end of the line. When he was through, Luthra replaced the receiver and said again: 'Ah ... Sukumaran ... '

Then suddenly, as if he remembered something just then, Luthra picked up the phone, dialed a number and talked to somebody. Sukumaran was used to all this waiting.

Perhaps I'm not sitting in this room at all, he thought. May be it's not really me who is sitting on this chair, but someone else. All this waiting, all this sliding down in priority in order to make room for the importance and urgency of calls ... all this is actually happening to someone else.

Luthra replaced the receiver and said: 'Sukumaran, we'll have to get a whole lot of reports ready. That's why I sent for you. And this man called Bajaj, he is in your unit, isn't he?'

'Yes Sir.'

'But he is always giving us the slip. One day I'll have to call him in and give him a sound warning,' said Luthra, pushing three swollen folders towards Sukumaran and continued: 'You see Sukumaran, I don't really enjoy giving warnings and stuff like that. Issuing a Memo, and then sending it through a peon-book and so on ... nonsense! All of you aren't school boys, surely? Well, I'm not a school master either, to yell orders at you, am I, hmm?' he asked, clearly annoyed about the whole situation.

'Sir, if you've no objection to the idea, then may I ask Bajaj to see you today?' Sukumaran offered.

'Thanks. Could you please do that? If everyone else in this office is as accountable as you are, then it can still survive. But some people seem to turn up for work only to waste our time,' sighed Luthra. Sukumaran gathered the folders and got up to go.

'Sir?' he said, standing.

'Yes?'

'There's something I ... '

'Tell me.'

'You're busy, Sir. And I really don't want to waste your time,' said Sukumaran.

'That's all right, Sukumaran. I have the time. Please take a seat and tell me,' said Luthra.

'Sir, I don't want to blow up anything beyond proportion or make trouble for anybody, believe me,' he began, but stopped.

'Hmm?' asked Luthra.

'Sir, for the past six or seven years now, some of us in this office have continued to work with the label of a 'Temporary Post' stuck on us. We feel very upset and helpless about this impermanent status. Seven years back, when we were interviewed for the post of 'Research Officers', we were given a grand assurance that 'only the post is nominally temporary. Where the UPSC is concerned, you're permanent for us because the government is planning to regularise the posts and make them permanent very soon. This is what we were told. It is another thing that we're supposed to be 'Research Officers' only by designation while there's absolutely no opportunity or incentive for us to do anything that could merit the word 'research'. And to make matters worse, our status at work is "permanently temporary". Just think of it, Sir,' said Sukumaran.

'Yes indeed. This has become a shameful anomaly and is a blot on the Commission. There seems to be a big flaw right at the core of our structure and policies and the way they've been formed,' observed Luthra, with a sigh.

'You know the whole picture, Sir, I don't have to tell you. We work almost in the pattern of daily labour and they keep 'extending' our term every year. Even the ones who joined on clerical posts after me, like in the ranks of LDCs (Lower Division Clerks) and UDCs (Upper Division Clerks) have been promoted to permanent positions now as Section Officers or Assistants to senior officers. We happen to be more qualified than them, we have more academic degrees, but what's the use? Where can you fault us, Sir?' asked Sukumaran.

'No, the fault is in the way you enter this organisation. Ironically, it's easier to climb your way up if you join the Commission as a clerk. Hell! It's too bad. This office doesn't know the worth of educated, knowledgeable young men like you,' said Luthra.

'Oh, there's nothing to write home about, Sir,' said Sukumaran, but Luthra interjected him:

'I know Sukumaran, I know very well. You're so erudite in Art History and are well known in the field. I've read some of your articles. They're so very good!' said Luthra, generously.

'Oh what's there in all that, Sir? I just write something to spend my time, that's all. About my service in the Commission Sir, I feel so very insecure at times. How can my family or I hope to ... ?'

'I have an idea,' said Luthra. 'Why don't you talk it over with our Secretary, Mr Shyam Sarup? He is not an ordinary IAS officer like the rest of us. I have heard that he is very scholarly and a learned man with a taste in art, theatre and so on. It seems he also writes occasionally. Go and meet him. I'll also put in a word about you to Mr Shyam Sarup,' offered Luthra.

'Thank you Sir, thanks very much.'

'You're welcome. As for the Reports ... '

'Don't worry Sir. I'll finish them fast,' said Sukumaran. He took the folders and left the room.

In the evening, there were the usual office commuters of Delhi milling around Sukumaran as he boarded the bus that took him home. People jostled, nudged and stumbled against each other on the steps of the bus. What a stampede on a daily basis! Sukumaran had eventually grown used to this dense crowd. He had become impervious to people pushing him around. Recently, there was the occasion of his birthday. When he woke up in the morning, his wife Vatsala greeted him with a blithe 'Happy Birthday!' He had turned thirty-two on that day but he had felt as if he had grown so much older, convinced that his end was near.

Vatsala had started rubbing it in right on the morning of his birthday. She had said, 'Here, I made some sweets especially for your birthday. I prayed to God that at least this year you should be made permanent in our office.' Instantly as it were, the birthday morning had turned to ash for Sukumaran.

I cannot blame Vatsala, he thought. It was my mistake to have agreed to this marriage. He had pleaded with his mother earnestly, 'I don't want to marry, not before my position is stabilised in office. I'm still temporary,' he had reasoned. But his mother would have none of it.

'Oh go on! You're always harping on the same tune that you're temporary ... temporary. But you should also realise that you're getting on in years. Don't you need someone to call your own, someone to set up a house for you? Consider your wife and your house as the permanent features of your life and be happy,' his mother had said firmly. And so his marriage had been fixed with Vatsala.

During the wedding ceremony, when he sat beside Vatsala on the ceremonial seat, his anguish reached a saturation point. Why am I entering into a bond with this girl? It is so meaningless. They, Sukumaran and Vatsala, had to exchange garlands and then hold hands. For one second, just a split second, the touch had seemed to germinate a tiny hope in his mind. Perhaps I'll come through this as a tangible, solid human being at least for this girl, my bride, he had thought.

But the ugly frictions started right on the day of the marriage. Vatsala's cousin Radha was the one to start it off. She had completed the old scheme of Intermediate Examination (a pre-graduation school certificate on a secondary level) and had joined the Canara Bank as a clerk. She was bragging about her job brazenly, 'Vatsala, now it's only you who can bring about some luck to your husband. At last he should be confirmed in his office and made 'permanent'. My best wishes to him,' she had said, insolently. Two months back her bank had made her 'permanent' in her post and that had gone to her head like wine. Then there was Chandru, Sukumaran's cousin. He worked with a private company. 'Sukumaran, this is atrocious!' he had remarked loudly, so that everybody heard him. 'You've been slogging for your office for so many years now and yet they don't confirm you in your post! For us in the corporate sector, even the period of probation is only for six months. This is terrible.'

It had provoked Sukumaran to such a degree that he was further infuriated with his mother that night.

'Why did you get me married Amma, *me*, of all the people, when I don't even have a future to look forward to? Perhaps I won't even be counted as being alive until I'm made permanent by the office,' he had exploded. 'What are you blabbering,' his mother had retorted. 'You're born as my son and that's a solid reality. It's the ultimate truth. And you're a husband to this girl here. Very soon, there may be a little one to call you "father". Who is that what's-his-name in your office who calls you "temporary" all the time and who dares to blow you away like vapour, hmm? Who the devil is he? Look Sukumaran, you're my son and to me, you're the ultimate truth. And that's all that matters!' his mother had asserted firmly. Sukumaran had felt a bit consoled after that. Before he had left for Delhi, he had touched his mother's feet in obeisance. At that moment, a small hope fluttered within him. Perhaps his wife Vatsala may also react like his mother? One day, she may, like his mother, acknowledge him as a solid, substantial man of some consequence, he hoped.

Solid? Substantial? The only things Vatsala looked upon as 'solid' and 'of consequence' were chunky gold jewellery, heavy silk sarees, money in 'fixed deposit' in the bank, her mother's house and the tickets she bought by the hundreds to see movies—all in that order. Like everyone else, Vatsala also constantly nagged Sukumaran about when he would become 'permanent'. When, when? God damn it! I should've listened to my inner voice, thought Sukumaran. The voice that rose from within again and again on the day I sat beside this woman during the wedding ceremony. It had warned me relentlessly. '*Hey, don't! Just don't get pulled into this unwanted ritual. Who's this woman? Why should you enter into a bond of relationship with her? It is all so unnecessary. Leave the place, detach yourself from all this rubbish and get up. Come on, get up and go!*'

It was an urgent, insistent voice, but he had disregarded it and gone ahead with the ceremony. He had agreed to marry, after all. Now I'm reaping the harvest of that mistake, he thought. A desolate sense of emptiness envelopes and smothers me as soon as I return home from office. I sense a complete void. 'You're my son, and to me you're the ultimate truth,' said his mother. He recalled her forceful words and her sturdy belief in him. 'Soon there'll be a little one to call you father,' she had said and sure enough, Sukumaran's baby daughter Uma Shankari was born.

Uma Shankari. When Sukumaran heard that his daughter was born, he was very thrilled. 'God be thanked! A tiny little baby girl, my very own girl. She is born with the trust that she has a father, me! I'm a father, her father!' he thought, happy after a long time. Suddenly, he felt the solidity of his own body as something real. He rushed to see the baby and Vatsala at her mother's place. 'Ha, my daughter,' he said, touching her wonderingly. When he touched her tiny hand, instantly the small, tender little fingers wrapped around his finger tightly. What a marvel! How do these delicate fingers get such a strong grip? From the soft, tiny little hand, a strong sense of trust flowed as if she had a certain tacit faith in him. His whole body quivered with excitement as he stood looking at the face of his baby.

He remembered the way Vatsala held his hand during the wedding in a weak, jelly-like grip. It was so wishy-washy compared to the unmistakable strength of this tiny hand. How strange, thought Sukumaran, that from an empty, meaningless social convention called 'marriage' there is an invigorating consequence such as a baby, his daughter Uma Shankari!

'Vatsala,' he said, eagerly. 'Just look at our Uma, she's such a darling. I'll show you how I'm going to bring her up.'

'Don't build castles in the air about her. After all, she is a girl, so how can we claim her as our own? When she grows up, we'll have to get her married and she'll just slip out of our life,' replied Vatsala, bluntly.

'What!'

'That's the way it'll be. If it had been a boy, we could've kept the child with us. She ... Uma ... doesn't really belong to us at all,' Vatsala reiterated as Sukumaran looked at her, aghast. How can she reduce womanhood *per se* so harshly, when she is a woman herself? How can she be so very retrograde in her thoughts, he wondered. Fuming, he left the room. But as he walked, the soft touch of the silky little finger lingered in his heart.

Sukumaran hesitated for a minute in front of the Secretary's room. Then he tapped on the door lightly and went in. Shyam Sarup was in his seat.

'Good morning Sir. I'm Sukumaran. I'm a Research Officer here,' he said.

'Uh ... ? Oh yes, Luthra told me about you. Please take a seat,' said Shyam Sarup.

'Thank you Sir.'

'Tell me. What can I do for you?' said Shyam Sarup, puffing at his pipe. Behind his seat was a gleaming bookcase, stacked to capacity with books that covered the entire wall.

Sukumaran briefly explained the way his position had stagnated over the past seven years in the office.

'You mean nothing has been done about it all this time?' asked Shyam Sarup.

'Nothing. Nothing at all, Sir. They've not made us permanent, and what's worse, they are using the excuse of "impermanence" to deny us even the promotions that are our due. Of course, we can't even talk or think about promotions,' said Sukumaran.

'Tch ... '

'Some of the departments in our office are taking undue advantage of our "temporary" status. They use our desk like a disposable garbage can and pile on all kinds of irrelevant work that takes the life out of us. We end up doing all that extra work without a single murmur of protest. But what do we get in return?' asked Sukumaran.

'Mr Sukumaran, that's nothing unusual. It's a very ordinary situation prevailing over certain posts in the government. No one can suddenly wish it away by waving a magic wand.'

'Sir, forgive me, but I don't mean to criticise anybody. Because I know that it has become a kind of a system in our government. But for how long can a man ... '

'It's hard on you, I know, particularly for someone as educated and scholarly as yourself. And someone who is an eminent art historian as well,' said Shyam Sarup.

'Sir!'

'I've heard a lot about you, Mr Sukumaran. Why, I've also read your articles, quite a few times. They're excellent, undoubtedly.'

'Oh it's no big deal, Sir. It's just something to keep me occupied. I wanted to consult with you on how to handle this knotty situation in the office, so ... '

'Have some patience, Mr Sukumaran.'

'Patience Sir? For seven long years we've been dragging our feet to this office and getting used to the drag. Perhaps that's exactly why we've been taken for granted by the office, all in the name of a 'routine' situation,' said Sukumaran, breathless with the effort of talking. His voice sounded loud to his own ears. The next minute, he cooled and apologised, 'I'm sorry, Sir,' he said.

'Mr Sukumaran, the way you speak English so fluently, it's beautiful. But why do you waste your language here? Preserve it for your writings,' said Shyam Sarup.

'Oh no Sir, all I meant was ... I mean ... '

'What do you mean then? Why should the government agree to a confirmation or give you a promotion the minute you ask for it? Because you're a renowned art historian with a flair for writing classy English?' laughed Shyam Sarup, placing his fuming cigar on a cut-glass ashtray.

'Don't worry Mr Sukumaran,' he continued. 'Leave it to us. We know what's to be done. All right?'

Sukumaran got up.

'Ah, one other thing, Mr Sukumaran. Please keep writing. Write a lot. It's good work. And all the best!' said Shyam Sarup, placing the pipe on his lips again.

Sukumaran came out of the room and walked in the long corridor, partially shadowed in darkness. There were many others in the corridor, jostling and brushing against him as they walked in the half darkness. Perhaps they can't see me at all, he thought. Or is it me who has become blind? He walked in a daze.

The dancing Nataraja in the temple of Valeeswara had Rishabharudra and the Devi on one side. He, Nataraja, was leaping out of the stone, alive. And on his face, there was a fascinatingly enigmatic smile that drew our eyes to speculate on its deep mystery. What a smile! It sent out so many different meanings each time one looked at it. What does the smile say now, wondered Sukumaran? Are the lips of Nataraja moving strangely in Russian, of all the languages?

The message that Sukumaran decoded from the smile was, 'How can you tell a man who is wrapped up in warmth and comfort that you're freezing and dying of the cold?' thinks Ivan Denisovich in the novel *One Day in the Life of Ivan Denisovich* by Alexander Solzhenitsyn. How does it matter whether Ivan says it in Russian or I absorb it in English translation, the colonial English that provokes a Shyam Sarup to fly into such a rage? And what, if for a moment, it is ingested by the Chola Nataraja in Tamil?

Savvyasachi Square*

'Do you have the key?'

'Hmm ... '

'Take the umbrella too. Come on, hurry up! I've to leave at once. It's getting late.'

'All right Vanaja. Bye.'

'Amuda, come on. We'll have to take two tube trains and then there's that bit of walking from the tube station to school. It's getting awfully late,' said Vanaja, pulling her daughter Amudavalli by the hand as she turned to go, handbag slung on her shoulder.

'The man forgets the key one day, his coat the next day.... If this old man catches a cold, then it's me who has to look after him, attend on him.... Hell, what a life having to deal with an infirm old man!' Vanaja cursed under her breath as she climbed down the stairs. Velayudam could hear her clearly. He heard every word.

He closed the front door and went to the kitchen to make some coffee on the electric stove. Oh, I forgot again, he told himself. Forgot to put on my sandals after my morning prayers. How it gave me a shock the other day when I touched this electric stove on bare feet. Perhaps my feet were wet. My son Arumugam had ganged up with my daughter-in-law Vanaja and had pounced upon me ... ! he recalled.

'Can't you be a little careful?' they had shouted. 'You should've some practical good sense,' Arumugam had chided. Carefully, Velayudam wiped his feet dry with a towel, pulled the socks over them and wore his shoes before switching on the electric stove. He

* Translated from the original Tamil "Savvyasachi Chattukkam" by the author, published in *Shubha Mangala*, Chennai. This translation first published in *Humanscape*, Mumbai.

made a hot cup of coffee for himself. After that, he put on a large overcoat and remembered to take the house key and the umbrella before stepping out of the apartment. He pulled the front door behind him and heard it locking itself firmly with a metallic 'click'. 'Thank heaven, God save me,' he muttered, taking a deep breath of relief. Every time Velayudam came out and heard the front door lock itself shut, he nearly lost his life for a moment and got it back all over again.

During the early days of his stay in London, there had been many instances when he had got confused about locking the main door. He would get flustered and finally forget that he had to take the house key every time before stepping out of the apartment. He would often lock himself out. Since he could not get into the flat, he would wander around the neighbourhood, then get back to the apartment to wait outside for hours for Arumugam and Vanaja to return from work. Predictably, they would be furious. 'How very silly of you to have forgotten the house key. Just look at the way you're standing, right in the middle of the road. It's so embarrassing. Everyone will laugh at us.'

Humph! Some big shame. Old hypocrites, the husband and wife. They put on a big front for the world and talk so euphemistically. On the rare occasions when they happened to talk to any of the Britons in the neighbourhood, how the two of them bragged about their so-called 'cultural values'.

'In our country, we always take care of our elderly parents well. Because that's the way we're conditioned. It's our culture, our duty too. In the West, elderly people are dumped in Old Age Homes so mercilessly. What a callous thing to do! We can't even imagine a situation like that,' they would go on, very pleased with themselves. And the Britons would make some polite noises of appreciation, just to keep up appearances.

Valliamma, my wife. She's gone now, peacefully. Only I'm left behind to suffer like this. I should've had the good sense to stay back in my own village in India. There's Kuttan in the village, Valliamma's brother. And then there's my uncle, my mother's brother, who is of course years older than I. I have so many relatives in the village. Whether we had internal family feuds raging within a household or not, there was always the comfort of being in one's own place.

The comfort of belonging. How can you hope to find that cosy feeling in a foreign land? But it was Arumugam who had nagged me continuously, without any respite. 'Appa, come and stay with us in London,' he had pleaded. 'We'll show you around. What does Tamil Nadu have to offer? It's so dry, dirty and dusty. Come and see what living in Britain is like. It's a land of plenty, it really is. All items—milk, fruits, vegetables, meat, down to housing is excellent,' he had said.

Arumugam had lured me with these words and here I am, a mere convenience. I look after their two small children, my granddaughter Amudavalli and my grandson Shanmugam until Vanaja, my daughter-in-law returns from the school where she teaches. I heat milk for the children, coax them to drink it up, I warm their food and serve them, tell them stories as I tuck them up in bed. Vanaja works as a teacher in a small, primary level school. What other job can she get with her indifferent academic background? A few Indians, Pakistanis and Bangladeshis of modest means got together and started a small nursery school in a house. And for that, Vanaja struts around and always talks about her 'career'! And that spineless Arumugam just hangs on her words, wagging his tail. How we wrapped him up with love and care when he was small, Valiamma and I.

Velayudam avoided the elevator and climbed down the stair. Bright sunlight greeted him outside. He did not open the umbrella. He walked across to the West Hampstead tube station and bought a ticket for himself. Following the direction of the route in the deep Pink Line, the Metropolitan Line, he boarded his usual train. In front of him was the usual morning scene of passengers in the train, deeply buried in the day's newspaper spread out in front of them. Only a few faces were visible in between the papers. Men and women with glassy eyes stared ahead without any expression on their faces, their bodies swaying to the rhythm of the train's movement. How do they live like this, without exchanging even a word with one another, Velayudam wondered. Travelling the whole day beneath the surface of the earth in this underground tube has perhaps robbed their faces of blood. They look so pale ...

Velayudam noted the names of the stations flitting through the windows. He got down at Baker Street and scanned the railway lines again, drawn in different colours on the wall. He followed the Brown Line, the Bakerloo Line, and slowly walked towards the platform. The train pulled up at the station. Velayudam boarded it and shortly afterwards got down at Embankment.

It was somewhat chilly. He bought coffee in a small kiosk. Yuck! It tastes like bitter medicine. They just kill the taste of coffee because they keep on boiling the coffee extract endlessly. Ah! The coffee Valliamma made. It was truly fit for the gods. And she would serve it along with *idlis*[1] soft and white as the flowers of *thumbai*[2]. She would tear off a piece of white cloth from an old, well-washed *dhotie*[3] and steam *idlis* in them expertly. Then she would percolate coffee and with the first extract, make coffee with freshly heated milk. As you sipped that coffee, the aroma would pierce your nostrils and a soothing warmth would wash over your whole body pervasively. It was a coffee that tapped alive the life force within you!

He looked at the remaining coffee in his paper cup, then crushing it threw it away in the waste bin. Climbing up the stairs of the tube station, he came out and strolled towards St. James's Park at a leisurely pace. Being a working day of the week, the streets were not too crowded although some people could be found walking briskly up and down the street. Nobody seems to notice me, thought Velayudam. I walk like a corpse, a living corpse. Even if people happen to see me, they dismiss me with just one sweep of a glance as if to say, 'oh, there goes yet another black man'.

Black or not, I'm real to myself. This colour which unsettles them, the colour of my dark skin, it's a truth. This skin feels the heat of the sun just as it feels the cold of the snow. It's a skin that smarts painfully from the stinging words of Vanaja, it's a skin that winces under the harsh words of Arumugam who always gangs up with his wife. But the skin is real. Real.

Velayudam's legs ached. The road to St. James's Park seems to be unusually long today. Or have I grown tired this early in the morning? I did a mistake in choosing to walk. After getting down at the Embankment, I should've caught a train on the Green Line. That would've brought me straight on to St. James's Park. It was foolhardy of me to opt for walking.

It was quiet in St. James's Park. There were only a few people around. Velayudam sat on a bench under a tree. In front of him

[1] *Idlis:* A breakfast dish made with rice and black gram.

[2] *Thumbai*: Soft white flowers of the white nettle.

[3] *Dhotie*: A loose piece of cloth worn waist-down by men.

was a small pond with ducks swimming to and fro. They dipped their bills in the water and quivered as they shook themselves free of the droplets of water, much to the delight of the small children who played around the pond, watching the scene. Their mothers had spread a cloth over the grass and taken things out of the picnic baskets. Sandwiches, rolls, apples, cartons of milk, chocolates and fruit juices were laid out on a cloth. Velayudam was surprised to see some of them throw crumpled paper on the grass. Oh dear, thought Velayudam, I've seen only Indians do that.

A few tourists strolled along the narrow pathway, cameras slung over their shoulders. On the bench next to Velayudam sat a Briton munching something, but deeply engrossed in reading his paper. It was pleasantly warm. Ah, what bliss! It is so peaceful to get out of the house to the great outdoors. But to reach this place every day one has to get into the tube train.

'It costs two pounds fifty cents for every return trip by the tube. Sheer waste of money. Why don't you sound him about it?' Vanaja had asked Arumugam.

'What? What're you saying? Who spends that much every day?' Arumugam had enquired.

'Your father, that's who!' was Vanaja's reply.

'Oh, father just goes out to get some fresh air. What will he do here, cooped up at home all day, with me returning home from office so late?' Arumugam had said.

'Now look here. We simply can't afford all this expense, let me make that very clear to you. Just think of the cost of living in London. Our house rent alone seems to swallow us up, whole. Then there's your father, occupying the living room the whole day. When my friends visit me, I can't find any place for them,' Vanaja had complained.

'But it was you who had been obstinate about our moving into a two-bedroom apartment. You're the one who planned that the children must've one bedroom for themselves, that we should have the other. That leaves only the living room for my father. Now you turn around and ... okay then. Shall we look for a three-bedroom flat?' Arumugam had said.

'What! Have you gone mad? Here I'm telling you that we can't even afford our present lifestyle.... Now listen to me. Are *you* going to talk to your father about the daily wasteful expenditure or shall I?' Vanaja had asked sternly.

'Oh no. I'll talk to him, I'll tell him Vanaja, leave it to me. I'll try to persuade him that it's enough if he goes out twice or three times in a week. All right?' Arumugam had said.

'Humph!' Vanaja had made a face at him and left the room in a huff.

Arumugam kept his promise to Vanaja. Gingerly, he broached the subject with his father. Velayudam could not absorb the words that dropped out of Arumugam's lips. He stood there as if he was struck deaf for a moment. Only his eyes noted how Arumugam gulped his words midway, how he repeatedly blinked his eyes.

'Appa ... Appa ...'

The small boy, Arumugam, tugged at the edge of his father's shirt.

'Yes my child?'

'Appa ... I ... I ...'

'Come on, tell me. What do you want, my child? Why do you hesitate so much?'

The small boy lowered his head and remained silent. Velayudam kneeled on the floor to bring himself at the level of the boy. He looked at him straight in the eyes and asked, 'Arumugam, what is it?'

Shyly, little Arumugam pointed at the ice-cream vendor.

'Is that all?' said Velayudam. He bought him an ice cream. Arumugam wolfed it down eagerly.

'Want to have another?' asked Velayudam. Arumugam remained silent. Velayudam bought him one more. Arumugam was delighted. Suddenly emboldened by the mood, he asked his father, 'Appa, there's something called cake in that shop, in light green, pink and white colours. What'll it be like?'

Instantly, Velayudam bought him the pastry. It cost him three rupees. He realised then that he did not have enough money left for the bus that would take them both home to Tambaram. Father and son walked their way back home that evening.

'Are you tired of walking, my child?'

The little boy just lowered his head and said nothing.

Velayudam kneeled down and looked at his son. 'Arumugam, are you tired in the legs?'

The boy shook his head. Velayudam pulled him close, gathered him up in his arms and hugged him. He lifted up the boy and made him sit on his shoulder. The boy's slender legs dangled on both sides of his father's strong, muscular shoulders. Making sure that the boy was secure on his perch, Velayudam walked, carrying Arumugam all the way home as if the child was light as a basket of flowers. On reaching home, he lifted Arumugam's head by his chin and said, 'Dear child, don't hesitate so much whenever you want to say something. I'm your father after all, am I not?' he said, patting him lightly. Arumugam flung his arms around his father's neck and buried his face on the strong shoulder.

Now, the adult Arumugam stuttered hesitantly in front of his father. He avoided meeting his eyes. But the same Arumugam could easily snap and bark like a dog, hiding behind Vanaja whenever she cared to shout at Velayudam.

'Excuse me, what did you say?' asked the Briton who sat on the bench next to his, reading a paper.

'What? But Sir, I never said anything!' replied Velayudam in English, beside himself with surprise.

'*Sir*? Why do you call *me* Sir? Anyway, I've been looking at you for sometime now. I noticed that you were saying something. I also thought that may be you spoke like that, without even looking at me because you have a problem with your vision. Do you?' said the man, rolling the paper in his hand.

Velayudam felt the blood rushing to his face. His body shrank back in embarrassment.

'No, no, there's nothing wrong with my vision. I can see properly,' he said. 'And I don't think I said anything, I mean, I didn't speak at all.'

'Very well, then. I just enquired to find out if you needed any help, that's all. Take care. Good day!' smiled the man and walked away from the place.

Velayudam looked at his retreating figure for a moment, then he shook himself. How very disgraceful. I've been sitting in this park, a public place, and talking aloud to myself. What utter idiocy! It's mainly the consequence of sitting in one place for a long time, with nothing to do. Let me walk around a bit, he thought, and got up from the bench.

Velayudam walked a bit and felt a dryness in his throat. He bought himself a cup of tea from a small kiosk and slowly strolled along the Birdcage Walk. Traffic flowed on the Horses Guard Road to his left. He walked towards the direction of the Spurt Road although his aching feet bothered him. In the park there were a few benches that lay unoccupied. He sat on one of them facing the Spurt Road, which was full of tourists walking towards Buckingham Palace, Queen Elizabeth's palace. He glanced at his wristwatch. There are still ten minutes to go for eleven o'clock. The 'Changing of the Guard' ceremony at the Buckingham Palace, complete with a music band, drums and what not will start in another ten minutes. That was one reason why the people on the road were hurrying towards the palace. When I was new to London, Arumugam had brought me over to this palace to see this ritual. What a grand spectacle it was!

Velayudam sat on a bench and closed his eyes. He could hear the music now. No, not the pomp and richness of the music from the 'Changing of the Guard' ceremony, for there were still five minutes to go. He heard another music now, a different kind of music, very quiet and soft as it swirled and echoed within his ears. He heard the sounds of a large cello. It wafted from a corner of Trafalgar Square where the roads met. A man stood, playing on the cello. He sang beautifully. People flung coins on the cloth spread in front of him and soon there was a pile of money over the floor. The music spread a sweet delirium, reverberating around the whole corner. Velayudam was amazed. What a gifted man. He sings so very well. He looked at him intently. Why, the man is old, he noted, quite old in fact. As Velayudam dragged himself away from the place and walked on, the music of the cello man followed him and wrapped around him with a soft, resonant presence.

Even now, sitting here in St. James's Park, it resounded in his ears so clearly. Has that old man splintered into many different men and have each of them occupied the different Squares in different parts of London, all those Squares where the roads meet, with a man playing music for every weary passerby? Has the man really split up into different men with different looks, playing different notes on different musical instruments across the various corners of London? Has he? If not, how then did I see another old man, different, yet somewhat similar to this one, near St. Westminster Bridge? On Sundays, occasionally even on Saturdays, if you walk past the Westminster Abbey and get into one of the smaller streets, then you can see for yourself. You'll find the man sitting in a large square, singing to the notes of his instrument, a triangular stringed musical instrument on which he played with a bow. It was something like the Russian balalaika except that it had a strange looking handle on the right. The man kept on turning the handle with one hand, while holding the bow with the other and sang in a way that softly caressed your heart. He rained music on anyone who came close enough. Who could say he was old at all? All the tired people, tired of walking endlessly, tired of stepping in and out of shops, felt refreshed by his music that rose and spread out, floating above and settling down on everyone like soft woolly clouds of melody.

Velayudam opened his eyes and cleared his throat. Carefully, he looked around in all directions. I mustn't talk aloud to myself again, oh no, I mustn't, he warned himself, closing his lips firmly. He closed his eyes again. I have half an hour for myself, after which I should leave for home. Come what may, I must go to the temple of Murugan[4] in Eastham at least once a week. It has been such a long time since I went there. And yet, whenever I go to Eastham I return with an incomplete feeling, as if something is missing. Is it enough to have a *darshan* of Murugan by seeing him? Shouldn't I complete my pledge to the god by walking barefoot on a hot, steaming asphalt road for miles on end with a *kaavadi*[5] on my shoulders, walk till my feet get blistered? How we walked in our village in India, carrying the *kaavadi* on our shoulders. First we stand in a row as milk is poured into a small container attached to our *kaavadi*. Once it is perched on our shoulders, we sing in chorus, 'Victory to god Murugan, victory to the valiant one who wields a spear!' And then we would set off on our long walk briskly, the milk in the small containers spilling over whenever our movements got jerky. We walked for miles on end, rows and rows of us, but actually we were really alone, each one of us. Every man walked alone, the *kaavadi* on his shoulders bearing his own private, secret wishes and goals. It was man alone with his individual pledge to god, even as he walked along with the rest of them.

[4] Murugan: Kartik, the young son of Shiva and Parvati, brother of Ganesh. He is a god of valour and strength.

[5] *Kaavadi*: A cylindrical wooden rod joined on top by a curved wooden strip. It is decorated on both sides with the feathers of peafowls. It is also used in folk dances.

The music resonated hauntingly. Velayudam could hear all kinds of sounds now. It was a blend of melodies from a harmonica, a synthesiser, the beat of drums. And that was not all. The melting sweetness of notes from a flute reached him. Knifing through the sound waves in between was the strong drone of Scottish bagpipes. They rang in his ears and inside his closed eyes a scene unfolded like a vivid picture. Has one man splintered into several different men who play on the instruments and sing in the squares of London where the roads meet? Or is it more accurate to think that all those different men have actually fused and welded into that one man who has magically gathered up their collective skills for his own incredible versatility? Have all the different skills of the men amalgamated into that one abundantly gifted man, a veritable conglomerate who handles a variety of musical instruments simultaneously and with such astonishing ease?

That man. He is unique. He always occupies a place on the square near Piccadilly where the four streets meet, the one beside the Green Park towards the direction of Piccadilly. It is a square which invariably vibrates with the notes of excellent music, thanks to him. It's not just the good music alone. It's also a splendid spectacle that fills your eyes. A visual delight. One day I edged closer and took a look. What a stunning display it was.

An enormous crowd milled around—an immense, surging crowd in which the children outnumbered the adults. And there stood a tall frame on which were fixed small colourful birds, ducks and many other things. The birds fluttered and flapped their tiny wings in answer to the sounds of harmonica coming from behind the wooden framework. Small ducks opened and closed their bills to the notes of the synthesiser. The birds and ducks, all of them quivered to the music, their body tingling to the notes. Then there were enchanting fairies too, along with elves, gnomes and dwarves that tuned into the music and danced together with admirable rhythm. There were also little pups, kittens, a baby bear, Mickey Mouse and so on. They moved to the beat of the drums and the soft, fluid notes of the flute, to every little movement of music from the various instruments. All of them—the birds, the ducks, the fairies, elves, gnomes, dwarves, pups, kittens, Mickey and the bear—all of them swayed, played, gamboled about, frolicked, clapped their hands and danced. What a splendid scene! An unforgettable experience.

It drew everyone, children, their young mothers, fathers and all others—who happened to walk that way. Attracted by the sheer force of the music and the spectacular display on the large wooden framework that dominated the whole square, they thronged, filling up the entire place. The man who conjured up this magical show was always concealed behind the wooden frame, working nimbly behind the scene, single-handed. Velayudam's eyes searched for him eagerly. There he was. The man who played on the harmonica, the synthesiser, the man who deftly turned to a side to do the drum beats, who again pulled out liquid melodies from the flute, or kept a sustained note of bagpipes threading through it all—the various 'hands' belonged to *one* man. It was one man after all who accomplished the feat of taking turns to handle all those instruments. And that one man functioned from behind the screen, the veins on his arms thick, and the veins on his neck swollen as if they may burst any moment, his face red and puffy. If he played on the harmonica and the synthesiser, the ducks in front of the wooden frame opened and closed their bills, scampered about playfully, and the little birds flapped their tiny wings friskily. When he played on the flute and the bagpipes while simultaneously beating on the drums below, tapping his feet to the beat, the rope that was fastened to his ankles set in motion the dance of the colourful fairies, elves, dwarves and gnomes who swayed rhythmically to the music. One could watch the show for hours.

After the musical show gave over, Velayudam swallowed his initial hesitation and approached the man.

'It's excellent, the way you play on so many instruments and also sing!' he remarked in English.

'Thanks. Thanks very much,' the man smiled and nodded.

'I just ... I wondered ... if ...' said Velayudam hesitantly.

'Yes?'

'I mean ... '

The man waited, wiping his instruments with a soft linen. 'Tell me,' he said.

'I mean ... I just wondered if it wouldn't be enough for you to play on one, or at the most two musical instruments, since you sing so well?' asked Velayudam.

'If I restrict myself like that, I could never hope to draw such a big crowd. Therefore, I wouldn't be able to earn this much money, you see?' he replied. He looked utterly exhausted by the exertion of the whole show.

'But ... but ... if you don't mind,' began Velayudam and stopped midway.

'Go ahead, tell me ...' the man smiled at Velayudam genially.

'You're wearing yourself out, aren't you, by handling so many instruments at the same time, not forgetting the drums as well. Must you work so very hard for money? Do you need this much money?' asked Velayudam.

'I've no choice really. This is London, a city of prohibitive prices. And I live alone, and have no one who'd care to spend even a penny on me. My children have distanced themselves from me. They don't even visit me anymore, nor do they bother to find out how I'm getting on. That's why I've to work hard to make a living,' he explained, as he wiped and cleaned the toys, the dolls and the instruments one by one. He stacked them up neatly in a box. The harmonica, the flute, the synthesiser, the drums along with the birds and the fairies were tucked into the box where they settled, still and quiescent, after that vibrant action just a while ago, drawing everyone magnetically as they stood in awe and wonder.

The fatigue on his face made him look even older from close. And yet, what an amazing person you are, thought Velayudam. You're highly skilled in doing so many different things. You are ... you are ... Savvyasachi. That's right! Savvyasachi, the ambidextrous. Savvyasachi, one of the many other illustrious names attributed to Arjun[6], might well be yours. Like Arjun who was adept in handling a variety of weapons with exceptional skill and nimbleness in the battlefield, handling them all as if he had twelve hands that sliced their way through a thick, pitched battle. That's how Arjun earned his name as Savvyasachi, the brave, indomitable warrior, incredibly adept at battle craft. You too, old man, you can handle so any instruments and sing for your birds and fairies with such nonchalant ease, you are a Savvyasachi. Indeed you are.

Battle-weary, utterly exhausted and embittered by the ravages of war, a much saddened Arjun asked Lord Krishna, 'To what purpose is all this? Must I go on killing my own relations so mercilessly?'

[6] Arjun: One of the Pandava brothers in the epic *Mahabharata*.

Looking at the peerless warrior, Krishna replied, 'Who or what do you think you're killing anyway? You don't wish to kill your relations, but don't you realise that you yourself are going to die eventually? In the final analysis, what can you hope to annihilate? You can only destroy this thing you recognise as a 'body', that's about all. And the body is just a garment O Savvyasachi. You are a glorious soldier who can use two hands like twelve with incredible skill. Even so, a fine body such as yours in only a garment, an old garment. Very soon you're going to throw it away as something too old for you. You'll shed your body like an old dress. In that case Savvyasachi, why do you lament for others?'

Under the darkening sky of Kurukshetra[7], Krishna's words from Bhagavad Gita pierced through the sombre overcast like a flash of brilliant lightning. The light bathed Savvyasachi in the battlefield. The light also bathed this nice old Briton, the musical wizard in the Piccadilly squares of London.

Velayudam raised his eyes and looked at the man, at the fine wrinkles on his face. How valiantly he struggled against the loneliness and infirmity of old age in the cold squares of London. Come my man, let's discard this old garment we still wear, he murmured. Come my Savvyasachi, let's both cast it off, then let's mingle with the air. Come ...

[7] Kurukshetra: The place where the legendary battle between the Pandavas and the Kauravas took place.

The Maze*

A wide variety of Leo toys lay scattered on the floor. There was a 'police car' with a red light swirling on top, an 'army jeep' in moss green, a monkey that did somersaults, a cute little engine going round and round over circular rails and many other toys. All of them looked bright and attractive but the little boy Vivek was totally engrossed in the new thing that his father had bought for him. It was a brand-new plaything and for the first time, it gave Vivek a novel kind of experience. He got a strange feeling that as soon as he made a move to play with this toy, it made a vigorous move in equal measure, to play with him, by actively provoking and teasing him, goading him on to a lively play of skill.

Actually, it was a very simple concept in plastic. It was a puzzle within a large, round, pink coloured disc that had concentric rows in white, forming a maze of narrow alleys with gaps here and there for exit or entrance. In the centre was a tiny circle. The entire maze was covered on top with a sheer, transparent plastic like glass through which one could clearly see the tiny balls of steel inside. Just as his father had taught him two days back, Vivek tried to slowly coax the small balls to get past the walls of the maze one by one and help them get into the small inner circle in the centre. But however patiently he tried to take the balls inside, at least three or four of them would be pushed out.

'Vivek! Come and have your lunch,' his mother Radha called out. 'What's this? You've sat down to play without even changing your school clothes. You have to eat now, come on, and hurry!'

* Translated from the original Tamil "Paadarasa Gundugal" by the author published in *Inge, Inru*, Bangalore. This translation first published in *Parijata and Other Stories*, New Delhi: National Publishing House, 1992.

Vivek noticed a slight irritation in his mother's voice. He got up, carrying the plastic 'puzzle' with him to the dining table. Placing it beside his plate, he kept looking at it as he started eating. The tiny balls of steel that had until now been rolling and groping about the maze like they had lost their way, now lay motionless within the white circular maze like trapped prisoners inside a jail.

'Amma, how to gather all these balls and put them inside the small circle?' asked Vivek.

'Hey Ram! Why are you taking a game so seriously? So what if you can't put the balls inside? Just let them be,' laughed Radha.

'No. I'll *have* to put them inside. I'm going to ask Appa in the evening. He can certainly teach me how to.'

Now Radha laughed aloud. 'Indeed! Your father has so much time, does he, to play this game? To top it all, he returns home so late. Come on now, hurry up and eat. Your food is getting cold.'

The tiny balls slid smoothly and slipped into the curving white rows of the maze inside the pink, plastic frame. Rajaraman tilted it very gently sideways, completely lost in the game. For someone who was oblivious of everything as he so intently watched the uniformly identical balls rolling around, Rajaraman was gripped by an illusion that he could identify and recognise a few balls. One particular ball was nimble and brisk. It ran along easily and was so smart that it was approaching the inner circle pretty fast. But, in a totally unexpected move, another ball gave it a small jerk on the side, nudged it out to glide smoothly till it slid itself into the inner circle. There was this other ball starting somewhere from the middle of the maze, it moved on slowly and lazily, inching its way, quite laid back in style. The other balls that tapped the 'lazy' one on their way, gave it a push till that 'lazy-bones' ball effortlessly and quite accidentally reached the inner circle. Amazing! What a victory this was!

'Oh God, look here Vivek, just look! I thought this is a "smart" ball but it is the "lazy bones" over there that slipped inside, instead!' cried out Rajaraman, excitedly.

'Appa, how can you separate "this ball" and "that ball" when all of them look alike?' asked Vivek, his eyes round with surprise.

'They may look alike at first glance, but one can recognise the traits and see which is an active ball but has an unlucky fate and which is the truly lazy one, but gifted with a blind luck!' explained Rajaraman as Vivek looked at his father wide-eyed.

'What's going on here? You've also become a child, sitting down for a game with Vivek without even changing your clothes? Ah ... just look at your coffee, it has gone cold. Shall I heat it up for you?' asked Radha.

'No.'

She looked at her husband with surprise, as he sat with his head bent low, all immersed in the game. She took the cold cup of coffee and went inside.

Rajaraman stood for some time looking at Vivek who was fast asleep on his bed. He smiled at the pink plastic puzzle that was beside his pillow. And then a thought hit him. He picked up the plaything and gently pushed the hair that strayed over the child's brow. Then he went to the living room with the plastic puzzle in his hand, switched on two lights and sat down to play under the bright light.

Balls that ambled, crawled, shuffled and rolled to run on even as they trundled and hit against each other to slip inside. The slightest movement by Rajaraman made the balls change their entire fate by the way they moved by the tilt of his hand. Rajaraman was completely engrossed in the game. He wilfully tried to defeat some balls but was himself defeated. Rows and rows of curving white hurdles obstructed the movement of the balls as they failed in their attempt to move and looked perplexed. Rajaraman watched the drama unfolding, his eyes riveted. Under his intent gaze, the shining balls of steel looked like balls of mercury mixing and merging with one another to grow big in size. Why, some of them even had 'heads' and 'faces' that he now recognised.

Rajaraman has been working for some four years now with a multinational company that manufactured batteries. That he was one amongst the four or five taller people in the office was something that he found accidentally and strangely useful one day in office. That day, he stood in his cabin for sometime, running his eyes over the office. In the layout of his office, all the cabins were without a roof, and they had short wooden boundaries that served as walls. As he stood there looking at them, a silent play unfolded in front of his eyes. From the room of the Secretary that was beside the Manager's, it looked like an important announcement was floated around that was discreetly reaching the ears of people till a point was reached when everyone got to know of it. There was a ripple of excitement now across the office. Quite a few people had left their cabins to approach their colleagues in other cabins and were now mutually engaged in deep conversations, whispering to each other. The news was—Varadappan had been promoted, superseding his senior Shekar Iyengar. Shekar is a sincere and extremely hard-working person but whoever wants his hard work? Not the office surely. Because, unlike Varadappan, Shekar did not know the art of sailing on whisky and rum till the wee hours of the morning in all the office parties, forgetting all about his wife and children languishing at home. During office hours, Varadappan would swoop down on the smaller globules of mercury working under him, chase them like a slave-driver till they ran scuttling across the floors. He would squeeze the life out of them by extracting a lot of work from them, and then claim all their work as his own in a Report, complete with his signature. Once the work was over, he would push the balls into the walls of their respective cabins once again, navigate and skate his own way with a smooth agility and then slip into the inner circle at the centre. That was Varadappan.

For how many years Shekar would have gone in and out of these cabins, functioning as the ever loyal employee? Rajaraman remembered his brisk movements in and around the maze that was the physical structure of the office. But it was Varadappan who knew how to crouch and hide and then spring forward in the corridors of power, skating his way through with a style unparalleled in the office! There were some other subsidiary balls of mercury always wanting to emulate Varadappan. There was Mehra, for instance. He had a way of speaking firmly with his head shaking vigorously all along as he cleverly piled lies upon glib lies with a self-assured air. Subir Gupta was another spherule who was sluggish to the core. He would yawn lazily without moving an inch from his place and move around with a supremely laid-back air. Why ever not? His father was the biggest shareholder of the company besides being a very big figure in the world of business. So what was the hurry for the Gupta ball? He was confident that he would be welcomed in the inner circle. And this other ball called Naresh? He had a knack of working with a lot of noise. Even if he moves just an inch forward, he would brag about his drive and his being proactive.

The cabin walls had secret twists and turns and invisible potholes and cold graves into which one could fall suddenly. The balls of mercury whirled around, rolled and ran along, testing themselves as they carried their transient fate on their heads. Some of them mingled, their forms bigger for the merging while others split up and thinned out.

Inside the sphere of the office was a force-field. Trapped within the dynamics of power, the balls moved about like trapped prisoners, getting past the blockades and the alleys around the maze. They hit against each other, collided and got bruised as they fell. Some focussed on the single target of reaching the circle at the centre and moved towards it with a single-minded motivation, but were swallowed up on the way. Some lost their way and got scattered as they ran within their lonely circles.

Daang!

The clock on the wall struck one. A few seconds later, there were swishing sounds of a saree.

'Oh God, what is this? You're still playing with that puzzle, like a child. It's past one now. I saw you in Vivek's room, stroking him to sleep and now here you are, playing with his toy.... Come on, get some sleep,' said Radha.

Having got up from the middle of her sleep, Radha's face looked drowsy. Yet, a small smile hovered over her lips as she saw her husband so deeply at play.

Rajaraman was shaken out of his concentrated play. He raised his head to look at her face. There was however, no answering smile on his face. His jaw had stiffened hard.

Just Think About It*

'And you thought there was no point in talking to someone like me, so you distanced yourself from me, didn't you?'

...

'What did you take me for, a plain stupid brute or something?'

...

'But I can understand you, in fact only too well. I understand your desires, your ideas, your objectives ... why, everything in fact.'

...

'A marriage, after all, is a bond that can show up a hundred little cracks on the surface. Is that a good enough reason for you to take such an extreme step, I mean your decision to ... Look, please forgive me my mistakes, won't you? Forgive me.'

...

'Just think it over. Give it one hard think. Even if I were to agree to this divorce after so many years of marriage, what are you going to achieve, all by yourself?'

...

'Sir, can I get you anything else? A plate of finger chips, perhaps? And another pot of hot coffee?' asked the waiter.

'What?'

'Sir, I just asked if I could get you another hot coffee and something to eat with it, may be?' said the waiter.

'But I've eaten already,' he replied, glancing down at the plate on his table. It had some left-over of the *dosa* that he had just eaten.

* Translated from the original Tamil "Neeye Yositthu Paar" by the author, included in an anthology *Inru Maalai, Enudan*, Narmada, Chennai. This translation first published in *Parijata and Other Stories*, New Delhi: National Publishing House, 1992.

He raised his head and said, 'All right, get a plate of cutlets along with some finger chips and some hot coffee to go with it.'

'Very well, Sir. In a moment, Sir,' said the waiter, picking up the used plate.

He sat for a while, looking at the retreating figure of the waiter. He pulled out a pack of cigarettes from his pocket, lit one and sat waiting as he blew out the smoke. And then he leaned forward over the table, lowered his head slightly and continued again in the same low voice:

'I gave you total freedom to do whatever you wanted to do—to work, to earn a salary, to dress as you please and to go gallivanting about with your friends. What more do you want?' he asked, smiling.

...

'Tell me. Why should you hesitate to tell me?'

...

'Hmm? So, why this divorce, it's so unnecessary! Why don't we continue to live together like before, you and I?'

...

'Just think it over calmly. That'll help you see things clearly.'

He drew in deeply and blew out through his lips till his face was totally covered by a cloud of smoke. When he looked through the smoke-screen, he could sense the way people were glancing at him every now and then. He drew in again and blew out a dense cloud of smoke. In between the fumes, he could see some other images now, although they were dim and appeared somewhat faded.

There was her face, staring back at him, dry-eyed. Even when he slapped her hard, he could not draw a drop of tear out of those eyes. They were sharp eyes that looked back at him wordlessly. *Che*! Is she a woman at all? All right, let me provoke her and see if she slaps me back in retaliation. That will give me an excuse to easily accuse her in return. So he would slap her harder, but she would hold his striking hand in a strong grip, push him firmly out of her way and leave the room. The same expression of a chilling remoteness would settle in her eyes. 'You're despicable to the core, I'll have nothing to do with you,' said her look. And then an oppressive silence weighed upon him. It erased and dismissed him. That enraged him even more. It becomes a woman to weep at least a little, doesn't it? She does not break down and cry, even once. Why doesn't she plead and beg me to forgive her and to accept her? Why?

Such things do not find a place in her life. She had already planned out a neat blueprint for her future and with that, she had slipped away somewhere far from him. She had arranged for her stay in a hostel for she wanted to pursue her studies. Her parents and relations had agreed for this divorce, an effective, successful lawyer had been hired to argue the case and she was surrounded by caring friends and colleagues in office. She was so capable, the way she faced problems with courage, the way she carried herself with equanimity and the way her intelligence manifested in every word and action of hers—he found it all disconcerting. She unnerved him. She had a style of holding on to her self-confidence without ever losing her innate sense of modesty. How his hands itched to beat her up till her bones broke and crumbled, to destroy her, and completely annihilate her.

He blew up the salary she brought home and squandered it away. And whenever she was at home, he broke her back by making her work endlessly. He drove away her parents and friends. He tore off the letters that came for her, without showing them to her. He quarrelled with her, scolded her, found fault with her and beat her up. And yet, what arrogance! Without the slightest hesitation, she took a bold decision to divorce and briskly got busy with the arrangements for this divorce ...

'Sir.'

'Hmm?'

'Sir, here's a plate of cutlets, some finger chips and a pot of hot coffee. Will that be all?' asked the waiter.

'Yes.'

He cut the cutlet with a knife, picked up a piece with a fork and started eating slowly.

'Do you think I'm your enemy? Whatever might have happened between us, I'm your husband! Just think about it at least once.'

...

'I'm also eager to see you grow in your career and to cultivate people in social circles. But naturally, why wouldn't I be eager?'

...

'I want to keep you happy. But by running away like this, you're not giving me a chance to make you happy. What can I do under the circumstances, tell me?'

He dipped the finger chips in tomato ketchup and put it in his mouth. He poured out the steaming coffee into a cup and sipped at it slowly.

'Listen to me. It's not too late even now. You can still save the situation, if only you cooperate. Withdraw your application for divorce from the court, all right?'

...

'Right. It's but normal for a husband and wife to have a hundred differences and fights between them. That's what makes the relationship truly sacred. Can't you be magnanimous enough to forgive me for the mistakes that happened in the past, an educated girl like yourself? Ah! Now you agree with me, I see a smile on your face.'

...

'I know. I know very well indeed that you'll eventually come to your good senses and won't make me lose my face in society by this bad word, "divorce". Good!'

'Sir.'

'Yes?'

'Would you like to have anything more, Sir?' asked the waiter.

'Hey, why are you pestering me like this? I didn't order for anything more, did I?'

'No Sir, but the plates on your table are empty, so I ... '

'So what? Do you think I should keep on ordering for more things? Are you trying to drive me out of this restaurant?' he asked in a voice that was very different now.

For one who had been talking all along in a low undertone, he now raised his voice till he could see the people at the tables around him watching him intently.

'Oh no Sir! Please do pardon me. I wasn't trying to drive you out at all. Since you were talking for so long, all by yourself, I thought I could perhaps get you a cool drink, that's all Sir,' said the waiter.

He pulled out his wallet and paid for his bill. The waiter stood for a while, looking at the man as he walked out of the restaurant. He laughed aloud. Now the people sitting at the other tables also relaxed and laughed along with the waiter. A few of them did not laugh but sat on, knitting their brows thoughtfully while a few others shrugged their shoulders and turned their attention to the food on their plates.

Simone de Beauvoir and the Manes*

'Oh yes, there's no doubt about it whatsoever. You're definitely going to grow up to be like the renowned French writer Simone de Beauvoir some day. All in the course of time.'

All of them said the same things, almost all of them. But when Uma heard it for the fifth time, it took her well beyond a jaded surprise to the annoyance caused by the repetition. The statement now seemed to stand in front of her where she could literally see the two ends of it visibly drooping with fatigue on both sides. She also got a creepy feeling that the ones who made bold to say this were doing so with a glib ease. Perhaps because what they said had the ring of a well-rehearsed line.

Uma was not getting any younger. She remembered how scared she was once, of the prospect of growing old. She was twenty-five then. She thought old age will catch up with her one day abruptly, like some terrible disease. Now she realised that ageing was more like a long, extended twilight that slowly, relentlessly crawled upon you. But even now, she continued to hear the same line, 'You too will be like Simone de Beauvoir.' She heard it again and yet again like a tune from the one-stringed *ektara*[1]. The only difference being the people who plucked at the solitary string in different ways to make different sounds.

* Originally published as "Neeyum Simone de Beauvoir Pola" in *Shakti*, Oslo, Norway. This translation first published in *A Storehouse of Tales*, ed. Jehanara Wasi, New Delhi: Shrishti Publications, 2001. *Manes* refer to ancestral spirits or the spirit of a dead person regarded as an object to be venerated or appeased.

[1] *Ektara*: A one stringed instrument used as a background for vocal music.

Uma flushed with embarrassment when she remembered her twenty-fifth year. She had written some shallow poems and some lightweight articles and she had carried them around in a basket on her head, hawking her wares in the market place of magazines and newspapers where there was a shrill sales-pitch. She remembered all those disquieting details. Once, something that she had written had been rejected three times in the same marketplace, shattering the very brittle thing called 'ego'. It was then that she heard the reference to Simone de Beauvoir for the first time. Uma remembered how she had collapsed on a chair, thoroughly demoralised by the third rejection slip for her writing. And Shekar had materialised in front of her, to sprinkle her back to life with refreshing rose water.

'Really Uma, you must believe a little more in yourself. At least believe me when I say that you'll certainly grow up to be like Simone de Beauvoir some day. I'm sure about that.'

She drank it in thirstily, and was eager for more.

'Yes indeed. Have some faith in yourself. Actually, what you need is a proper climate for your writing. And a congenial companion who understands what writing is all about. Given these conditions, your writing will bloom and flourish. You'll then see for yourself how you'll develop into yet another Simone ... '

Shekar was thirty-seven. His words spilled out firm and rounded. A firmness that supported her young spine like a strong pillar. He took her hand resting on the table and held it in his.

'Uma, your writing is like you, very, very delicate. Both need to be protected.'

Holding on to her hand, he had continued: 'All these things—a family, parents, a home, uncles, aunts, festivals, weddings—they make such a din that your writing will wither away if you allow yourself to be overcome by all that. Entrust yourself to the care of a suitable companion, like Simone de Beauvoir did.'

This man Shekar. He has written three full-length novels, a play and many short stories. He is already well-known as a writer. And yet he respects me, *me*! And my writing ... Uma mused over his words. A small voice protested from a corner of her head. *Fool, you can't hold a candle to Simone,* it whispered. *How can you be compared to Simone? Why, it's so absurd, you greenhorn. You're much too young yet and have a long way to go. And you'll have to work a lot, lot more to develop into anything like Simone.*

Besides, you need to be creative about your very life, like her. You will have to dissolve your self in life, like Simone did. Experimentally? May be. She dug in deep with courage and, to be sure, surfaced with some bitter truths. Look at you. You're still imprisoned within the narrow confines of what you call 'beautiful poems'. You're locked up in your petty little ideals, petty little objectives. It is a trap. Learn to suspect the very ideals you've set for yourself. They merely protect you from what is unknown. Break those dwarfish walls, smash them down and put your neck out into the wide world, even if it hurts. Come on!

'What are you thinking about, Uma? Do you think I'm extravagant in drawing parallels?' asked Shekar.

Uma was stumped by his shrewd guess.

'Look Uma, let's make a pact. From now on at least, let's dedicate ourselves to writing. Totally. Don't look upon my wife or your parents as big hurdles. Let each of them stay in his/her/their own context. We'll keep them as a kind of background music. You and I are gifted to create. We'll have to distance ourselves from these mundane social roles and lead our lives independently.'

Back home, Uma's mother Mangalam came down hard on her husband.

'But I told you a long time back, don't you remember? This boy Rajan, he comes from the family of Sundaram's father-in-law. I came to know that he is highly educated. Has good professional prospects too. In addition to all this, he is good looking. What's more, his family looked so eager when they asked for our Uma in marriage. Why don't you clinch the matter quickly before the coming month of *Thaiye*?[2] You drag your feet so sluggishly,' she chided him.

'But Mangalam, Uma wants to complete her PhD before she gets married. She also wants to go abroad on a scholarship. That's why ... ,' her father could not complete his sentence, for Mangalam interrupted him: 'Ask your daughter to complete her PhD *after* marriage. And tell her we'll allow her to go abroad only after she has had her first child,' said Mangalam, firm as ever.

[2] *Thaiye*: Name of the tenth Tamil month from mid-January to mid-February, considered auspicious for marriage.

'O Mangalam, then everything will get so complicated for the poor girl,' her father remonstrated with his wife.

'I know what's best for her,' said Mangalam. 'We can't afford to slacken the reins. The very continuity of our family lineage depends on Uma. Moreover, a lively, educated girl like her needs to be protected even more than a girl who stays at home. Don't you know even this simple truth, as a father? You've no wisdom whatsoever.' Familiar noises. They now reached Uma with a fading exigency. Was Shekar right after all, about the way things recede as some kind of background music when one withdraws from life? Does everything float then like music, mild but dispensable? From now on, let me just live for my writing and nothing else, thought Uma. She recalled how Shekar said, 'Uma, life is short, very short indeed. Don't waste your time.' His voice was low as he bent forward to hold her hand in his. She did not pull back her hand.

'No I won't,' she nodded, her expression earnest. 'I promise that I'll never waste my time.'

Uma imagined that she was writing copiously. The sheets fluttered and flew around her. She stayed awake for long hours at night and wrote page after page. She dreamed that she toured all around the country and met with people from different walks of life. The name 'Uma' was splashed in every newspaper and magazine and it shone luminously. She was determined to write more and bring out full-length books one by one, like this Shekar here.

Back from work, Uma hardly had the time to eat her meals or rest. She could not sit down to write or even spend a few quiet moments thinking about what she wanted to write. As soon as she reached home, her telephone would ring. And ring incessantly. It was one such call from Shekar. His voice at the other end of the wire was snappy and crackled with annoyance.

'Where on earth have you been? And when can we meet? I never find you in the university. Where do you hide yourself?' he demanded.

Eventually, Shekar took to hijacking Uma when she was on the way home from work.

'It's been a long time since we met. You're always in a great hurry to go home, saying that your father will be angry if you're late. Hell, what a life,' he said.

'Shekar, I'm working on a book. I've been busy ... '

'O shut up. Come, let's get out of this damn place. I have a suggestion. I'm going to Jammu next month on work. Join me there and we'll go up to Kashmir. I'll book a cottage for the two of us in Pahalgam,' he said.

'Really Shekar, what wild, impossible ideas you have! I can't do that. Besides, I've just started writing something and how can *you*, of all the people, ask me to drop this work and ... '

'Ha! Composing a great epic, are you? Tell me once and for all. What's more important for you? Me or your silly scribbles?'

Uma was speechless with shock. She left for home.

Simone, Simone, Simone. And Sartre. Why should I allow myself to be led on to build dreams around this couple and the two of us, Shekar and me? Why did I nurse notions about Sartre and Simone when I know next to nothing about their personal lives, when I haven't even bothered to read about them beyond their books? I just went along with whatever Shekar said and today my half-baked knowledge is responsible for this impasse. I can only blame myself for that, thought Uma.

In the next two weeks, something egged her on to hunt for materials regarding Simone de Beauvoir and Jean-Paul Sartre. Uma went to various libraries and gathered all that she could lay her hands on—their works, the critical works on their books, their lives, their memoires, their articles, interviews and autobiographical excerpts. Gripped by an enormous hunger to devour the details and facts culled from the books, Uma immersed herself in the accounts of their lives. She ignored the telephone that continued to ring maddeningly. Her parents exchanged curious glances whenever the phone rang out hysterically in the silence of the room and she made no move to take the calls.

Her mother Mangalam asked her, 'Uma, why do you pore over books all day and night? You're ruining your eyes. Just look at your face, it looks so tired. You don't have to do research like this, at the cost of your health,' said Mangalam.

'Your mother is right,' said her father. 'Be more outgoing, Uma. Meet your friends and enjoy yourself. You're much too young to be cooped up indoors all day with books,' said her father.

Uma absorbed what her parents said, just as she absorbed every single detail that she could get about Simone and Sartre culled from books and old journals.

In 1929 Simone de Beauvoir shone as a star student of philosophy at the University of Sorbonne in France. Sartre was in the same department. Steadily, the two of them held on to their top positions in their classes and evolved as fine, articulate intellectuals.

Avidly, Uma assimilated the other details of their personal lives. How Simone and Sartre got acquainted with each other, and then became close friends who eventually decided to live together without the ritual of marriage, an institution they scorned. She read about how they lived together for a long time as an exemplary literary couple who faced the inevitable problems that came with the unorthodox lifestyle they had opted for. Uma noted some familiar paradigms that surfaced. Sartre could always depend upon Simone even as he gathered many girlfriends on the side. Simone accepted his affairs with these women in a stoic, wifely manner. As a gesture of equality, Sartre suggested that Simone could also have relationships with other men if she wanted, but Simone could not/did not/would not compete with Sartre in this. She remained choosy and mature about the friends she made, whether it was a man or a woman.

Sartre got his women easily and tired of them just as easily. Some of them were his 'conquests' but he had no hesitation in shaking them off unceremoniously in order to resume his writing again without any disturbance. When he felt the need for women again, he found them.

Meanwhile, Simone got very attached to the American writer Nelson Algren. She respected his work and was happy in his company. Whenever she was with him, she sensed her own womanhood as something that bloomed alive with fullness. Nelson Algren. Within his embrace, she enjoyed the new freshness of her own body, the curious feeling it gave her of stepping away from herself to experience a new tangible womanhood within her being. A small universe that was lovely, clean and gentle germinated magically between them. But then there came a day. It was a day that saw even Nelson Algren burst out in exasperation. 'I don't like this arrangement at all,' he exploded. 'The way you come from Paris so casually to visit me in the US, like it's a holiday or something. You come to spend a couple of days after which it's time for you to return to Paris. This is no good,' he protested.

'What else can I do, Nelson? I've a house in France. I've my work too,' said Simone.

'You have your Sartre in France, say that. I know you go back only for him. I know that only too well.'

'Nelson, please ... '

'Look, I can't stand this any more. It's agonising. Sartre possesses you totally. You only throw the crumbs of life at me. You belittle me,' said Algren.

'How can I leave Sartre ... ?'

'See, I was right in my guess, wasn't I? You go on as if you're his wedded wife. Simone, listen to me. Forget about Sartre and move over to the US. Live with me.'

'O, but how can you suggest ... '

'Fine then. If you don't agree to that, don't visit me like this. There's no point. Don't torture me like this. Unshackle me Simone, please.'

Simone had steeled her heart and returned to Paris. She resolved not to meet Algren ever again. All through her journey the questions chased and haunted her. Actually what urged her to continue living with Sartre? Was it dependence, or a kind of bondage, or merely a force of habit? What is the nature of this relationship? Some answers surfaced but her mind refused to accept them. The answers winked at her surreptitiously, even as they went about their convoluted ways to soften the edges for her comfort.

The truth surfaced more naturally for Simone, through her body. It expressed itself in her health. The same truth exploded in subtle, subterranean ways in her novel *The Mandarins*. In the novel, a woman who is nearing middle age has a young daughter who is much disturbed by what happens to her. The woman returns home after bidding a last and final farewell to her lover, after they come to a mutual decision not to meet again. The woman reaches home, locks herself inside her room for days on end and sits within, brooding over her life. Her young daughter tries her best to comfort her. She serves her meals, makes tea, pours wine and talks to her soothingly. But the woman seeks the privacy of her room and shuts herself in for a few days. When she comes out of the room, her appearance alarms her daughter. Is *this* my mother, she wonders. My mother who is in her late forties, who until now looked so very youthful and attractive? God, whatever has happened to my mother?

Outside that novel Sartre does not fail to notice the drastic change that has come over Simone. However, he turns to his women and pursues his writing. And he writes extensively. The Nobel Prize comes his way. He rejects it and by doing so, becomes more famous than he has ever been. Half of the western world gets hooked on to his philosophy of Existentialism. He writes on, struggling with his failing health. When he falls sick, Simone nurses him tenderly, like a wife, a mother, a sister, or a faithful nurse and maid. Again the questions rose from within her and were quelled: what is this relationship? Is there anything 'special' about it? Is there any difference at all between living like this and living within the sanction of marriage, as husband and wife? Perhaps a man-woman relationship runs on a familiar, beaten path with these recognisable patterns and paradigms?

Simone gathered the silent questions together with the silent answers and offered them up to the future generations to evaluate her as they pleased. She offered to posterity her remarkable books—*The Second Sex*, *The Prime of Life*, *Force of Circumstances* and many more before she finally went to sleep.

'Uma, why are you nibbling at your food?' demanded her mother Mangalam angrily. 'At this age you should be eating well and have a lot of milk, butter, yoghurt, sweets and so on. Just look at you. Your face has a pinched look and you've become dark and thin. Is this what your 'great' research is all about?'

'You've become rather listless, my child,' said her father. 'What's the matter?' he asked anxiously. 'Take a break from work. Let's all go out. Come, I'll take you to some beautiful temples.'

'It's all because of you,' said Mangalam, descending on her husband furiously. 'I asked you to get her married by the month of

Thaiye when we had such an excellent offer, but you wouldn't. You crawl through life and look what it has done to Uma,' she fumed.

Backstage sounds? They were as loud and clear as the onstage ones.

The telephone rang relentlessly.

'What are you scratching your head about,' asked an irate Shekar. 'If you don't like the idea of Kashmir, then let's go elsewhere. But leave the choice to me. I'll think of some nice, cool getaway.'

'That's a wild, impossible idea,' said Uma.

'What now? Here I am, thinking that you'll be like another Simone de Beauvoir, independent and bold. Hell! You're just a very ordinary girl, as ordinary as they come. Damn!'

Eventually, it was *his* voice and *his* phone calls that retreated and faded off as background music, or more precisely, background sounds.

It was the late seventies. Feminism as an 'ism' was still an emerging movement that had started surfacing in different ways in different places. Various seminars and conferences were organised by departments of sociology, economics, literature, psychology and other streams. In the literary forums, one repeatedly heard the names of Germaine Greer, Kate Millet, Gloria Steinem, Simone de Beauvoir among others. Literary scholars wrote about Simone as a fine example of one who lived her life like her books, and as one who followed a unique lifestyle. Quite a few men joined in presenting papers and participating in discussions. That is how Uma happened to meet Mohan Mehta at a seminar in Chandigarh and later again, in Pune. He was a lecturer in English and could easily hide behind nice words.

'Uma-ji, I've read some of your stories,' he said. 'As for your poems, I've even learnt a few of them by rote,' he declared and went on to recite one of her poems smoothly, the lines flowing out without a single mistake.

Uma felt the prickle of her goose-flesh.

'Don't, please don't,' she protested.

'Sorry. I know how you feel. It would be embarrassing if someone were to hear me. Shall we go to the lounge? It's quiet in there,' he suggested.

They ordered for tea.

'How do you like this seminar?' he asked. 'You know, I wanted to get up and ask the speakers why they go on and on citing western examples—Germaine Greer, Kate Millet, Simone de Beauvoir and what have you. Why don't they cite Indian women?' he said, his face intense.

'Perhaps our women don't have an international reach yet,' said Uma. 'There are some good writers of course, but no one has written anything that stimulates or provokes the consciousness of an entire nation, let alone the world. At least, not yet.'

'No, no, Uma-ji. Time will tell. Ours is a young country, but I've full confidence in our women. Let's take you, for example. If writers like you try, you can really achieve this reach that you talk about. Then you'll also be like a Simone de Beauvoir some day,' he said.

Uma laughed.

'Why do you laugh? Because you haven't found a Sartre?'

Uma laughed even more, her shoulders shaking as she tried to control her laughter. She flicked away a tear that threatened to spill with her laughter.

'Mohan-ji, I'm surprised. Because you just now objected to our servile dependence on western models and western examples and now, you ... '

'Heh ... heh ... ' he laughed sheepishly. 'What I meant to say is that we should acknowledge our own writers and our literature, first of all, although there is a lot to be learned from the west. One can learn valuable things from the lives of Sartre and Simone. Come to think of it Uma-ji, that we are born as Indians is a mere accident, a freak of fate. True, we've our familial ties here, husband, wife, children, and parents and so on. But to attain a quality in both writing and in our life, we need to protect and preserve our individuality, you see. If you've no serious objection to the idea, we ... '

Since then, Uma has counted many birthdays. It had been a time of search and it had also been a time of reckoning. Patterns appeared, they got rearranged with an altered complexion, and there were also changing equations and changing values. The various seminars pushed into the front seasoned speakers who were articulate, smooth and glib talkers. They invariably received a loud cheering and applause by the audience because the speakers said what the audience liked to hear.

For Uma as for her peers, there was the usual pressure of work, of career, of research and family. Things blew around her and her contemporaries, but she got a strange feeling that she was standing at the centre of it all, and that she was severely, absolutely alone. The 1970s rolled on towards the eighties and the eighties unfolded with its share of confusions and half-truths. Even for Mehta here, it must've been a time of uncertainties and uneasy truths, conceded Uma silently.

'I can understand your hesitation, Uma-ji. I think I can guess the reason too, if I may say so. You may have perhaps heard this several times, right?'

'Oh no, it's the very first time I am hearing anything like this,' said Uma. 'It's just that I could never even dream of being like Simone de Beauvoir,' she added as calmly as she could.

'What about me? Do you think I can be like Sartre? Still, if we have the imagination and the will ... '

Swallowing the seventies, the eighties reached the nineties. Now the 'ism' of feminism took a foothold as a fierce movement. Newly recorded facts and insights emerged from various disciplines—from clinical psychology, agro-economics, eco-feminism, social anthropology, literature and the arts. They ignited sparks of cognition everywhere. The prescribed curricula in schools and colleges, the works of writers, films and just about everything came under the scanner for a merciless re-evaluation. Everything was examined, analysed and judged unsparingly. Few areas escaped the new scrutiny.

Inside Levi's jeans, *Blue Lagoons*, inside trousers, skirts, shorts, salwar-suits or sarees a young femininity with stylishly trimmed hair woke up on the strength of its own innate forces and impulses. Young women from different walks of life, with different cultural and professional conditioning, articulated their reactions with a hard headed clarity.

'Kate Millet really opened our eyes,' said a young girl. 'Now we can never see D. H. Lawrence, Henry Miller or Jean Genet with the same eyes as before. We can't. Millet has stripped these writers stark naked and they now stand defenseless.'

Her friends agreed with her. These young women had no problem getting on with men they worked with or went out with. When they discussed things among themselves, one could see that Simone was a remote figure for them.

'It was a fatal mistake on the part of Simone to have given herself up and her entire life to Sartre on those terms,' argued a young woman, hotly.

'Yes. A gifted woman doesn't need a crutch to lean on in order to grow or develop in her art or in her writing. If only Simone had decided to stay alone, independent of Sartre, she would've evolved in more strikingly original ways,' said the girl.

'May be she would've then ushered in the new times much earlier than she did.'

'Yes. Even so, Simone was a fine intellectual. She was an excellent writer who not only had what's commonly termed as "intellectual honesty", but in addition she had that rare thing, an emotional honesty. Sartre's oppressive presence somewhat eclipsed her and dimmed her natural luster. Simone should've got married to Nelson Algren who was a damn decent guy. That would've been sensible. Then Sartre would've realised what "Existentialism" was all about!'

'Correct. We see this anomaly in our everyday life too. These men are torn apart by a paradox within themselves. I wonder how they handle it? Won't they just split apart someday?'

'Hmm ... But they keep trying nevertheless. When I was in the Mussourie Academy for my IAS training, a guy told me that I was "smart, talented" and that if I pair up with him, the two of us can show the world that we are "yet another Simone-Sartre"! I smashed the mouldy myth that had wrapped around this couple and showed him what it was like for Simone, in reality. Know how he reacted to that? He stopped talking to me, he even stopped greeting me with a "Hi" whenever we met,' said the girl, laughing.

Sounds of hearty laughter from the rest of the young women wafted on the air, borne aloft by the wind changing its course.

Even now, Simone continues to be a disconcerting presence, in her 'tangible' absence. She is analysed, probed, examined and argued about. Many of the younger women are angry *for* her. They are angry with the decisions she took in life. They are angry too that a fine intellectual and a sensitive writer like her should have lived with Sartre as less than a wife and with such a blind devotion. It is all so unnecessary, they argue.

Slowly, time rolls out the balls of *pindam*[3] on the smooth banana leaf. They show Simone in different colours as she retreats into some far-off point in the distant past. In between the rolling balls of *pindam*, whenever an occasion presents itself, Simone keeps tempting and seducing a Shekar or a Mehta or a young potential bureaucrat in the Mussourie Academy or wherever. She appears and re-appears.

[3] *Pindam*: Balls of cooked rice offered to the manes in the Hindu ritual of obsequies in Tamil Nadu. The manes, i.e., the spirits of the dead ancestors, are worshipped as guardian angels.

A Word with You, Father*

I stood at the counter with my token. A man heaped *uppuma* on a plate and poured something that passed for chutney. It was scorching hot. I looked around for a table and chair under the ceiling fan but no luck. All of them were occupied. I only got a table without any chair in a stuffy corner at the far end, away from the fan. I kept my plate of *uppuma* on the table and went again to the counter with my token for coffee to ask if he would take it back and give me a token for some cold drink instead. Just as I expected, he shook his head to indicate 'No.' I cursed myself for my stupidity in buying a token for coffee in this blazing heat and returned to my table with the coffee in hand. I pushed away the insipid chutney and swallowed the *uppuma*. Sipping the hot coffee, I looked around with envy at all those people who had been smart enough to grab tables under the fans. When they planned to build this 'Coffee Home' at Baba Khadak Singh Marg, some perverted person must have also planned to play a game of 'Musical Chairs' with the customers who came in droves. Which is why he had structured it this way. Because always, but always, there were more people than chairs in here. Come summer or winter, in sweltering heat or shivering cold, a majority of the people ate and drank their beverages standing.

There were crowds of women with huge parcels and shopping bags. The bounty from their shopping jaunts in all the rows and rows of Emporia dotting the Baba Khadak Singh Marg were stuffed into their parcels. I looked at the chic looking crowd that already

* Translated from the original Tamil "Appa, Ungaludan Oru Vaarthai" by the author, published in *Unnatham, Kaavandapaadi*, Chennai. This translation first published in *Muse India*, no. 30, March–April 2010, Special Issue on Tamil literature.

had the stamp of an 'Emporium' on the sarees they wore, and on their salwar-suits and dresses. They did look like women who were given to squandering their husband's money or the money they earned.

There were others who were the 'regulars' here, and most of them were the elderly ones. Like in the US now they are also referred to as 'Senior Citizens'. The last time the owners of Coffee Home who had devised the 'musical chairs' system of 'less chairs and more people' wanted to further reduce the number of chairs, it was this assertive group of senior citizens who got organised to strongly oppose the cruel move. 'We don't have any place to sit and relax in this large capital. Where else can we go to chat with our friends if there wasn't a "Coffee Home"? All of us are past sixty in age. How can you ask us to eat our snacks and have coffee standing?' they hotly argued. They finally got their way. The authorities did not reduce the number of chairs. Even so, there were always fewer chairs and more people.

There were large circles of these senior citizens talking fiercely about rising prices, about social evil, the current political scenario and so on. 'There were such excellent statesmen in the political arena during our times,' they mused nostalgically and talked about Ram Manohar Lohia, Jayaprakash Narain and others. 'They were capable men and were so effective in implementing whatever they did. The Nehru era had such earnestly held ideologies and values. Now all those values are vanishing,' they lamented. The cheerful and enthusiastic interactions of these senior citizens reflected the mutual warmth and affection of a friendship that had endured over the years. They spent their time laughing heartily, freely teasing each other and cracking jokes. Their laughter rang out loud and clear. It seemed to make them shed a good ten or fifteen years from their faces. Only one elderly man sat a little aloof and away from this robust crowd. He had his back turned towards me as I stood at my table, eating. The man sat quietly, his right hand wrapped around one unoccupied chair. Surprising. How rare to find a chair unoccupied. From an angle on the side one could see a section of his glasses perched on his sharp nose and one could also see half of his lips. Well-shaped, chiselled lips they were. But his hair was not thick. Although there was a youthful crop of thick hair on top of his head and on the sides, there was a slight balding patch on the back of his head. All things considered, there was that same detached standoffish look, the same familiar way of cutting himself off with a 'leave me alone' message that I recognised so well.

My heart started pounding within me. The sounds also echoed in my ears loudly. I gulped the coffee down hurriedly like it was some poisonous potion I had bought with good money. I went closer to that man who sat calm and aloof and felt the pounding again. I felt the throbbing in my ears.

I pretended elaborately that I hadn't seen him and went past him towards the place where one could have cold water. I drank three-fourths of a glass of chilled water. It fell on the hot coffee that I had just gulped down and a bizarre, unsuitable mixture of the hot and the cold was happening inside me. Perhaps it may quieten the mounting agitation I felt within, that seemed to increase with every second ... ?

Now, from where I stood, if I turn my head ever so little to look at that man, I can look at him straight, face to face. Just one tilt of my head will make it clear for me, if he is the man I think he is. A mere turn of the head will confirm it for me. So, I need not turn my head. I can refuse to look at his face and just walk out of this place. I can then avoid the agony that will come with the recognition. There is every possibility that I may be right in my guess.

The same features of the face, the same lips, and the same serene look as he sat there. I am familiar with all of that. Certainly it is he—but then, how can that be possible?

I drank up some more chilled water. Something had blocked my ears but I could still hear the loud pounding of my heart. I gathered all my courage and slowly tilted my head to look at him from the corner of my eyes. Beyond any doubt, that is he. That *is* he. There was that same expression of a slight fatigue on the face. And sitting lightly on the face, like a wispy mist was the sadness I recognised. It was a sadness, a light, gentle melancholy, that lent a certain inexplicable dignity to the elegantly handsome face. That is father. My father. After twenty years he had not aged, how amazing. That he is remarkably handsome is unambiguous and beyond doubt. Then as now. He is just the way he was when he died. He looks the same ...

I was nearing the phase called 'middle age'. Whoever thought of this prefix 'middle' has hit upon an apt word. The phase actually does make you stop a bit on the track, sort of pause in the middle of the frantic pace of life. It is an age that provokes us to ask some inconvenient questions. Naturally, inconvenient questions earn inconvenient answers.

'You are getting more and more foolish by the day,' warned a voice within me. 'You are also getting wild. What utter madness,' said the voice. I disregarded the voice and decided to approach the man who sat alone.

He raised his head for a minute to look at me. Instantly as it were, he removed his arm that was around the vacant chair.

'May I sit here?' I asked.

'But of course,' he replied.

The same low, well-bred voice. It was a voice that had the astonishing capacity to maintain the same tone even if it has to severely censure somebody. He could scold severely without raising his voice or shouting, he could just shake up a person.

'Do you recognise me? Don't you know me?' I asked, holding back the word 'Father' with great difficulty. I swallowed the word.

'Uh ... Recognise? Excuse me, have we met before?' he asked.

Again, how amazing, the way he had preserved his voice. The same familiar undercurrent of threat that I knew floated through that polished voice. In the midst of this din, the noise of the Coffee Home and the collective voices of the people, the voice could magically create a cool watery pool of quiet and tranquility. He drew me into this cool vortex of untroubled peacefulness in the corner.

'You *really* don't recognise me then?' I asked. 'I'm Venky. Your son Venkatesh. Can't you see who I am, Appa?' The word 'Appa' tumbled out in spite of me.

'"*Appa*"? It means "Father", doesn't it?' he asked. I realised in a trice that he was not a Tamilian. Perhaps his mother tongue is Hindi.

'Yes, yes. Appa means Father,' I said.

He gave me a steady gaze for a minute and said 'Hmm ... ?' thoughtfully.

'But surely I'm not old enough to have a son of your age? That apart, I don't have children, for I'm not married,' he declared.

A smile shot through the chiselled lips for a moment and the face became pensive again as he was plunged into thought.

God, why did the day turn out like this? There is this blistering heat on the one hand. And there are some unbearably shocking happenings on the other. Here I am, insisting to my father who died twenty years ago that I am his son Venkatesh. I have drawn a chair close to him informally, like a friend, and am sitting on it. But how? I have never done a thing like this when he was alive? I would sense the controlled anger in his low, well-bred voice and get very scared. I would see the hatred spilling out of the eyes from that dignified face and would just shrink back. Or I would stand wondering in confusion how a father could hate his own son, his own daughter. How could he hate the children he fathered, I would ruminate, unable to believe it or take it.

When he died, I did not weep or grieve for him. My sister too did not grieve. Both of us thought that something very unnatural had occurred in our lives. It was so strange a happening that it could not be easily explained to others. Something in me died along with Appa on that day. But the end was not so neat. Because after that, my sister and I nursed a lot of bitterness for him. 'How could a father dislike his own children?' was a question that we threw out like a ball, endlessly. We never got a comforting answer. Our bitterness evoked memories of a father whose eyes never concealed the disappointment he felt about his children.

Our relations and friends however were unanimous in their admiration: 'You have a father with such a majestic and youthful appearance. He is indeed a rare person', they had marvelled. And yet ...

Now here I am, melting like this, trying to get close to father. As for him, he is *not* my father. What is more, in a very civilised way he said emphatically that he is nobody's father, for that matter. We were gripped by a heavy silence. Then he cleared his throat and looked at me with compassion when he said gently, 'Sometimes one comes across a person with a strong resemblance to someone we know, isn't it? The resemblance could be amazing, yes?'

Oh, it's him, it's him all right. It *is* Appa. By the grace of God I got him here. By the same grace he is sitting here, beside me. What an unusual chance to tell him what I had always wanted to tell him, all that I kept corked up within me.

Appa, Appa, now I can understand what you thought about me and your daughter. Now I understand very well why you were cross with us.

Should I say this aloud or not, I wondered. I kept quiet.

'Shall we have some coffee?' he asked.

'No, no. Oh, I mean I find this heat unbearable. Besides, it's when I gulped down the coffee that was like a poison when I happened to ... to see you ... '

'What?'

'Oh I'm extremely sorry, do excuse me. Let me get *you* a coffee, may I Sir?' I asked.

He smiled.

'I'm surprised at you. First you called me "Father". And now you address me with a "Sir". Come to think of it, I'm not so much older than you, am I? Please don't misunderstand me, though,' he said, his voice soft and silky.

'Yes, yes, I think I'm roughly of your age. I just said "Sir" out of respect', I explained.

Having reached your age I now realise that, how children change into problems once they grow up. Children are a mixed blessing, that is, if they're a blessing at all, in the first place. They become so headstrong and at times, they also ... become ugly. They're so vulgar! They have no respect for elders. Do you remember Meenu and Shankar? How affectionately you made them recline on your knees and played with them, moving your legs up and down, up and down? Then you would toss them up in the air and catch them with superb ease as they shrieked away in delight. Now the same Meenu and Shankar have become so monstrous. Appa, I'm afraid I don't like them any more, I don't like them at all.

'No thanks, I don't want coffee,' he was saying.

The same scrupulously clean clothes like the ones father always wore. I noted too the same smell in this close proximity. The smell of unsoiled purity, the smell of the immaculately clean. How very amazing! If you bend down to look, he had that very same, incongruously fat, large-sized big toe, totally unmatched with the four other slim toes in his feet. I seem to have inherited that from father (of all the things!), so I was always took care to hide my feet.

'Shall I get a cold drink instead?' he offered. 'Why are you perspiring so much? I hope you're doing well?' he enquired gently.

'No Sir, I'm fine.'

'Can I ask you something, if you don't mind?' he said.

'Not at all. Please go ahead,' I said.

'Do you have a father?' he asked.

'No.'

'Oh, I'm sorry. But I never knew that a grown up man like you could remember a father so intensely as to.... I lost my father when I was very small,' he said and continued: 'Then, after I grew up I decided not to marry. Because if one married one will have children to contend with. It'll be a sweet experience in the beginning but as they grow older they'll change drastically. They'll have no softness to speak of and may turn out rough and repulsive. Some become even vulgar! I wanted none of that, so I steered clear of marriage,' he said.

There was again a pounding noise in my ears. I felt my heart palpitating wildly. The words that I had not spoken aloud, the same words were amplified in sound and seemed to be thrown out of some microphone as it rushed back into my ears.

My forehead throbbed. The tongue went dry. The inside of my palms were sweating. And my legs, oh my legs gave way and I felt a cramp. God, am I going to faint and fall down here? Let me have an icy cold drink to stabilise myself. Let me go out in the excuse of getting a cold drink for both of us.

'Sir, come let's have a cold drink. I'll get it for both of us,' I said and rushed out without waiting for his reply.

I returned with two bottles of Fanta orange. What now? Is it the game of 'musical chairs' again? Did he go in search of another chair? Why has he changed the place? I looked around but could not find him. I took just five minutes to get this drink, where could he go and how far can he go in this short time? I went to the Gents' Toilet to check. Then I rushed out of the Coffee Home and looked around at the shopping mall.

Why did he leave like that, without even saying a 'Bye' to me? We were talking to each other for such a long time, why did he disappear so suddenly?

Appa, I had so much more to tell you? I want to tell you that ...

Guava with a Red Heart[*]

In Tamil, it is a common practice to refer to an honest and innocent individual as a person who has a 'white heart'. But when it comes to the rare variety of the red guava, the fruit, we describe it in English as 'a guava with a red heart'. It is also an innocent term that insinuates nothing whatsoever.

Come winter every year, guavas ripen when the mist spreads out. Starting from the month of *Kartikai*[1], the guava goes on through the months of *Margazhi*[2] and *Thaiye*[3], all along changing its colour in subtle ways. It comes wearing a pale green colour that gradually deepens with time and turns golden yellow as it ripens, dazzling the eye with its changing hues. With that begins my long hunt for the red guava.

It is not just a hunt, you can call it a quest, a tireless quest. My family may laugh at me, the younger members of the family may smirk and chuckle behind my back but I really don't care. I carry on with my search for that guava, the one that has 'a red heart' and I never give up my hunt, no matter where I am. Be it Mumbai, Kolkata, Hyderabad, Bangalore, Delhi, Chandigarh or Chennai, my legs will take me in my search for the variety of guava that has 'a red heart'. In the process, I fall prey to the many cheating games of the guava sellers with all their cunning guiles. Yet my quest for the red guava continues.

[*] Translated from the original Tamil "Sivanda Ullam" by the author, published in *Kanavu*, Thiruppur, Tamil Nadu. This translation first published in *Chandrabhaaga*, Winter Issue 12, 2005, Cuttack, Orissa.

[1] *Kartik*: Tamil name for the month from mid-November to mid-December.

[2] *Margazhi*: Mid-December to mid-January.

[3] *Thaiye*: Mid-January to mid-February.

Let us take Chennai, for instance. What a bustling crowd there is on the kerb in Luz Corner. It is always teeming with people. Filling the pavement and kerb were heaps of fruits piled on like mountains—bananas, apples, pomegranates, *chikoo*s (sapodilla plum) and of course, guava. What attracted me first was that spectacle. Perched on top of a pile of guava was a single guava, cut out in an artistic flowery pattern with curving petal-like cuts, showing its 'red heart' within. How it sat on top, that guava with a 'red heart'. A fruit just made for grabbing and eating with relish!

I asked the guava fruit seller: 'Are all the rest of the guavas under this cut red guava, of the red variety?'

'Yes of course, Amma. How much do you want? Two kilos or three?' he enquired, taking up the scales to weigh the fruit.

'Give me a kilo.'

'Is one kilo enough Amma? It's a superior variety,' he said.

'One kilo is quite enough.'

'Very well, Amma. Here you are,' he said, placing the fruits on his scale.

'*Aiyyo*! You bastard!'

Startled, I reeled around toward the direction of that voice.

At some distance on the same pavement, there was a woman selling sapodilla plums. It was she who had cried out like that.

She now spat out the red juice of the betel leaves that she was chewing, and exclaimed '*Chee*! Hey you, do you have even an iota of shame or honour in you, eh? I'm asking you. You're lying to this lady so outrageously?' she asked angrily.

'Hey, just shut up, okay? Just mind your own business and don't interfere with mine. Yes, I warn you!' the guava seller shouted back at the woman. He kept the weights on the scale and lifted it to see the weight.

'Hey you, I'm talking to *you*, do you hear? Just put that guava down, I tell you. Yes, keep them down, the whole lot of that guava, you good-for-nothing fellow,' hissed the woman, furious.

'Now look here woman, you won't listen, is that it? If you create any more trouble, I'll throw the entire pile of your *chikoo*s onto the road, yes! So beware!' the guava seller threatened.

'Aha? You'll throw them out, would you?' the *chikoo* woman retorted, shaking her right hand and mimicking him. Then she turned to me and said, 'Amma?'

What a steady, unwavering look. It was disconcerting.

'Amma, you want only the red variety of guava, don't you?' she asked.

'Yes,' I replied.

'In that case, would you buy guava that is not red, but is white inside?' she asked, as if she wanted to grill me.

'Nn ... no ... I won't,' I dragged but followed it up by shaking my head. I was flabbergasted by the way her direct questions matched her unwavering look. I just couldn't understand the situation.

'You won't buy, would you? Hey you, did you hear that?' she said, turning to the guava man. She looked at me and continued, 'Then don't buy this lot of guava, Amma. This creature lies through his teeth. He has just carved out a single red guava decoratively and displayed it above the heap to attract innocent customers like you. He is such an outrageous cheat. *Chee!* Deceiving people has become a way of life for this chap. The entire lot of guava he has in there is the ordinary, white variety. I know that only too well,' she said with conviction.

'Is that so?' I remarked.

'But of course, what else?' she replied and then turned to him. 'You rowdy liar, may your entire house fall into ruin,' she cursed the man vehemently.

I stood dumbfounded. What a fluent, unfaltering stream of invective.

'Hey woman, don't mess around with me, I warn you again. What to speak of your *chikoo*s, I'll throw you out too along with your fruit and get rid of you. Got it?' shouted back the guava man.

'Oh yes? Let's see you do it then?' the woman challenged. 'Hey, who do you think you are anyway? Is this pavement your father's property, I ask you, you son of a bitch!' she spat out. The guava man got up.

'Are you going to shut up? Or else ... ' he began.

I hurried out of the place.

'Amma, Amma, take your guava with you. So what if it's the white variety? It tastes like honey and is sweet as sugar. Just have a bite and see for yourself Amma,' the guava man entreated. My back absorbed the sounds of his cry.

I walked on for some time till I came upon a small restaurant on the way with a name board hanging out. It said 'Parimala'. It seemed to have been freshly painted. When I looked at it intently, I could read the faded old name of the restaurant underneath the new one. The faded letters said 'Karpagam Kaappi Club'.

'Kaappi Club'.

Until the fifties, one might say even during the sixties, one could see this term 'Kaappi Club' which in fact meant 'Coffee Club' used by modest eateries that were without any ostentation. This little eatery, wanting to be upwardly mobile, had 'modernised' its image. It has thrown off 'Kaappi Club' and now wears a new name over the old one, 'Parimala'. I went inside.

I went over to a small table and gently pulled out the wrought iron chair to sit down. It made a grating sound. I sat down. The table was littered with all kinds of things and was very dirty. I asked the small boy who hovered around to clean it up. He brought a dirty old rag, wiped the table with it and gave me a mocking smile.

'What'll you have?' he enquired.

My senses were assailed by the stench that rose from the table wiped by a dirty rag. I pressed my handkerchief to my nose and covered it.

'One coffee. And bring it soon,' I ordered.

'In just a minute,' said the small boy and ran to get it.

A housefly repeatedly circled the table. The coffee came piping hot, steam spiralling up from a tumbler frothing on top. I sipped at the coffee. It went down my throat soothingly, warming my blood, leaving a pure and pervasive taste on my palate. What a wholesome taste. And how very aromatic it was, the coffee in this shabby, dirty little eatery called 'Parimala'. The word 'parimala' means that which is fragrant. How surprising! What a flawlessly brewed, pure genuine coffee from this humble little 'Kaappi Club'.

'Genuine' coffee?

'Genuine' coffee as against the 'false, fake' guava.

No, no. It was not 'false', nor was it a 'fake'. It was just the white variety of guava, that is about all. How indignant the woman who sold *chikoo*s was over the fact that the guava man had lied to me, that it was all 'red guava'. What a righteous, moral indignation! She is such an upright woman.

After I had the pure coffee from that small tumbler dented in places, I paid a generous tip to the boy. He pressed his palms together in a 'Namaste' and beamed a bright smile. I went out, took an auto-rickshaw and asked the driver to take me to the place where I stayed.

Even here, one could see some auto-rickshaws winding their way through narrow streets, or negotiating in between big buses and speeding across cycle rickshaws that crawled on the roads slowly. I took an auto-rickshaw to reach this place, Ameenabad in Lucknow. And it would be more appropriate to call this narrow street a lane. It was flanked by the back walls of crowded houses built in close proximity to each other. The walls were used most carelessly by adults and children alike who urinated on them as if they were the prime target. The entire lane reeked of the stink of urine. Through the offensive, foul odour, a delicate fragrance sharply pierced through and reached my nostrils. It was a fragrance that I would recognise anywhere in the world by its subtle, nectarous redolence. The scent that is so special to the red guava.

I looked at the old man who was selling guava on the lane. He too, like the fruit seller in Chennai, had carved out a red guava like a flower and had placed it strategically for all to see, on a heap of guava. He wore an ordinary pyjama and kurta. His small basket had just a few guavas, about twenty or twenty-five at the most. Perhaps all the fruits were sold out. In that narrow lane, he was selling his fruits quietly, without shouting out his wares, and without any of the usual cries of the vendors.

I asked him the same question, 'Are all the guavas in your basket the red variety or only some of them are red?'

'Yes, this entire lot is the red variety,' he said in a matter of fact tone, stating the fact without any undue emphasis. It was like giving an ordinary, obvious piece of information about the place, like 'yes, this is Ameenabad.'

'Buy if you want to, or don't'—that was his nonchalant attitude. For some reason, his attitude gave me hope. Even so, I wanted to check it out first, I wanted to sort of test him.

'Give me a quarter kilo of guava,' I said.

He weighed them on the scale, put them in a bag and gave it to me. I took it from him, and then pretending as if an idea had struck me suddenly, I asked him, 'Cut the guava for me, each one of them.'

He looked up at me.

'Hmm. Come on. I'm hungry. I want to eat them now,' I urged.

'Very well Madam,' he said and calmly cut the fruits one by one. His knife glided through the fruits smoothly. With his cut, each one of the guavas revealed its red inner portion and a delicate fragrance, unparalleled and unique to the red guava, wafted out of the cut fruits.

I took one guava, bit into it and enjoyed it.

'Aha! Give me one more kilo of it,' I said.

After weighing one kilo of guavas, he asked, 'Should I cut them too, Madam?'

I was taken aback. Is this man teasing me?

'No, no. Put them in a bag. I'll eat them later,' I said. I took the bag of guava and paid him. There were only a few guavas in the basket. Let me buy the rest of them, I thought for a moment. No, let others also get a chance to enjoy red guavas, I told myself and walked on that narrow street, biting into a guava.

The fragrant sweetness of the fruit exploded within my mouth. It tapped alive my palate as I tingled to that familiar taste and that familiar smell. The narrow lane of Ameenabad expanded into a wide road with *gulmohar* trees on both sides dripping with flowers. The cool shade of the trees in Mysore's Ontikappal spread all around us. And now, big cars whizzed past carts pulled by oxen. I walked on the wide road, enjoying my guava. Then I turned near the Kempe Gowda circle of Bangalore and walked on a shaded road.

After that I stood at the outer gate of Lal Bagh in Bangalore. I searched for the road that went towards Cantonment. I found it and slowly started walking towards that direction.

They were a bunch of girls who giggled without any apparent reason. There was much boisterous merry making, again for no particular reason. The only excuse for laughter was laughter. Find a chance to laugh. Even in the cold weather of December and January we would stuff our sweaters into our school satchel and get deliberately soaked to the skin in the rain by our unhurried walk on that wide road, chatting and yapping happily. The Bangalore sky seemed to be showering us with the raindrops especially for us. Laughing and giggling, the small school girls lifted their faces and looked up at the sky. Damp faces glistening with rain, hair all wet, blue skirts that reached up to the knees, a matching tie around the white top, twin braids of long hair fastened by black ribbons. Each little girl had a guava in her hand. Not an ordinary guava, but a red guava. They reached their houses.

'Oh, why did you get drenched in rain, and in this cold month? You'll catch a cold!' mother may scold. The very thought of a mother's wrath made them pull out the sweaters from their satchels and wear them. They wiped off the water from their faces and their hair and swallowed the red guava.

How the red guava opens its heart out the minute a knife slices through it. The fragrance and taste is so distinct it pierces right through your ears too and thrills as it transports you to some place far off, to some place beyond the present. The unique red guava.

A Political Colour*

At last the game gave over. Kalyani wiped her tennis racket, slid it inside the cover and waited for her friends. The last set of tennis seemed to be over in the adjoining court as well, for Robert, Anna, George and Dulcey came over to where she stood waiting. Margaret, Jim and Sahira also walked across from the first court and joined them.

'Whew!' Jim let off a sigh.

'Today we could play two sets to our heart's content,' smiled Dulcey.

'We can do that only for a while now. This is after all, our first week. From next week onwards classes will be on in full swing. There will be seminars in the department, project meetings, this, that and the other. We'll all become very busy,' said George.

Around the same time last year when she started her term, Kalyani would often long for her home in India. Now she was thoroughly used to the University of London, and generally felt at home in England. So completely immersed was she in her studies now, and in all the related projects that she did not even find the time to go to India on her last vacation. She found a job in a computer center and went through a training that involved learning new skills. This year, if possible, I should go home, she mused...

'All right, now let's have some chilled beer, come on!' said Robert, hustling everybody.

They walked towards their favourite watering hole.

'I want a lemon-soda,' said Kalyani.

* Translated from the original Tamil "Nirami" by the author, published in *Puthiya Paarvai*, Chennai. This translation first published in *The IUP Journal of Commonwealth Literature*, vol. II, no. 2, Hyderabad: IUP Publications, 2010.

'Why, don't you have beer, ever?' asked Margaret.

'No.'

'Wine?'

'Not wine either.'

'So, you're a total teetotaler,' smiled Margaret. 'Do all girls in India follow your practice of not drinking or is it just you who has resolved not to?' she asked.

'Ah, you can see many girls like me in India,' said Kalyani.

'What about your family?' asked Jim. 'Doesn't anyone drink in your home?'

'No, even my father doesn't touch alcohol,' said Kalyani.

'Good! I too want to give up drinking totally, some day,' said Anna.

'That is one thing I can't do,' said Robert. 'But I'm trying to reduce my intake of meat and fish little by little.'

'Why? Are you going to become a vegetarian?' asked Dulcey.

'That's my goal. Let me at least try to become a veggie ... ,' replied Robert.

Chilled beer was served to everyone and Kalyani got her lemon-soda.

'Ha! After a brisk game, it's great to cool oneself with chilled beer,' said George, licking the froth around his lips with his tongue.

'First class!' agreed Sahira enthusiastically.

'Can I ask you something? Don't people object to women drinking, in Pakistan?' asked Jim.

'They do. They object to not just women drinking, they also disapprove of men having alcohol,' said Sahira.

'I suppose you're not bothered about all that,' remarked George.

'Yes. There are lots of people in my family who drink, and I'm one of them!' laughed Sahira.

'Out here in England, and in Trinidad where we were born and we grew up, we've been drinking for generations now. As for beer, it's as good as drinking water for us,' smiled Dulcey. Kalyani was amazed at the attractive way her flawless set of milk-white teeth sparkled against the soft and smooth texture of her black face. Dulcey had a special beauty. An unusual black beauty! But will anyone in India, especially in Tamil Nadu, easily agree that she is beautiful? 'Oh, she is so black,' they would dismiss, with one word.

'Kalyani! Don't roam around in the sun too much, or you'll get dark.'

'Why are you always playing tennis or basket ball? Your face has become dark and has shrunk like a dried up ginger. Enough of games, now just stop playing, will you?'

During holidays and at least once in a week, people in her family would force her to apply a face-pack of sandalwood or almonds with cream and honey on her face.

'Just listen to me! Make a nice face-pack from the paste of sandalwood, cream and honey or rose water, or the paste of almond and cream, and apply it all over your face. Keep it on for half an hour and then rinse it off with warm water. It'll lighten your complexion a little, and it'll lend a glow to your skin,' they would advise. They continued with their suggestions till she left for England.

'You must continue to take care of your skin in England as well. Don't be careless and roam around under the summer even in England. You'll get sun burnt. Soak almonds in hot water, peel off the skin and then grind it to a smooth paste. Mix it with the cream of milk, add rose water or honey and apply it all over your face and then after half an hour ... '

What a lot of advice! Kalyani laughed as she thought about it. Everybody seemed to be driven by just one fear—that Kalyani should not become dark. Because Kalyani is a girl who has reached an age when she is primed for marriage. If someone were to comment on her looks with the words, 'O, this girl is slightly on the darker side,' her parents would feel much traumatised about it.

Coming to think of it, Kalyani did have what could be termed as a 'questionable colour'. Anybody who had eyes to see can never slight her as a dark girl. No, no way! Nobody can call her 'dark'. At the same time, nobody can generously call her 'fair' either. Because she was born with the ambiguous complexion that was somewhere between dark and fair, a colour that was suspended between the two points in an uncertain hue that forever puzzled people and made them wonder how to classify her. In Tamil, her complexion went by the common term '*maaniram*', a term that was always accompanied by a discontented, ungratified feeling. Actually, her colour was a shade of brown that was tinged with gold. It was a variety of '*maaniram*' that often caused her parents, close relations and her community profound anguish. If Kalyani selects the colours of her dresses thoughtfully and teams them up tastefully, then she looked very elegant indeed. But if she was forgetful even for a moment and wore just any garment in certain colours, instantly as it were, her complexion would stick out like a problem.

During her early days in London, Kalyani obediently followed the advice of her parents, her grandmother, aunt and went through what was like a 'ritual' for her skin. She made a face-pack of sandalwood paste and the cream of milk, mixed it with rose water and meticulously applied it over her face. During her first year, she had to share her room with Anna Polambi, a girl from Spain. So, whenever Anna went out of the room on some work, Kalyani would grab the chance to pamper her skin with this beauty treatment. Before Anna could return to the room, she would take care to thoroughly wash off the almond-rose water face-pack from her face until there was no trace of it left.

A few months rolled on like this. Outside the room of course, there was another Kalyani—a normal girl who studied with her peers, who played with them, sang and danced with them and shared her meals with them. She was a Kalyani who all day long, moved with everybody in the cosmopolitan atmosphere of the University of London that absorbed people coming over from all the corners of the world with different complexions, different physiognomies, different cultures, speaking different languages.

But the moment she returned to her room and bolted the door from within, the moment she was alone, she became the Kalyani who would take out the sandalwood and grind it on a round slab of stone to a smooth paste, mix it with the cream of milk and apply it on her face with rose water. Again, when she opened the door to step out into the multicultural ambience of the campus, Kalyani was yet another young Indian girl who was accepted by everybody on her terms, for what she was.

By returning to her room and closing the door, she often felt like she was shutting the door on the face of this Western world. She also felt a change come over her. It seemed to be such an utter lack of confidence, in the gold-brown colour of her complexion. Kalyani had a serious doubt now. Do the entire lot of students and professors—who represent so many other cultures and countries—accept me *because* I meticulously follow this beauty ritual, or have I, in fact, placed a pair of South Indian spectacles on their nose for them to look at me through those glasses?

The Kalyani who opened the doors of her room and went out into a large world to attend many a forum that took up issues against colour discrimination, racial discrimination and apartheid and who often spoke intensely against such discrimination, turned into someone so different the minute she stepped inside her room and closed the doors. She became another girl, a rather confused girl who tried to lighten her skin by this ritual on her face. Kalyani told herself that even if she could not go home to India on her last vacation, she should at least write about her feelings to her parents, grandmother and elder sister in a letter. And how will they react on reading her letter? They may just get very puzzled, or agitated, who knows? They may even order her to 'return to India immediately!'

The doors of her room fell like a curtain.

One day, she had miscalculated the time. On that day, Anna had retuned to the room before her time and had chanced upon Kalyani with that sandalwood face-pack.

'Oh my goodness! What happened, what ... ?' screamed Anna, very scared as if she had seen a ghost. The incident made Kalyani burst out laughing every time she remembered it.

Dear Anna. Anna Polambi. She is Spanish. Sharing a room with her for one year was a new experience for Kalyani. What an adorable girl Anna is—happy, vivacious, forever actively engaged in something or the other and full of pranks. In short, very alive. When she was not studying or playing games, one could see her singing all the time or dancing and learning new dance styles. Whenever she sang or danced, her face would go through such an amazing transformation that Kalyani was very surprised to see this change. In other moments, when Anna was not singing or dancing, her face would look quite plain. She had a fair skin, a slim figure but other than that there was nothing on her face to merit the word 'pretty' or 'lovely'. Still, I suppose the people in Tamil Nadu would appreciate her and say, 'ah, she is fair!'

Anna would play a song on her music system, sing along with it and dance as if she was in a trance. She would then turn into a mesmerising figure. The plain face would be gone and now she would attract everybody's attention with her extraordinary radiance and beauty. Men and women alike would vie with each other to dance with her on the floor. She was extremely popular with everybody.

After beer, they fully woke up to the reality of their classes and written projects for the following day. Everybody got up to go.

'Come, let's sit for some time in the bar,' said Robert to George. 'This watery beer isn't enough for us.'

'Hey Robert! You promised to help me plan about the Rally we're organising next month. Are you giving me a slip?' Dulcey exhorted him.

'I'm ready. Why don't you join us? We'll talk about it over drinks in the bar,' said Robert.

'All right,' said Dulcey, picking up her hand bag. 'Just a minute,' she said, searching for her room key in her handbag.

'You didn't get the key?' asked Kalyani. 'Don't worry. I'm heading straight for our room. I'll be there when you return,' she assured Dulcey.

'Oh thanks. All right, come along,' said Dulcey.

'Bye.'

'See you,' they said to each other as they dispersed.

Kalyani walked towards the students' apartments. It was cold. She pulled her overcoat till it covered her neck. Last year, she had shared a room with Anna and this year Dulcey was her roommate. Both were different, but Kalyani had had some interesting experiences. Last year ...

How shocked Anna was to see Kalyani with a mask of sandalwood-and-cream on her face! Kalyani recalled the incident again.

'Oh my goodness, what happened, what ... ?' Anna had cried out. It was all so funny.

After Kalyani handled the situation somewhat, Anna had persisted on asking her: 'Kalyani, why do you apply this stuff on your face and suffer like this? It's all so unnecessary.'

'I wanted to lighten my complexion a bit,' Kalyani sought to explain when Anna interrupted her. 'No, no! I said it's all so unnecessary. You're attractive as you are. Why should you go into all this trouble and smear this face-pack on?' she asked.

Kalyani noticed how genuinely concerned she was about her. She swallowed her hesitation and told her, 'What can I do, Anna? In my country, people get very disturbed about my complexion.'

'What! How very absurd!' cried Anna. She went over and sat next to Kalyani.

'Kalyani, your complexion is such a nice shade of golden-wheat brown,' she remarked, her face very earnest. 'And it suits you too, because you're an Indian. After all, the complexion you have is natural to most other Indians. Anything that is natural in appearance has a special beauty of its own. It has an innate power to draw us by its quiet, decent allure. You're already blessed with that kind of a charm. Why then do you go through this agony of applying all kinds of things on your face?' asked Anna.

'Do you really think all this is unnecessary?' asked Kalyani.

'Definitely! Do you know how many people appreciate you and talk about you so positively—men, women, Europeans, Britons, professors—the whole lot of them? When you come through to all of them as perfectly normal, as someone who is very graceful in fact, why are your own people in your country so sightless and blind?' asked Anna, with some heat.

Kalyani had no answer for that.

'Listen Kalyani, your entire appearance, right from your dress, your complexion ... everything goes to show that you're Indian. It makes a clear statement about where you come from. Why then should you do something to wilfully obliterate your Indian-ness and slowly make your colour fade off? I really don't understand,' said a vexed Anna.

But the case in India ... ?

'Let's offer a proposal for our Kalyani, for the second son of that family. He studied abroad and has a good job too.'

'All that is fine, but did you take a good look at the boy?'

'Why?'

'He is extremely dark, like *saandhu*.'[1]

Another time ...

[1] *Saandhu*: A black pigment used as a cosmetic dot on the forehead by women, or as a mark for warding off 'the evil eye'.

'The Srinivasan family is really a high class one. Good education, a good status and they're very civilised too. That family will really be suitable for Kalyani who studies in London and has earned a good name. Ask them to come and meet our girl one day,' said Kalyani's mother.

'It seems they've already seen Kalyani. Madhavan, who works in our office, told me. He is distantly related to that family,' said her father.

'Is that so? Where did they see her?'

'At some wedding. It seems they appreciated her a lot and remarked "Ah, such a charming girl and very intelligent too"... '

'How nice! And why have you taken your own sweet time to scratch your head and tell me this good news only now?' said Kalyani's mother.

'How could I have told you? Madhavan also said another thing.'

'What?'

'He said they were still hesitant because Kalyani is not very fair.'

'What do you mean by this? It's like you're offering me something with one hand and taking it away with the other,' said her mother.

'Now you understand why I never talked about them?' justified her father.

Kalyani could remember each and every word of her parents. She unlocked the door of her room and went in. There were lots of flyers, papers and letters strewn on the floor. They had been pushed in through the slit under the door.

Kalyani ate the meal that she had cooked for herself and studied for some time. No sign of Dulcey yet. She got up, washed her face, hands and legs and sat in front of the mirror to brush her hair. The ordinary cotton sleep-wear that she always put on before going to bed felt comfortable on the body. At this moment, with the privacy granted by the locked doors of her room, the mirror reflected a face that was calm and without any mask or posture. It was an Indian face. What was termed here in the West as a 'coloured' face, a naturally brown face. Why should I torture this face all the time and protect it from getting darker by subjecting it to all kinds of rituals? What a nuisance it is to have this uncertain, wheat colour, the '*maaniram*'. She brushed her hair and waited up for a while for Dulcey and soon felt sleepy. She lay down on her bed and stared at the ceiling. *There is a sky above the roof. It is a sky that looks blue as usual, to the whole world. And there is a cool moon on the sky, round as usual. In India, my parents, grandmother, elder sister and everybody must've looked at the same moon last night. It must be noon now, in India. The sun must be scorching. It will burn the skin of people and make them dark. Over here in England, the sun will put its head out only after ten more hours of night. Yet, the sun will not darken anybody's skin except mine. And Dulcey's. And Robert's. Because we're the 'blacks'.*

The 'Blacks'.

At first, Kalyani thought the term—'Blacks'—only referred to the African race. She got very shocked by the way Dulcey and Robert talked.

Dulcey has chaired and been the keynote speaker in many seminars that addressed the issue of racial discrimination or apartheid, in the capacity of being a 'Black' woman. As a fellow Black and as her good friend and companion, Robert would help Dulcey a lot with the organisational work. He would help in arranging for the seminars, in carrying out the sessions, in mobilising and gathering men and women students of the university and in also persuading professors to attend the events—Robert was Dulcey's trusted lieutenant and worked very hard. Everybody supported him with enthusiasm. How he would leap across the tennis court agilely in a game with his strong physique and tall figure. The minute he took a tennis racket in his hand, he would be greeted with whistles and clapping by an eager, cheering crowd.

Dulcey too had plenty of friends. Everybody including the faculty members was very impressed by the way she had totally dedicated herself to the cause of issues such as 'Racial' or 'Cultural Discrimination' and the way she would go all out to work very sincerely for these causes. Dulcey and Robert had managed to gather an enormous crowd of fellow Blacks—as well as Whites—to support them in their struggle for this cause and their friends were innumerable. 'Down with Discrimination *per se*' was their ideal and true to the spirit of this ideology, they forged a warm, friendly relationship with the Whites on the campus.

From the second year of her stay in the university, Kalyani has been sharing the room with Dulcey. During this one year, Kalyani came to realise that the black complexion of Dulcey was a very pure, undefiled and absolute truth. So smooth and unblemished was the texture of her black skin that it reached the eyes and registered in the mind and heart as something genuine. Yes, the glowing blackness of her skin was genuine. It had a natural radiance, the radiance of the real. It was such an honest colour.

Kalyani remembered the day when Dulcey had approached her for the first time to give her a hand with the forum on 'Colour and Race'. Kalyani now laughed at herself as she recalled how very shocked she had been on that day. She also felt very embarrassed.

'Kalyani, will you take part in this forum and speak on behalf of the Blacks in South Africa?' Dulcey had asked.

'Who, me? Isn't it a forum for the Blacks?' Kalyani had enquired.

'Yes it is.'

'Then how can I ... ?'

'Why, aren't you one of us?' Dulcey had asked.

'Ah Dulcey, but I'm Indian you see.'

'So what? Does that make you a white woman?'

'No, no! Definitely not!' Kalyani had said.

'In which case, you belong to the Blacks. In this country, whoever is not a White, is a Black, simple! In this world, and in this century, people like you and I can understand only two races—one is Black and the other is White!' Dulcey had said, laughing heartily.

Then she had briskly set about gathering the posters and notices that were prepared by her friends and colleagues and got ready to leave.

'It's okay Kalyani. Whether you wish to speak or not speak in these colloquiums is of course entirely up to you. Follow your heart. I don't mind. And listen, I'll be late today so don't wait up for me. Have your dinner. After I return I'll have some dessert with you. I'll get some fruits, ice cream or something for us. And then I'll tell you all about what happened in the colloquium today, all right? Bye!' Dulcey had said with a smile that was beyond compare as she stood for a moment at the doorway, waving her hand. Her blackness was soft as silk and her flawless set of pearly white teeth competed with the rest of her face. Like a flash of lightning, Dulcey was gone.

After Dulcey left, an oppressive silence had descended on the room. It pressed upon Kalyani. She remembered her mother using a Modern Tamil dictionary in Chennai that explained the 'Blacks' as Africans. Kalyani got up. She opened her wardrobe and took out the round slab of stone and the sandalwood piece that she would rub on to make a smooth paste. She also took out the bottle of rose water and the jar with almonds. She opened her suitcase, removed a few of her clothes and things to make space for all the things. Then she placed the round slab of stone, the sandalwood, almonds and rose water at the very bottom of the suitcase and covered them with clothes. She tidied up the top pile of clothes in the suitcase, closed the lid, locked it and put it away. She scrubbed her face with soap and water, wore a freshly washed pair of jeans and a T-shirt and let herself out. Locking the door behind her, she went in search of Dulcey.

There they are, Amma, Appa! Kalyani waved her hands at them vigorously but they didn't seem to notice her. There were heavy glass panes of windows all around. A huge number of passengers had just got down from the plane. Kalyani's suitcases were yet to be cleared by the Customs. She could see many heads and she peered through the gaps to search for her parents again. 'Wow! There is Grandma! Even she has come. Poor lady, at this age she has taken all the trouble to come. There's Sis, standing beside them. The entire family has come in full strength! God, I'm coming back to India after two years, and this is indeed a rousing welcome!

Checking over at the Customs', Kalyani piled her boxes on a cart and moved on. Now her family could see her clearly through the glass. They smiled at her and waved their hands. When she came out with the luggage cart, her parents rushed forward and hugged her.

'Welcome home, my darling,' said her grandmother. Kalyani bent down and touched her feet.

'Just look at our child, how she has changed,' said her grandmother. 'Her complexion has become so fair and she is glowing all over!'

Her mother and father thirstily drank up what Grandma said, clearly delighted to see the change in their daughter.

'Yes Amma, Kalyani has really become fair. The glory of it goes to England!' agreed Kalyani's mother.

'Hmm!' said Kalyani's father, pride lacing his smile.

Kalyani's elder sister beamed at her and gave her a secret wink.

'All right. Now come on, hurry everybody,' said Grandma. 'Our child has crossed so many seas to reach us. We've to take an *aarti*[2] the first thing. And after that, we have to remove the evil eye. How lovely our child looks now, all fair and radiant. Who knows, somebody may cast an evil eye upon her. Hurry up, we must go home,' said Grandma bustling everybody.

Suddenly, Kalyani felt a bitter taste in her mouth. She swallowed the moisture within her mouth.

'No Patti[3], I haven't become fair. I'm also a Black woman!' she said, laughing.

The family stared at her, aghast.

[2] *Aarti*: A plate containing water mixed with turmeric and lime, waved in a circular motion to welcome a person.

[3] *Patti*: Grandmother

Because...*

Kamala washed her hands after dinner and rushed into her Pattu Athai's[1] room. She bumped against her mother on the way.

'Hey, look where you're going?' laughed her mother. 'So? You're rushing in to your Athai's to hear a story again. At least wait till Akka[2] has her dinner.'

Kamala went inside her Athai's room. She knew that her Pattu Athai will not take long for she only ate *palagaram*[3] at night. She looked at the garlanded photograph of her Athai's husband on the wall. Such a nice face. A large book rested on Athai's single bed. It was *Ramayanam*. What will Athai read out for me tonight, she wondered.

Kamala walked over to a small table on the side. A mirror hung over the table on the wall. On the table was a bottle of hair oil, talcum powder, some letters, a large comb, a smaller comb in ivory and a few hair pins. Athai's comb is so very wide, noted Kamala. Naturally, for she has to brush her luxuriously thick, long hair that reached well below her waist. But Pattu Athai always gathered her hair tightly and secured it with these pins. On the occasions she let it down, how Kamala loved to run her fingers through her glossy, raven hair admiringly. Has Athai not eaten her *palagaram* yet?

Kamala moved away from the table to a corner where a *veena*[4] slumbered inside a cloth cover. She lifted the cover and peered inside.

* Translated from the original Tamil "Enenral" by the author.

[1] Athai: Father's sister

[2] Akka: Elder sister. Here, husband's elder sister.

[3] *Palagaram*: Light snacks and fruits eaten as a custom observed by widows who avoid a full meal.

[4] *Veena*: A seven-stringed musical instrument used in classical Carnatic music.

Oh, it's so dusty, in spite of the cover. Kamala smoothed away the dust with her hand. *Nang*! The sound stole out of a string in the *veena* like a secret. Nobody in the house played on this *veena*. If Kamala asked why, she got a standard reply: 'because who can ever have the nerve to play on the *veena* when Pattamma (her Athai) is around. Oh no! All of us are half-baked amateurs, Pattamma is the real maestro.'

'When you praise Athai so much, why don't you ask her to play the *veena*?' Kamala would ask her family but nobody cared to answer her question.

Why? Why doesn't Athai play on the *veena*? Kamala strummed on the *veena* slowly. *Saa ... paa ... ree ...*

'Naughty girl!'

Kamala turned around to see her Athai laughing.

'Want to learn the *veena*?' asked Pattamma.

'Yes Athai!'

'All right. Now cover the *veena* properly and come. Hurry, for it'll soon be time for you to go to bed.'

Kamala settled down comfortably beside her aunt on the bed. She lifted the large *Ramayanam* and placed it on her lap.

'What story will you tell me tonight, Athai?' she asked.

'I told you so many times my child, that Ramayanam is a single, long story. So we read it in continuity.'

'All right Athai.'

Pattamma opened the book on the page that had a book mark.

'Remember last time, I told you about how Kaikeyi asked King Dasharath for that boon?' said Pattamma.

'Yes. The wicked queen said Sri Rama should be banished to a wild forest for fourteen long years,' said Kamala.

'And then?'

'And then Sita said she'd also go along with Rama. Even Lakshmana said he'd go to the forest with his big brother Rama,' said Kamala.

'Right. So all of them get ready to go to the forest. The two queens Kausalya and Sumitra in particular are very sad to see their sons go. Rama says goodbye to his parents. Lakshmana also says goodbye to them and to Urmila,' said Pattamma.

'Who's Urmila?'

'Oh, I forgot to tell you. Urmila is Lakshmana's wife.'

'Is Lakshmana married?'

'But of course.'

'Then why doesn't Lakshmana take his wife Urmila to the forest, just as Rama takes Sita with him?' asked Kamala.

'Oh ... er ... you see, because it's very tough to live in the forest,' said Pattamma.

'Isn't it tough for Sita as well? Then why does Rama take Sita with him?'

'Because, my child, can anyone ever separate that couple? Sita is a devoted wife, a *pativrata*[5] who always maintained that wherever Rama is, that's Ayodhya for her,' explained Pattamma.

'Didn't Urmila ever get a chance to say that wherever Lakshmana lives, that's Ayodhya for her?' countered Kamala.

'Mischievous girl! Even if she said so, Lakshmana would've left her behind.'

'Why?'

'Because he is a rare person who is utterly devoted to his brother Rama.'

'Then why did he marry Urmila?'

'Kamala! If you keep on cross questioning like this, the story won't move at all.'

Kamala wrapped her arms around her aunt's neck.

'I'm sorry Athai, I only asked because poor Urmila would be so bored and lonely.'

Pattamma cupped her hands around the small girl's face and smiled at her.

'Just look at the way your mind works! No, Urmila wouldn't be bored at all. She'll be busy serving her mothers-in-law and father-in-law. She is a noble soul who sacrificed her married life for the sake of Rama and Sita. You must understand that.'

'Yes Athai.'

They heard the rustle of a saree and turned around.

It was Maitreyi, Kamala's mother.

'Is she pestering you again Akka, with endless questions? Why, where, how, what ... and so on. She does the same thing with me too,' said Maitreyi.

'No Maitreyi, she doesn't pester me. She is very intelligent. It's we who sometimes lose our patience,' smiled Pattamma.

[5] *Pativrata*: A wife who is totally devoted to her husband.

'Come Kamala, it's time you went to bed,' said Maitreyi. 'You need to get up early in the morning for school.'

'Good night Athai,' said Kamala, hugging her aunt. Pattamma kissed her on the brow.

'Oh god, what's this? Kamala, Kamala!'

'Coming Amma, I'm brushing my teeth,' replied Kamala from the washroom. When she came out, Maitreyi asked her, 'Kamala, your bed is wet. Why?'

The girl's face flushed with embarrassment. Maitreyi gathered her close and placed her hand on her forehead and her neck to check if she had fever. She noted that her eyes were swollen and red, her face puffy.

'Do you feel sick? But you don't seem to have fever. Then why this ... ?'

Kamala's face flushed again. She buried her face in the folds of her mother's saree.

'Tell me, my dear. What's the matter? You can tell *me*.'

'I got a bad dream Amma. I got very scared.'

'Really? Why didn't you run over to me or to your Appa?'

Kamala was quiet; she did not answer. Maitreyi stroked her head.

'What was the dream about? Tell me.'

'I saw a devil, right from a distance. He had ugly teeth jutting out of his mouth. I tried to run away and escape, but he took a deep breath that sucked me in like a strong wind and swept me up to him. You know Amma, then he laughed in a terrible way. With a cackling sound and in his hand, he ... '

'That's enough, my child. Just forget about it for you know it was just a dream after all,' said Maitreyi. She gathered the bedsheet along with the mattress and took it inside to the back portion of the house, to soak the bedsheet in soap water and to put out the mattress to dry in the sun. Kalyani, her mother-in-law was busy making coffee.

'Hasn't Muniyakka come as yet, Amma?' asked Maitreyi.

'There's no sign of her,' said Kalyani.

'She seems to be late today.'

'But I'm *not* late 'Mma. Here I am!' said Muniyakka, standing at the back door.

'You're exactly forty-five minutes late, do you know that?' said Kalyani.

'What can I do 'Mma? There was dense fog all around. My ageing eyes have gone all bleary, so I couldn't notice him lurking around. If I had, I'd have given him a slip and come through the Ulsoor road,' explained Muniyakka.

'Now don't reel off your yarn about the devil, Muniyakka. Who was it this time anyway? The *Kettu Pichachi* or the *Olle Pichachi*[6],' asked Kalyani, smiling in spite of herself.

'What can I tell you 'Mma, for you it's all a joke. Damn that fellow, if he was *Olle Pichachi* why would I feel like taking another street to avoid him? I would've greeted him and shared my tobacco with him, surely?' said Muniyakka.

Kalyani and Maitreyi exchanged glances and smiled.

'So you say that it was your *Kettu Pichachi*?' asked Maitreyi.

'Indeed it was. The devil. He had hidden himself in the fog. Suddenly, he pounced on me and pulled my hair. Oh Lord, how it pained me. "Let me go, leave me alone," I pleaded. "I'll have to go to Amma's house on time for my work, you swine, or they'll get angry," I begged but nothing doing. The stinker held on to my hair. "Give me coconut, give me a large piece of jaggery," he demanded,' said Muniyakka, picking up the unwashed vessels for cleaning. She swore under her breath all the while in fluent Kannada.

Vishalam, the woman who worked as a cook, came out of the kitchen and said, 'Muniyakka, wash those big vessels first and give them to me. I have to hurry with my cooking today.'

On the way to the backyard, Muniyakka glanced at Pattamma saying her prayers in the *puja* room. She bowed before the gods and hurried out with the vessels.

'Has our child gone to school?' asked Muniyakka, coming into the hall.

'Long ago,' said Maitreyi. 'Her bus came on time. It's you who is late.'

'But I told you why I got late 'Mma,' said Muniyakka. 'From tomorrow onwards, I'm going to carry some camphor with me and a bunch of *neem* leaves in my hands. That'll chase the bad devil away,' she said, carrying a large number of unwashed vessels with

[6] *Pichachi* is devil in Kannada. *Kettu Pichachi* is a bad devil. *Olle Pichachi* refers to the good devil. Rural people believed in them.

absolute ease, like they were feathers. Maitreyi wondered if the woman was really seventy years old or if she had lost count of her age. Just look at her body, she thought, it was like the taut string of a bow. Compared to her, all of us look old well before our prime.

Maitreyi went to the kitchen to help the cook Vishalam Mami who was planning to go out after the day's cooking.

'When do you have to go Mami?' asked Maitreyi.

'I should reach the place by eleven. We're four of us. We'll take a bus. The Acharya is expected to come a little before twelve. I hope we can see him with God's grace. You'll have to serve the food today, so sorry for the inconvenience,' said Vishalam.

'No problem Mami. Pattu Akka and I'll manage,' smiled Maitreyi, helping her with the vegetables. She grated the coconut for her and noticed how fresh Vishalam looked, wearing a washed silk saree that was off-white in colour. She had draped it tightly around her head. The sacred ash shone on her brow.

Kamala returned from school and sat down for lunch in the big hall where the family usually gathered for their meals and for a chat. Maitreyi and Pattamma served her.

'Where's Vishalam Mami?' asked Kamala.

'She has gone to see the Acharya,' said Maitreyi.

'Which Acharya?'

'I told you yesterday, about the Big Acharya, Shankaracharya Peiryavar who is visiting the city.'

'Didn't you go to see him Amma?'

'No.'

'How about you, Athai?'

'The Acharya won't see me, my dear,' said Pattamma.

'What!'

'Yes, he won't.'

'Mma, I'm going home now,' said Muniyakka, coming into the hall. 'I've finished all my work. I filled up the bath water, washed the utensils, swept and swabbed. Now I must hurry and cook something for myself. Chinnamma,' she called out to Kamala. 'So, you're back from school, are you? Eat well and get some sleep,' she said, smiling affectionately at Kamala.

'Kamala, why are you pecking at your food? Do you want some vegetables?' asked Maitreyi.

'No,' said Kamala, her eyes focused on her aunt. 'Why wouldn't the Acharya see you Athai? Hmm?' she asked again.

'Oh let it be,' said Pattamma, with a shrug.

'Now look here Pattu,' said her mother Kalyani from where she sat, on a lounge chair. 'You simply shouldn't care. Live in peace within the culture and mores of your family.'

'Yes Akka,' agreed Maitreyi. 'By the standards of our times, you're already living like an ascetic. That in itself is a bit too much. Just ignore the Acharya. All this is ... is ... sheer cruelty.'

'That's right!' said Kalyani. 'You can say that again. A man who says that he will "see" or grant an audience to only those widows who've tonsured their heads is indeed very cruel. If he refuses to see widows who have hair, then let him go his way ... ,' fumed Kalyani, her face flushed with anger.

'In this point I seem to have a status in his eyes that is even lower than that of our cook, Vishalam Mami,' said Pattamma, with a wry smile.

'What on earth do you mean, Pattu?' Kalyani shot back angrily. 'You're very young and yet you get confused by these outdated ideas? To think of the days when you were small.... How people adored you and would remark that you're exquisite as silk. That's why we called you "Pattu" for silk and brought you up most tenderly. God gave you the gift of music and you played on the *veena* in a way that enchanted everybody. But tragedy struck our family. We lost our young son-in-law. After this sad event we, your father and I, had to give in to a lot of restrictions for the sake of society. According to the dictates of convention, you had to give up *kumkum*[7] and with that went flowers and ornaments too. The damned society laid down another lame rule that you shouldn't play a musical instrument, so you stopped playing on the *veena*. So many "shouldn'ts"! You shouldn't participate in festivals, shouldn't wear new clothes before washing them first, shouldn't do this, and shouldn't do that ... *che*!' Kalyani gasped for breath, her nose flared in anger. Maitreyi placed her hand gently on her mother-in-law's shoulder.

Pattamma rushed into her room and locked the door from inside.

[7] *Kumkum*: The vermillion used by married women.

Muniyakka, who stood there listening to all of them, now joined in the argument.

'*Ayye*, just forget about this Acharya 'Mma,' she said. 'Is he a man at all, I ask you? A male who cannot admire a woman for her lovely, luxurious black hair ... how can you call him a man, in the first place, I ask you!'

'*Aey* Muniyakka,' warned Maitreyi, trying to make her more temperate in her reactions, but Kalyani forgot her anger for a moment and laughed aloud at her maid's remark. Emboldened to see Kalyani's anger fading off, Muniyakka walked up to her and accosted her, 'What's all this, 'Mma? Why didn't you get Pattu Amma married again as soon as your son-in-law died? You spent sweet time scratching your head in hesitation, thinking and thinking. Pattu Amma was so very young then and such a pretty little bird she was, very lovely to look at!'

'Ssh! Not so loudly, Muniyakka. She'll get angry if she hears you,' whispered Kalyani. The vegetables, rice and *papad* on Kamala's plate remained untouched. Suddenly she felt something tugging at her stomach, pulling it in. She did not feel like eating. Everyone around her was arguing hotly. In a swift move, she hid her plate laden with food and went out. Washing her hands, she went to her own room and flung herself on the bed, feeling very tired.

The cook, Vishalam Mami. Once a week a barber came to the house furtively, walking along the side of the house to reach the back portion. Vishalam Mami would bend her head to this barber, offering the few wisps of hair in a growth of two weeks for him to shave. After that, she would have a bath and appear again in her white saree tightly swathed over her head, complete with the sacred ash on her brow and no change at all on her usual placid face. What could be the connection between *her* and Pattu Athai, wondered Kamala.

Pattu Athai is a tall young woman with a fine, impressive figure. She has a serene beauty that is further enhanced by her thick, glossy hair, so long that it flows below her waist. Her brow is clean with no trace of *kumkum* in it. She looks like the picture of Mumtaz, wife of Emperor Shah Jahan that Kamala saw in a picture book. What were they all talking about? Why shouldn't Athai play the *veena*?

It was pouring outside. The rain was so typical of Bangalore, the way it always pours down in the afternoons and evenings. I can't play outdoors today, thought Kamala, closing her eyes. She fell asleep. Urmila stands at the palace door, waving goodbye to her husband Lakshmana as he leaves for the forest with Rama and Sita. Then she goes in and serves lunch to her mothers-in-law. At night, she massages their feet. But Urmila gets bored. She goes out and stands in the garden but there is no one to talk to. Then she puts on her shoes and starts walking on the street in search of another palace, in another country.

On the way, she comes across a queen.

'Ah ... isn't that Urmila? How're you, my dear?' the queen greets her.

'Er ... forgive me your Highness, but I don't recognise you,' says Urmila hesitantly.

'Don't you know me? I'm Gandhari.'

'Queen Gandhari?'

'Yes.'

'Oh, do forgive me,' says Urmila, bending low to touch the queen's feet. 'You haven't tied that piece of cloth over your eyes, you see, that's why I couldn't recognise you,' she explained.

'It doesn't matter. I threw away the piece of cloth around my eyes because I wanted to see the splendour of the trees in the forest, I wanted to see the flowers and the birds. I wanted to see people too,' she smiled.

Urmila smiled back and nodded in agreement. Together they walked for some time. They could see a devil from a distance, baring his teeth. There were long, ugly incisors protruding over his lips, but he joined in their laughter whenever the two ladies laughed about something. The devil helped them throughout their travel in the wild forest.

Once a big tree had fallen on the path that the royal ladies were walking on. Instantly as it were, the devil had removed the tree and cleared it for them. Next, they came across a river and wondered how they were going to cross it for there were no boats around. The devil sucked in the water, drank up the whole river and created a path for them on the dry riverbed.

Soon, a storm gathered and lashed around them. The devil stopped it with a mere gesture of his left hand, and with his right, he gave a signal to the storm and diverted its course. The storm turned and went towards a different direction. The devil with his rough, matted hair, his long tongue that was red as blood, and his protruding teeth, helped Queen Gandhari and Princess Urmila all through the way, because he was the Good Devil.

The *Olle Pichachi*.

Kamala tossed on the bed. There was a continuous patter of rain outside and the room was plunged in darkness. She got up and looked out the window. All the trees and plants in the garden stood dripping water. She gazed through the screen of water and thought, what a funny dream I had. Urmila meets Gandhari, like *Ramanyanam* meets *Mahabharatam*! Shall I tell Pattu Athai about my dream?

No ... I better not. The other day when Athai was telling me the story of Gandhari in *Mahabharatam*, I had asked her why she should blindfold herself just because her husband, King Dritharashtra was blind. I had pointed out that Gandhari would trip over things while walking if she were blindfolded. But Athai had become angry. 'Gandhari is a virtuous queen, do you realise that?' she had retorted. 'So why should a queen cover her eyes?' I had still demanded. Then she had said, 'Oh you poor thing, you don't get the point at all. You don't understand the meaning of purity or virtue, because you're much too small now, for all those things. One day when you grow up, you'll understand, you certainly will. Because you're also a *kamala*, a pure lotus that blooms in water,' she had said, cupping my face in her hands. I hadn't known what to say. I had just stared dumbly at her lovely face.

'Have you got up Kamala? Here, have your Bourn Vita,' said Maitreyi, coming into the room with a steaming cup of the beverage.

'Amma, today I can't go out and play,' pouted Kamala.

'That's right. See how it's raining cats and dogs,' said Maitreyi, giving her the cup.

'What shall I do then?'

'Finish your homework. Then draw some pictures and colour them,' said Maitreyi.

'I've no homework for today, Amma. Why don't you read me a story from the book of fairy tales?'

'All right. Once my work is done, I'll be back for your stories,' said Maitreyi, going out of the room.

'Tell me, what shall I read for you? You know all the stories by heart,' laughed Maitreyi.

'Still, I like to hear you read.'

Maitreyi read from *The Grimm's Fairy Tales*.

'The wicked witch snatched the small girl Rapunzel from her parents and locked her up in a high tower. There was no door to the tower. No stairway either. It only had a small window.

In course of time, Rapunzel grew up into a beautiful young girl. She had lovely, long hair, blonde and lustrous as spun gold. It was so very long that whenever the witch wanted to go up to the tower, she would call out,

"Rapunzel, Rapunzel, let down your hair."

Rapunzel would then let down her hair through the window. The witch would hold on to her long hair and climb up the tower to reach her. Then she ... '

'Amma, why do girls with long hair always suffer so much?' interrupted Kamala.

'What do you mean?'

'Just think about it. Even our Pattu Athai seems to suffer a lot and she too has thick, lovely long hair. Today all of you were talking about not removing her hair. Horrors! Just imagine removing Athai's beautiful hair! But even Athai was equally strange in her behaviour, for she didn't seem to know the value of her own hair. She argued with Patti about something, and then she became very sad and locked herself up in her room. Amma, I knocked on her door and called out "it's me", but she didn't open the door, even for me!' said Kamala.

Maitreyi was at a loss for words. She sat in silence for a while, and then she said, 'Kamala, I thought you sharpen your ears only for stories. But you seem to eavesdrop on everything we say! You don't *have to know* about all those things. You're a small child yet. Now let's return to the story.'

'But first tell me Amma. Is it wrong to have long, beautiful hair? Look at Rapunzel, for example. She too suffers a lot because of her long hair. And in addition, she is also stupid.'

'What!'

'But of course! She is a perfect fool. She knows very well, doesn't she, that the wicked witch will climb up the tower by holding on to her hair? Then why does she let down her hair at all, silly girl!'

'What's this Kamala? First, you eagerly ask for stories, and then you start questioning the stories, even the good ones,' said Maitreyi.

'How do you call this a "good" story? Rapunzel has to wait till the end for some nice young Prince to come on his own and set her free from the tower. Besides, the Prince just happens to see her, by chance. And he only *happens* to hear Rapunzel sing.'

'And so?'

'Suppose the Prince didn't come that way at all? What would've happened then?'

'He *will* come. Because Rapunzel is such a sweet, innocent young girl.'

'Ah! So, for that she has to be shut in a tower. It's the same even in the story of Snow White,' said Kamala.

'Now what's your complaint about Snow White?'

'She is also quite dumb, like Rapunzel. The seven dwarfs who are so nice and friendly, warn Snow White so many times not to open the door to any stranger in their absence. Still she opens it again and yet again for that old witch and gets into trouble. Finally, when she swoons and is put inside a coffin, she too has to wait like Rapunzel for a young Prince to save her and bring her back to life. Both Rapunzel and Snow White are unable to do anything on their own.'

'Kamala, why do you argue so much about these stories? If that's the way you think, then why don't you go ahead and *write your own stories* the way you want? I'm not going to read any more stories for you. Come along now and have your tiffin,' said Maitreyi, getting up.

They found Vishalam Mami explaining everything in great detail to Kalyani—how she got a *darshan* of the Acharya, what a wonderful radiance he had on his face, how an immense crowd had milled around him and so on.

'Mami,' said Maitreyi, coming into the large hall with Kamala in tow, 'Muniyakka has kept some more washed vessels outside, in the corridor.'

'I've already taken them,' replied Vishalam. 'She has scrubbed them so clean and shiny that you can see your face on them. She is thorough, our Muniyakka, we can't find fault in her work,' she said generously.

'She is very strong for her age too,' said Kalyani from where she sat, on her favourite lounge chair. 'Just calculate her age. She has been working in this house even before I came in as a bride. She is very much older than I and yet it's me who gets easily tired. I drag my feet around, bogged down with respiratory problems and what not. But look at Muniyakka. She is alone in life, her husband is dead. Her three sons have abandoned her and fled somewhere. Yet, she is so undefeated by life! She is such a cheerful soul too, who eats heartily, laughs heartily. The very picture of confidence!' said Kalyani, admiringly.

'Yes indeed,' agreed Vishalam. 'She has tremendous vitality even at this age. If only she gives up her habit of coming late for work, and telling us those peculiar tales of devils and ghosts as lame excuses for her getting late, then she would be a gem of a person,' said Vishalam, heading for the kitchen.

'Maitreyi,' said Kalyani, in a low voice. 'Vishalam knows very little about Muniyakka. For some of us who've really grown old and who've been around for too long, we often get a feeling that we've ourselves become somewhat like "ghosts". A feeling gets hold of us that we're haunting this house like spirits!'

'Really Patti? Are we ourselves like ghosts then?' asked Kamala, nestling up close to her grandmother.

'There you are, my curious cat!' smiled Kalyani, hugging the child.

'Amma, here's coffee for you,' said Maitreyi, handing her a tumbler of steaming coffee inside a *davara*[8]. 'Where's Pattu Akka?' she asked.

'She is probably resting. You have your coffee Maitreyi,' said Kalyani.

[8] *Davara*: A small utensil in steel used to hold a hot tumbler of coffee.

'Amma! Ammaaa ... vv!'

'Who is it? Why, it's Muniyakka. You're right on time today!' said Kalyani.

'Yes 'Mma, heh ... heh ...'

'Did you get drenched in the rain?' asked Kalyani. 'This is amazing! It's still pouring outside and your saree, blouse and your hair ... they're all so dry, Muniyakka?'

'I just escaped the rains 'Mma, all by the grace of the *Olle Pichachi*. Throughout the way as I walked, he pulled a piece of clear blue sky right over my head. It was like an umbrella!' said Muniyakka, with a broad grin.

'Indeed!' said Kalyani smiling, vastly amused at the familiar yarn she heard.

'Yes 'Mma. Not only that, he stopped the cold winds for me with his hand. That's why I could run over to your house on time,' she said, picking up a bucket of water and a broom. She briskly went over to the front of the house.

'Kamala, come over here and eat your *dosa*,' said Maitreyi, hovering over her plate on the table.

Muniyakka returned with the bucket and the broom.

'Muniyakka, will you have some *dosa*?' asked Maitreyi.

'Do you have some *kuzhambu*[9] to go with it, 'Mma?' asked Muniyakka.

'Why a little? You can have a lot of *kuzhambu*.'

'You see 'Mma, I brought some green gram sprouts with me. I thought I would swallow it down with some *kuzhambu*, that's why I asked.'

'Sure.'

Kamala finished eating her dosa and went over to the porch used by the maids and helpers of the household to have their food. She found Muniyakka sitting in a corner, engrossed in eating. Dipping half a *dosa* in *kuzhambu*, she put it in her mouth and swallowed it in one gulp. She dipped the other half and in it went, smoothly. Another ... and another. Beside her was an aluminium utensil with a dent on it.

[9] *Kuzhambu*: A tasty, spicy dish prepared with tamarind juice.

Muniyakka opened it and poured the green gram sprouts on to her plate. Mixing it with *kuzhambu*, she rolled them into tight balls in her fist and threw them into her waiting mouth. Ball after ball of food shot in accurately, into her eager mouth. Kamala watched fascinated as Muniyakka wolfed down her food, smacking her lips appreciatively with sounds of *chup*, *chup*, gorging herself on a meal of green gram sprouts. Perhaps her kind of food is very tasty, thought Kamala as she watched, eyes riveted.

After she finished eating, Muniyakka noticed Kamala standing at some distance.

'What're you looking at, my child? Come, come here,' she beckoned.

Kamala went closer and sat beside Muniyakka on the floor.

'Did you have your *dosa*, my little one?' asked Muniyakka.

'Yes.'

'What did you study in school today?'

'Something. Er ... Muniyakka?'

'Yes, sweetheart?'

'Have you really seen a devil?'

'But of course. Several times. Did you think I lied?' she said, laughing.

'Muniyakka, don't you get scared?'

'Why should I get scared my child, when a devil is also someone like us?'

'Oh no! How can that be?'

'Because even amongst people there are some who are good and some who are evil, don't you think? So in a way, we're also like devils and ghosts. Like them, we'll also vanish someday,' smiled Muniyakka.

'Then why do you complain about your *Kettu Pichachi*?' asked Kamala.

'What can I do, you tell me. He is such a big nuisance. Sometimes he harasses me wherever I go and I get fed up! The other day I told you in detail, didn't I, about how the *Kettu Pichachi* troubles me, remember?'

'Aah ... ? You mean the one that suddenly jumps on your back from a tree?'

'Yes, yes, the same one,' nodded Muniyakka.

'Then you said he pricks your feet painfully.'

'He does.'

'And ... and then you said he has eyes as red as ripe, red chillies which he rolls about to frighten you?'

'You're a smart little one. What a marvellous memory you have!' she said.

'Muniyakka, after that you said the *Kettu Pichachi* gets into the body of a tree and makes the branches swing and sway wildly in the windstorm, in a devil's dance. Remember, how you said the tree conspires with the devil and howls and sighs making sounds like *hoosh*! *Huoy*! *Hoosh*!'

'Exactly! That damned fellow is capable of all kinds of mischief. I'll teach him a lesson someday. I must get even with him,' declared Muniyakka.

'Can you really? Is that possible?' asked Kamala.

'Why ever not? I'll cut a lemon into two, mix some old rice with the red *kumkum* of Goddess Mariamma and put it on the way of the devil when he comes. If he ever happens to step over it ... '

'What'll happen? Tell me!'

'Why, he'll simply shrink and shrivel up to nine inches or even less, wouldn't he? If even that doesn't work, I'll practise sorcery. I'll tie a black thread around my neck and if he comes near me, I'll give him a tight slap on his cheek!'

'*Aiyyo*!'

'What else? Do you think I'll embrace him with love? I know all the grand, fustian ways of that rogue, all his pompous tricks, his cheap jugglery. I know them so well that as days went by, I too learnt some of his tricks, my child,' said Muniyakka, suddenly lowering her voice to whisper secretly to Kamala.

'Oh, good heavens! Then will you also become like the *Kettu Pichachi*, Muniyakka?'

The old woman laughed merrily.

'Isn't that the right thing to do, my child? Only when I become a little like him can I hit him back on his own terms, you see?' she reasoned.

Kamala slowly sidled away from Muniyakka and sat at a safe distance.

'Muni ... Muniyakka ... ' she said, hesitantly. 'You ... who are you? I mean, are you a woman or a devil?'

'My dearest child,' laughed Muniyakka. 'Did you get scared? I'm your very own Muniyakka, my little one. I'm the loyal, faithful maid of this household, have been so for years now. I was working in this house even before your grandmother came into this family. And when you arrived, I carried you as a tiny baby, cradled you on my lap, and played with you, my precious, golden infant,' smiled Muniyakka.

Kamala smiled back at her.

'But, if ever that worthless devil crosses my way, I'll just rip him apart. Only then will his arrogance be tamed. In order to do that, we should also have some wickedness within us. Otherwise the rogue will devour us. You must realise that, my little one,' she said, with a broad grin.

Kamala looked at Muniyakka and her nicotine-stained teeth. There was a gap in the middle where she had lost a tooth. With that, she flashed a captivating smile that lit up her eyes. Her face was innocent and open, like that of a child. That's our very own Muniyakka. She belongs to our home.

Kamala moved closer to her and sat beside her till their shoulders and arms touched. A smell of *kuzhambu* mixed with tobacco wafted from her body. She could also smell dried betel leaves and areca nut. Kamala placed her hand on Muniyakka's lap. It was so comfortable. Snug and cushiony. Ah ... what a very safe place this is, beside Muniyakka, thought Kamala. She is so strong that she doesn't care about old customs and traditions. She can even take on the devil! One can always be secure and unharmed with Muniyakka around.

A Sky All Around*

'The pulse is very low,' said the soft voice.

'Not again?' said the firm voice.

'Take a look at the screen. According to the head nurse Sujatha, he seems to have been all right at night.'

On the monitor, a flat thread of a line ran along staggeringly.

'Feel his pulse, please,' said the silky voice. It was the same soft voice that had spoken first.

That voice drew Varadarajan into a blue, watery expanse. On the water, he floated weightlessly. Then swam. There was this sky above. It was there anywhere he looked. A sky that rippled with water. The water touched the sky. Varadarajan looked around him. There was not the faintest line that could be identified as the horizon to separate the water from the sky. The sky was all liquid, with the lustrous sheen of water.

'But what about the rest of his vital functions?' said a third voice. It was a female voice, definitely female although it was coarse. *That woman cannot sing. She better not. Even if she were to obstinately open her lips to sing, everybody will get up and leave, that's for sure.*

Out in the open. What an aqueous spread of a sky. Am I floating on it, or am I swimming? Couldn't say with certainty. Such an unsoiled blue, this open stretch of space, of ether.

'Sister Sujatha.' It was the female doctor's coarse voice.

'Yes Doctor, Madam?' Nurse Sujatha rushed to her side.

'Sister, did this patient pass urine properly?'

'He was passing urine properly until yesterday,' she replied.

* Based on a real near-death-experience. Translated from the original Tamil "Engum Vaanam" by the author, published in *Kanaiyuzhi*, Chennai.

'Until yesterday? What do you mean?'

The vibrations of the two voices were caught in the whirlpools of the waters. They drowned, and then floated up again, reaching Varadarajan in muffled fragments.

'Did he pass urine today? It's now three in the afternoon,' said the female doctor.

'Afternoon'. What's 'after' noon? Out here, the colour of the sky is spread out, unchanging.

'The last time he passed urine was yesterday, in the morning,' said Sujatha.

'Oh! Remove the sheets. I want to see his legs,' ordered the coarse voice.

The three doctors gathered around the foot of the bed. Vardarajan's legs were spread out when the sheets were removed.

'See that?' said the coarse voice. 'There's a lot of swelling on both the legs,' she remarked.

Fingers pressed hard on the feet, instep, ankles and the fleshy portions of the calves.

'He has edema. The legs have swollen up such a lot, *tcch*,' said the soft voice.

'Yes indeed. Wherever we press, the fingers leave a deep pit as an impression,' remarked the firm voice.

'Perhaps this case is moving towards renal failure.'

'Before we hasten to that conclusion, let's try a dialysis on him. Sister, who is on duty today, during visitors' time?' asked the firm voice.

'Hmm ... ' Nurse Sujatha thought for a moment. 'It's Dr Mani, and then there'll be Dr Desai to assist him,' she said.

'All right. We'll call them and tell them about what we discussed amongst ourselves regarding this patient. In the evening, when the patient's family visits him, you too should explain the condition to them clearly. Ask them to get organised immediately for the money required for dialysis. Then the duty-doctors can go ahead with the arrangements,' said the coarse voice.

'Sister Sujatha, would you be off in the evening, after the change of duty?' asked the firm voice. 'This case has turned serious. He has not only been in a coma for several days now, he has this edema now. I'd like you to look after him. Leave him under the care of someone for a while, then you go, freshen up, have your meal and come back,' said the firm voice.

'Yes Sister,' the soft voice chimed in. 'When I look at the swelling in his legs ... Aah, I've a small doubt. Does he have sensation?'

Aiyyo! It's paining. No, No! Please don't do that. Leave me alone. Who's pinching me like this, is it the man with the soft voice who just spoke? How can someone with such a delicate voice have these rough hands that press and pinch so hurtfully ... it doesn't match his voice? Aiyyo! Amma! That's enough, stop it for God's sake, STOP! Now all of you are not just pressing my legs, you're also turning and twisting my toes so mercilessly. Amma, I'm in agony. This pain ... now they're pinching my arms too, any which way.

Varadarajan tried to open his mouth to cry out. Something filled up his mouth instantly and blocked it. Suppose I remove that 'something' and open my mouth? Will the water on which I'm floating rush into my mouth?

'Hmm. He has no sensation at all. Let's look at the heart monitor for a moment.'

'Doctor, has he really lost his sensation?' asked Sister Sujatha.

'Ye ... es? And so?' there was an edge in the coarse voice as if Sister Sujatha had said something impertinent and out of turn.

'Oh, nothing Madam. I just noticed that when all of you were pressing and pinching his legs and toes, his face seemed to wince with pain. I mean it got all twisted up. That's why I wondered ... ' Sister Sujatha spoke hesitantly.

Suddenly, there was laughter all around.

'Sister, perhaps your imagination is running wild. Take some rest. And if you want to be eligible for the nursing profession, you'll have to leave all this unnecessary baggage of sentiments and emotions. Only then you can serve a patient well,' said the firm voice.

'Yes doctor.'

The voices faded off. Nurse Sujatha sponged Varadarajan on the brow with a damp towel. *Aah, it is so cool and soothing.* She sponged the jaw, then the area around the nose. *Ooh, that hurts. Something has blocked the nostril.* Very gently, she removed the tube for the nasal feed that was blocking the nostril, to wipe around the upper lip. Yet how it hurt. *It's unbearable.*

Suddenly, Sister Sujatha stopped sponging. She placed her palm over his forehead and stroked his brow gently with her hand. 'There, there,' she whispered. Even so, the pain that began with the nostril suddenly spread, erupting in pockets of pain in different places of the body. *Aiyyo, Amma, save me from this torture. Come. Come soon ...*

'*I'm coming, my precious. Varad, listen Varad ...* '

The name echoed across the sky. It was the voice of a young girl. Her thick black hair was long and braided. She had a sharp nose and her lustrous eyes exuded love.

'*Varad ... Varad ...*' she called out, smiling. Her teeth shot through the sky like lightning.

'*Amma, where were you? I've been searching for you all the while.*'

'*Just where did you search for me, my precious? Did you also look for me inside the wardrobe?*' *she laughed.*

Once again her smile lit up the sky.

Amma is so very tall! Even her face seems to spread itself all over the sky. What a very large face. Yet the small boy Varadarajan, dressed in shorts and a T-shirt, did not feel scared. For Amma's eyes were two tender pools of compassion. She bent down to gather her little boy in her arms. Then she hugged him. The boy rested his head on her cheek.

'*What's the matter Varad?*'

'*It's paining a lot, Amma.*'

'*Where exactly is the pain? What happened? Did you get hurt?*' she asked, agitated.

'*No, they pinched me. They pinched my ankles, thighs and my arms as well. And they twisted and turned my toes so hard it was very painful.*'

'*My God, but who did all that?*'

'*They, the doctors.*'

Her arms stretched out like long white clouds and embraced him.

'*Let them be. From now on, nothing can hurt you. Come over to me, Varad. Nothing can hurt you ever.*'

'*Amma, how can I come? They'll be waiting for me.*'

'*Who are 'they'?*'

'*Kanaka, Ganesh, Revathi, little Anu, then Chitra ... everybody.*'

'Come away from everything. Come to me. Then nothing will hurt you any more. Nothing whatever.'

Above him, the waters rippled and swished. How come this water does not fall down from above? What kind of an upside-down gravitational force is this?

'Amma ... Amma.'

He searched for her in the sky. And searched for her in the waters. But he could not see the young girl with the long braided hair. And the lustrous eyes exuding love.

They were small, beady eyes instead. And a somewhat plump figure. The hair was not long or braided. It was sparse and wispy. That was Kanaka, his wife. She was cooking something in the kitchen. Varadarajan wanted to go in and ask her what she was cooking, but he restrained himself. What if she takes one look at this little boy in shorts intruding, and admonishes him, 'Hey, who are you? How did you stray in here?' He could recognise Kanaka, but can *she* recognise him, as a small boy? The sky was spread all around in a uniform shade of blue.

'Thatha, Thatha.[1]'

'Hush Anu, keep quiet. I just told you that you shouldn't speak loudly in the Intensive Care. They'll drive us out,' warned Ganesh.

'Amma, why is Thatha sleeping all the time? Does he sleep in the evenings too?' asked Anu.

'Thatha is not well, my dear,' said Revathi. 'Keep quiet. You mustn't talk in the ICU', said Revathi.

'All right. Amma?'

'Ssh! I just asked you to keep quiet, didn't I?'

'Look, Patti[2] is weeping. Chitra Athai[3] is also weeping. Why?'

'Come on Anu, let's go out of this ICU.'

No Revathi, no! Let the child stay here for some more time. Allow her to touch me.

[1] Thatha: Grandfather

[2] Patti: Grandmother

[3] Athai: Father's sister

'Manni[4], do take Anu outside the ICU. I'll see the duty-doctor with Ganesh and Sister Sujatha. Manni, O Manni,' Chitra broke down.

'Take heart, Chitra. Be brave. Everything will be fine. Come Anu, let's go out.'

'Ganesh, what's happening? Has Appa finally ended up with renal failure, as they hinted? He's going to let us down in the end, is he?' said Kanaka, her voice choking.

'Amma please, please don't weep like that. Let's attend to what has to be done now. I'll go with Sister Sujatha to see Dr Mani,' said Ganesh.

'Ganesh, they say a dialysis costs a lot, a lot. See these milagu[5] bangles? They're heavy and can fetch a good price. I'll sell a pair of them, or may be sell two pairs. You can use that money for dialysis,' said Kanaka.

'What nonsense Amma. How can you talk like that? I'm thinking of approaching the Rotary Club for help,' said Ganesh.

'Good idea,' said Chitra. 'I'll ask Indraneel too about it. He knows a few people in the Rotary.'

'Then hurry up and ask around. I'll call Indraneel around ten at night or eleven, may I?' asked Ganesh.

'Oh you can call us at any time. How do you measure time now? Let's do whatever needs to be done, and fast,' said Chitra.

'Oh God, only you can save him,' said Kanaka, sobbing.

Kanaka, Kanaka, don't cry. Don't. If you cry, then Ganesh and Chitra will get very demoralised. Gently, Varadarajan moved the bangles on her arms back and forth. He stroked them. *These bangles should always be on your arms. Don't ever sell them, don't! Can you hear what I'm saying, Kanaka?*

'Amma, I tried stopping her but she just wiggled out of my hands and ran inside,' said Revathi trailing behind Anu.

'Thatha, Thatha.'

Varadarajan felt Anu's small hands stroking his cheeks.

'Thatha, get up. Play with me.'

'Now look here Anu, listen to me. You must. Let's get out of this place, come,' said Revathi. Turning to Kanaka, she said, 'Amma,

[4] Manni: Wife of elder brother

[5] *Milagu*: Pepper in Tamil; here it refers to a popular 'pepper pattern' for heavy gold bangles.

come, let's go home. He said we should all go home as soon as he sees the duty-doctor. Because we have to do our *Gongyo*[6] prayers together.'

'Oh yes. We should do *Gongyo* the first thing on reaching home. Come Revathi, let's get going. After *Gongyo*, we should chant *daimoku*[7] with all our heart. Anu sweetheart, come,' said Kanaka.

Swirling currents of water caught the voices, and then they cleared and reached his ears.

Don't go away, all of you. Don't go. Let the child stay by the side of me for some time.... Please don't leave. Do your Gongyo prayers right here so that I can hear it too. I want to chant with you all....

'*Namaskar* Doctor.'

'*Namaskar*. So what did you decide?'

'I'll arrange for the money for my father's dialysis, and then I'll come early tomorrow, Doctor,' said Ganesh.

'Good. We wanted to give a chance to Mr Varadarajan. Let's try the dialysis. Okay, good luck!' said Dr Mani.

In the beginning, it could be heard as a faint vibration. Eventually, the sounds seemed to reverberate with a clear continuity. It was the Buddha's peerless Lotus Sutra, also called the *Saddharma Pundarika Sutra*. Gautama Buddha, affectionately called Shakyamuni, gifted

[6] *Gongyo*: The daily prayers done in the mornings and evenings by reciting parts of the 2nd and the 16th chapters of the Lotus Sutra by the Buddha. It is based on the Mahayana school of philosophy that enables ordinary lay people to develop qualities necessary to combat the enormous problems in life. Buddha, the Shakyamuni from India, had predicted that out of the confusions of our present times (he called it the Latter Day) a great teacher would appear and expound the philosophy of Buddhism based on Lotus Sutra. Centuries later, Nichiren Daishonin, a thirteenth century Buddhist sage from Japan, revived and defined the essence of this teaching of Shakyamuni with a relevance to the present times.

[7] *Daimoku*: Chanting of the supreme Law of Buddhism, *Nam-myoho-renge-kyo*, that stands for the oneness of the Person and the Law. It is the title of Lotus Sutra, originally written in Sanskrit as *Saddharma Pundarika Sutra*. It was rendered into classical Chinese by the great Buddhist scholar Kumarajiva.

this Sutra to the world and it was unfolding in the metric, stanzaic regularity and orderly rhythmic cadence of a *Gongyo*. It was followed by the unbroken flow of *daimoku*.

'*Nam-myoho-renge-kyo* ... '

'*Nam-myoho-renge-kyo* ... '

'*Nam-myoho-renge-kyo* ... '

Tirelessly, they chanted. Waves and waves of sounds rose and wrapped around Varadarajan pervasively. The voices of Kanaka, Ganesh, and Chitra, Revathi and in between, the voice of little Anu could be heard in a harmonious blend. The sounds carried their life breath, rising high, reaching the sky till it misted over with their breath. They condensed like pearly drops of dew, as if the sky had burst out in perspiration. Although the chanting voices chimed in an orchestrated harmony, Varadarajan could identify and recognise some individual voices. The strong baritone of Ganesh. Revathi's sweet voice. Kanaka's came through like the uniform thrumming of a *tanpura*[8], clear and steady as it gave them all the main *shruti*[9] support. Kanaka's voice had the cultivated control and maturity that came with her years of training as a vocalist. Anu's young voice could be heard in between, rising, fading.

Varadarajan opened his mouth to join them in the prayers. He tried to chant *daimoku*. Small bubbles of water came out of his mouth and floated upward. No sound came out of his lips. *What's happened to me? Have I become mute?*

'*Nam-myoho-renge-kyo* ... '

My ears can hear that very well indeed. But what's happened to my voice, my mouth?

'Thank you very much Sister Sujatha. Actually, we can't thank you enough for this favour,' said Chitra.

'But nobody should come to know about this,' warned Sister Sujatha.

'But of course, Sister. You've gone so far as to allow us to chant our prayers in this Intensive Care, however softly we did it. You have a big heart; we are indebted to you. We'll never tell anybody about this,' assured Ganesh.

[8] *Tanpura*: A four-stringed instrument for supporting and maintaining the basic notes.

[9] *Shruti*: The basic note to which both the instrument and the musician have to be synchronised.

'All right, you better leave now. It's time for the duty-doctor's visit. Go out quietly, without making a noise,' said Sister Sujatha.

'Come out, everybody,' gestured Ganesh, leading the way.

It was a long corridor. Not one or two but many, many corridors. Each one of them was flanked by high walls with lights burning on them. They were walking to and fro in the corridors, and walking very fast. *No one seems to walk normally here. Why is that? All of them walked as if hurrying on in some great rush. What was so urgent for them? What are they searching for, to be scampering around like this?*

Varadarajan started walking in the corridor. Some people pushed him from behind and jostled him as if to say, come on, move on, and hurry! Some others hit him on the sides and pushed their way through. *If I don't make way for them instantly, they stamp on my legs hurtfully and move ahead. Aiyyo! Don't stamp on me like that*, he cried out but as soon as he opened his mouth, small bubbles of water came out and floated around. They glittered. No sound came out even as he cried out, so people continued stamping on him unheedingly, hitting and jostling around as they rushed on.

So many corridors. Some were narrow, long and curved in such a way that you did not know when you would come upon the next turn. He could not make out which was the beginning of the corridor, and which the end. Some corridors were broad and brightened up by many lights. But all the corridors thronged with the same kind of people, rushing, hurrying on. Most of them were strangers. Some made you feel that you have seen them before somewhere. Yet, even as you thought that you may have met them and observed them keenly, the resemblance faded and the faces froze into strangers again.

There, see over there? See the man who is literally 'running' along the corridor? His face looks familiar. Perhaps he would also turn into a stranger even as I look at him? At a fleeting glance, he looks like Bhaskaran. The figure walked rapidly along the corner near the wall. He turned his head to push a man who crossed his way. *Ah! I'm right. That's Bhaskar for sure. No doubt about it.*

'Bhaskaran, hey Bhaskar!'

Even while working in the office Bhaskaran always used to rush around like this. On his way to lick the boots of someone, or to fawn over and ingratiate himself with the Senior Vice-President of the company. Crafty to the core, he would deceive the VP with his sweet speech. He was consumed by an ambition to move upward in the profession faster than anyone else and that eventually landed him with a problem. Hypertension. He suffered a lot and yet, hypertension notwithstanding, he never gave up the compulsive habit of chasing big-time personalities. He continued running after them, pushing himself, not heeding his doctor's warnings. He rushed headlong in all four directions and one day had a heart attack and died.

'Hey Bhaskar, why're you rushing around hurriedly like this, even after coming to this place? Who do you want to catch and what can you possibly achieve by that? At least now you can stay calm and be at peace. Haven't you learnt a lesson at long last? Bhaskar, hey Bhaskar! Look here, it's me, Varadarajan.'

Bhaskaran suddenly turned and went into a corridor that was on the right side. Varadarajan hurriedly followed him inside the corridor. *Must catch up with him somehow. This place is very strange. You see a familiar looking face, and it not only fades the very minute you recognise it, you too tend to forget who it is. Take for example that man, I mean the ninth one walking on the same row as Bhaskaran. I remember having played with him in a house, some house that I can't remember for sure, try as I might. But I do remember having grown up together with this man in the same house, I remember having played with him, having studied with him, I remember having quarrelled with him. I'm not clear about where that house was, I mean in which city. Let it be. Bhaskaran is the only person here about whom I can surely say 'I know him'. So let me catch hold of him and ask, hey old fellow, why are you hurrying around crazily even after coming to this place?*

Varadarajan walked rapidly within the corridor. He feared that Bhaskaran might at any moment suddenly get into some other corridor, so he walked faster. *This chap Bhaskaran, he always belonged to the tribe of burglars who smear oil all over their body. He is the slimy kind of thief who can slither and slip through and cannot be caught by anybody. But I'm going to catch him anyhow. I must confront him, pin him down till he is stymied and then ask him: what crafty strategies are you up to, even out here, eh?*

Bhaskaran walked on, breathless. At last, Varadarajan caught up with him. He tapped him on the shoulder and asked: *'Hello*

Bhaskar, where're you rushing off to, in such a great hurry? Are you on your office work, even here?' he smiled at him with a wink. Bhaskaran turned around and looked at Varadarajan appraisingly. He brushed off Varadarajan's hand from his shoulder and retorted: '*Who're you? And what do you want?*' he said, glaring at him.

Aiyyo, have I approached a wrong man? Like the others around here, has Bhaskaran also turned into a stranger?

'Aren't you Bhaskaran?' asked Varadarajan.

'I am Bhaskaran, but who're you? I don't know you,' he said.

'Don't you recognise me? I'm Varadarajan. Remember, we worked for the same company?'

'I don't know,' said Bhaskaran again and in a trice, as if impelled by some force which pushed him forward, he walked through the corridor very rapidly, suddenly turned his direction and disappeared.

How amazing! For so many years we've worked together in the same office. He had died of a heart attack only recently. Has he already forgotten me? I even went to his house with Kanaka, for the condolence meeting.

Varadarajan felt suffocated by the crowd jostling in the corridor. He could see a spot of brightness at the far end. Could it be sunlight? Is it the mouth of this corridor which is stretching long like a tunnel?

Varadarajan speeded up towards that direction. He kept walking. Eventually, he could see the end of the corridor. Aah, at last. Let me breathe in the fresh air outside, he thought and came out eagerly. He reached the blue expanse of the sky. A sky cooled by a watery shine. He swam in it. He flew in it. He floated in it weightlessly.

There were clouds all around. Clouds that are conventionally described as 'fleecy' in books. They did not caress his cheeks or his body, like he expected them to do. He could not even feel them as he went inside them and came out, untouched by anything. Anything at all.

What a wide expanse. There was not the faintest hint of a line that could be taken as a 'horizon'. One could not tell which was the sky and which the water and which the centre. It was an immense stretch of something. The water rippled and gurgled. On the water he saw the reflection of the young girl's face again. The same sharp nose and large, lustrous eyes. Her teeth had a whiteness that dazzled like lightning. He remembered having seen this young girl somewhere. She too seemed to remember, for she smiled at him. How the waters lit up with her smile.

'*Varad, Varad,*' she called out softly. Oh, she knows my family name and she is calling out my name with such familiarity, this young girl. She is right about my name though. Everybody at home used to call me 'Varad'. Perhaps she has mistaken me for some other man called 'Varad'? Just like Bhaskar couldn't recognise me.... This place *is* queer. It is very strange. It makes everybody falter in recognising people. It is a place that plays tricky games by conjuring deceptive appearances. Poor girl, how eagerly and affectionately she looks at me and calls out my name.

'*Varad, Varad my precious, I'm there for you. Come. Come over to your mother,*' she said.

Mother! Is she my mother? I'm the grandfather of Anu and for someone as old as me, how can this young girl be my mother, when she is years younger than I? Poor thing, this girl is very confused. She is of course right about my name. And I must admit that I too faintly remember having seen her in my family some time, somewhere. Yes, it's true. I have seen her somewhere ... yet, how can I be the son of such a very young girl? All this is happening because of this strange place. It has an atmosphere that creates confusions. I feel very sorry for this girl.

'*There, there, my girl, you're mistaken. I'm very much older than you ...* ' Varadarajan tried to explain it to her. He opened his mouth to talk. Tiny bubbles of water came out of his mouth. They rose and glistened and shimmered as they floated. Let me go closer to her and explain through my gestures and signs, he thought. She may then understand. He began to swim towards her image which was reflected in the waters. Films of waters flowed over the face of the young girl like you see on a screen. The face was fading away even as he swam towards her eagerly. But he could not find her.

'Dr Mani, did you follow up this case?' enquired the firm voice.

'Yes. It's really a bad case. I came to the ICU two times at night to see him. His condition is serious. In spite of all that we do for him, he seems to slip away somewhere,' said Dr Mani.

'He has been on dialysis but it's of no use whatever. From now on, it's going to be very difficult to save him,' said the soft voice.

'Hmm ... it's a total renal failure. He is almost dead,' remarked the firm voice.

'Not 'almost', it wouldn't be wrong to say that he is dead. He has a pulse beat only because of the life support system, the ventilator. It'll stop the minute we switch it off. And that'll be the end of him,' said Dr Mani.

'Have you informed his family?'

'They were informed four days back. But they stubbornly refuse to accept the truth. They said, "we'll pray for him. He'll survive". They're so simplistic in their belief but I felt sorry for them.'

'Things have gone past that time now. Prayers can't help.'

'Besides, this bed in the ICU is being wasted. After him, we can allot this bed to yet another critical case. Only *we* know how difficult it is for us to find beds for terminal cases. Sister Sujatha, explain all this to the family somehow.'

'Yes doctor.'

'Call the family over phone, ask them to come and see me in my chamber as soon as they can,' said the firm voice.

'Very well, doctor.'

'They can't keep on deceiving themselves any more.'

'You see doctor ... '

'What?' His voice expressed shock.

'Oh nothing Sir. That is ... I meant to say that his family still has faith that he'll somehow survive and come through. They pray so much for him everyday.'

'Humph! How can he survive after this ... ' began the doctor, and then lapsed into silence for a minute. 'I can understand the agony the family is going through only too well. Everyone will pray of course for somebody who has reached this stage. It's but natural. But so far as this gentleman is concerned, his pulse beat is only mechanical, like a clock that works on a cell. And only because of this life support system. He can't breathe on his own without the ventilator.'

'We're sorry. We tried our best but couldn't save him,' said the soft voice.

No, no!

I'll come through this alive! I can hear Kanaka's prayers. I can hear the chanting of Ganesh, Chitra, and Revathi. Please have faith in the prayers of my family,' Varadarajan cried out silently.

'*Nam-myoho-renge-kyo* ... *Nam-myoho-renge-kyo* ... *Nam-myoho-renge-kyo* ... '

'What a lifeless chanting. The lines are so tired they seem to droop down at both ends. Come on, gather some strength and do some vibrant chanting!' said Kanaka.

The rhythmic chanting picked up a pace and went on. Somewhere in the middle of the chanting, Chitra's voice broke. They waited for her to collect herself and resumed the chanting. Ganesh's voice went hoarse. He cleared his throat but stood silent.

'Now Ganesh, take heart,' said Kanaka. 'Whatever the doctors say, let's keep it on hold. Let's chant *daimoku* without any disruption and with complete faith in the *Gohonzon*. Come, let's surrender your father to the hands of Buddha and chant. Let *daimoku* surround him and encircle him,' said Kanaka, encouragingly.

'*Nam-myoho-renge-kyo*, *Nam-myoho-renge-kyo*, *Nam-myoho-renge-kyo* ... '

The sounds reverberated for a very long time.

On a low table to the left of the television, there was a framed photograph of Ganesh and Revathi on one side, with a separate photograph of their child Anu. On another side, there was a photograph of Chitra and Indraneel. Beside the television was a picture of Varadarajan and Kanaka, obviously taken when they were young. '*How slim we look in this, the two of us!*' thought Varadarajan.

Hanging on the wall was a large photograph with a garland around it. The young woman in the picture had a sharp nose, lustrous eyes and pearly white teeth. That's Amma. Beside Amma stood Appa, the very picture of dignity. Within a year after Amma died, Appa followed her as if he could not stand the grief of her absence.

Aha, the comfort of lying down on my own bed, in my own room and in my own house—it's beyond compare, thought Varadarajan. Kanaka took a spoon and fed him small pieces of stewed apple sprinkled with sugar. She fed him little by little.

'Eat slowly,' she said.

After stewed apple she gave him half a glass of warm milk. Varadarajan took it from her and sipped at it slowly. The milk went down his throat with a soothing warmth.

Kanaka tidied up and arranged the newspapers and magazines on the small table. Sipping his warm milk, Varadarajan noted how the *milagu* bangles slid up and down her arms as Kanaka arranged the papers.

From the room adjacent to his, the sounds of *Gongyo* from Ganesh and Revathi floated in. Varadarajan finished drinking the milk. Kanaka took the tumbler from him. Varadarajan reclined on the bed, rested his head sideways on the pillow and said: 'You know Kanaka, I could hear the sounds of your *Gongyo* and the chanting very well indeed.'

'Oh, you can hear the sounds well, can you? Wait a minute. I'll ask them not to be so loud. I'll ask them to chant a bit softly, all right? You sleep peacefully,' said Kanaka.

She took the bowl, picked up the tumbler and was about to leave the room when Varadarajan said, 'No, no, Kanaka, I wasn't talking about them. I want to hear their chanting.'

Kanaka turned from the doorway and looked at him questioningly. Holding the bowl and the tumbler in her hand, she came back to his bedside.

'No, don't restrict them, let them do their *Gongyo*,' said Varadarajan. 'What I said was, I could hear your *Gongyo* and chanting very clearly, even there. That's what I wanted to say.'

'What do you mean by "even there"?'

'I mean over there, at the hospital. Kanaka. I could hear every single line that all of you recited and chanted. I could hear the doctors too. They were saying about me, "It's of no use, it's really a bad case", then they said "this man is almost dead"... I could hear all that too, quite, quite clearly.'

'What! You could ... you ...' Kanaka got a bit agitated. She placed the bowl and tumbler on the table, leaned over and placed her palm over his brow. Anxiously, she asked:

'Do you have a fever?'

'No Kanaka, no! I'm telling you the truth. I could hear everything. *Everything*. I also wanted to join you all in Gongyo and chanting. But whenever I opened my mouth ... I don't know why ... my words changed into rounded bubbles of water.'

Maria*

That was way back in 1987 but even now things are vivid in my memory.

She shook my hands with great enthusiasm and held them for a while, a broad smile brightening up her face.

'Are you Lakshmi? From India? I knew, I knew, I can tell,' she said.

'Oh? Have we met before? I don't remember where... ' I said.

'No, no. We're meeting for the very first time now, in the US. But back in Manila, when I received the names of selected writers for the International Writing Program at Iowa, I could instantly guess that "Lakshmi" must be the name of a woman, even though there was no prefix like "Mr" or "Ms" or "Mrs" to any name. See how right I was in my guess?' she smiled, shaking my hand again.

'I'm also very happy to meet you Salina,' I said.

'Aguinaldo. Salina Aguinaldo. But you can call me Maria. That's my mother's name for me,' she said.

I looked at her with surprise. It was hardly ten minutes since we had met and she was asking me to call her by her pet name used within her family. How can I be on such familiar terms with her, we've just met?

Salina had a fair complexion and was very short. She managed with two inches of heels in her sandals. Her small, sunken eyes seemed to be merely two slits to see through. Her nose was blunt

* Translated from the original Tamil by the author. This translation first published in *Parijata and Other Stories*, New Delhi: National Publishing House, 1992.

and her mouth rather flat. She had styled her hair in a close-cropped way that gave her a young, boyish look. It was a borderline 'punk' hairstyle but the rest of her was dressed in a proper skirt and top. The red of her lipstick was so loud that it screamed out of her face. I smiled at her and asked an unnecessary question: 'Salina, are you based in Manila, in Philippines?'

'Maria!' she cried out, raising her voice. 'I just asked you to call me Maria.'

'Oh, I'm so sorry. Maria then, Maria, okay?' I said, somewhat taken aback by her reaction.

She looked a bit pacified as she walked with me to the big bus that was waiting for us. She sat next to me in the bus, chatting away about a variety of things. Since I was spared of the effort of participating in the conversation, I divided my attention by alternately looking at the city of Washington speeding through the window and turning my head occasionally to smile and nod at her.

'I knew, I knew beforehand,' said Maria again.

'Knew what? That Lakshmi is a female name?' I asked.

'Not just that. I knew that the number of male writers in the International Writing Program is always staggeringly huge in comparison with the number of female writers. See that woman writer over there, from Bulgaria? She is actually a substitute for the man who was originally selected. It seems he fell ill and they sent this lady instead. If she hadn't come, then it would've been just you and I, with over twenty-five male writers in this program, imagine!' she remarked, pointing out the men sitting in the bus.

True. The large number of men in the Iowa International program filled the bus almost entirely. What a relief, I thought, to have this woman from Philippines here. 'Thank God that you came, Maria,' I said aloud.

'Ah, at least this time you called me Maria. Good, good!' she said, eagerly clasping my hand. She held on to my hands and smiled, her small, beady eyes shining brightly. When was the last time I sat close to a girl like this, holding hands? Way back when I was school, may be ... ? But Maria is a grown woman. And it is less than an hour since we met. How she bubbles over like a school girl, it's amazing! Or could it be the other way round? Perhaps it's me who has hurried through the stages a bit too fast, and also hurried into an old age prematurely?

After completing a week-long program in Washington with the International Institute of Education, we left for Iowa. And with that began the system of living in individually allotted apartments in Mayflower Residence Hall that had twin-set apartments split between two writers. Each one of us had a study and a living-cum-bedroom to ourselves but the kitchen and the rest rooms were common to both and had to be shared with the occupant in the adjoining half of the apartment.

As expected, many of us felt rather uneasy about this arrangement. Having reached an age where privacy was a given, a normal way of living, we had grown used to our own individual 'space'. Now we found it difficult to revert again to the lifestyle of young college students in a Residence Hall. Also, each one of us had distinct tastes and preferences in food, our individual customs and habits that we followed.

The stubborn fact that there were three more months to go for this program forced us to look at the positive side of it. Here was a good chance to get to know the rest of the writers, a chance to observe other cultures. Thus gradually, we learnt to live the Mayflower way, for there was no way out. It was a system that had frozen into a convention in the Iowa program.

The Bulgarian lady was given a twin apartment that she shared with a couple from Europe. That left Maria and me as the only two women. Naturally, we were asked to share a twin-set as no woman would be asked to share an accommodation with a man. Maria's happiness knew no bounds.

We were soon pulled into a schedule of meetings, talks, mini-courses, conferences, readings and some very enjoyable field-trips that took us out of Iowa city. For some of us at least, it was perhaps the first time we got so much time to ourselves for writing. We luxuriated in that exclusive, undisturbed time for our writing and plunged into our projects with our full concentration, having discarded all the problems and responsibilities that plagued us back home in our countries. It was going to be writing, writing and more writing all the way for the next few months here. It was a rare chance too, to continue working beyond midnight until the wee hours of the morning, a chance to linger in bed the following morning and sleep till ten or eleven! I could never afford to do that in my own country. So I spent hours writing and scribbling away.

Every morning we would make coffee together, Maria and I. And then we would prepare our breakfast and meals. When she came to know that I was a strict vegetarian, Maria always took care to stack her meat at the far end of a corner in the fridge. I noticed with some discomfiture that gradually, Maria's consumption of meat and fish began to decrease.

'I too want to become a complete vegetarian like you,' she would often say, as she went about the work in the apartment singing songs in her native Filipino language, Tagalog. She would settle down to work at night.

'Maria, when and how did you become a writer?' I asked her one day.

'I'm the eldest child in the family,' she said. 'I had to keep my younger sister and brother occupied by telling them stories. I used to narrate all the stories I knew until I finished all that was in my stock! I wondered what I should do next. Then I hit upon an idea. I took some paper and cut out figures of a boy, girl, child, animals, trees, houses and other things with scissors, like this ... ,' she said, and quickly, deftly, demonstrated with a piece of paper. Her scissors sliced through the paper accurately, without the help of any penciled diagram. Small figures of animals, people and trees dropped out of the paper so neatly!

'There, see what I mean?' she continued. 'I'd then give the people some names and use my imagination to weave a story around them and the other things. Or make them 'act' in a play by staging one. Doing all this got me into the habit of weaving stories,' she said.

'Really! And then?'

'And then, as I grew older ... '

'Yes Maria?'

'It was hell! I was tossed about roughly in life, I was so badly crushed and bruised. That is when I began to write poetry. Also fiction. I won a lot of awards from the government,' she said and her eyes brightened up for a moment. However, the next instance, her face changed and turned gloomy.

'Maria, all the twenty-seven people here must've been shaped and moulded as writers by their share of grief and pain,' I said.

Suddenly, she got up, came over to where I sat and hugged me.

'Oh Lakshmi, I feel like telling you a lot, but when I see how busy you always are, I get a feeling that I might be wasting your time. Tell me one thing, why do you always function like a machine, why do you keep on writing intensely as if you're under some compulsion to finish?'

'What else can I do? I get very little time for myself in India. There's such a lot of pressure all around me. Office work, house work and so on. In addition, I've to look after my two children too, you see. What about you?' I asked.

'I didn't marry. Who wants to get tied down to one man, not me! I just don't like it. But I've plenty of lovers. After I've tasted each one of them, I simply kick them out of my life and resume my free life,' she remarked.

'!'

'That is, till I get another man,' she added, laughing cheerfully.

'Why are you suddenly so quiet Lakshmi?' she asked, lighting a cigarette. 'How about you and your husband? It seems some married couples eventually become so very placid after years of living together that they become almost like a sister and a brother?' she asked.

This unmarried woman, how did she get such notions about marriage, I thought, smiling at her in silence.

'Oh, I just said that I've a lot to tell you,' she resumed. 'My father was a damn fool. He gambled and played cards while my mother would break her back and work so we could eat. The useless fellow would gamble away all her hard-earned money and dissolve it in his drinks. One day he left my mother and all of us and ran off somewhere, that son of a prostitute!' she cursed, pulling at her cigarette, her jaw set hard.

'How sad!'

'Indeed yes, for my mother. Poor woman, she brought up the three of us with enormous difficulty. But I used to help her a lot. She on her part, loaded me with a lot of responsibility, her excuse being I am the eldest of the lot. So I grew up without even a childhood, Lakshmi.'

'Tch!'

She puffed away at her cigarette and blew out the smoke.

'Do you know,' she said. 'Our staple food in Philippines is rice. So there were vast expanses of rice fields all around. Everyday, when my mother resumed her work in the afternoon, she would ask me to cook some rice in a pot, see that it is properly done and then remove the pot from the fire, cover it well and so on. These were her instructions before leaving for work. I would keep some water in the pot, wash the rice before putting it into the pot and then come out of the backyard to stand for a while in the rice fields.'

Maria raised her glass, sipped at her whisky and continued.

'Soon the sun would set. Like a huge Maltese orange, the sun would descend and slide down the sky at dusk, lacing the fresh, green horizon of the rice fields with gold. My god, what breath taking beauty! As a small girl I would get totally engrossed in the luminous, wondrous beauty of the scene. Then slowly, as darkness spread, I would run into the house. And what would I see there?'

'What?'

'All the water in the pot dried up and the rice burnt to a cinder! Then when my mother returned and found out the mistake, she would give me such a sound beating that it almost peeled the skin off my flesh ... I wince with pain even now when I remember that,' she said, laughing heartily.

She fully drained her glass of whisky and got up.

'Maria, that's enough for today. Eat something and go to bed,' I protested.

'No! I want another glass. How about you? Ah, you don't need anything, do you, a perfect damper!' she said, going in.

She came back with a full glass and continued.

'Do you know why I laughed, Lakshmi? My mother was quite justified in getting angry over the wasted, burnt rice and in giving me a sound beating. Because it happened so often. But what I still don't understand is—why didn't I think of cooking rice either an hour *before* sunset, or an hour *after*? I haven't been able to figure that out till now!' she said, laughing at herself.

'Ssh! Don't laugh so loudly Maria. These Mayflower walls are like thin cardboard,' I warned. She laughed uncaringly.

'Hail Mary! The sublime beauty of a sunset, it's so magnificent! It's worth receiving any amount of beating.'

'It was that setting sun that made you a writer,' I said.

'Correct! I still had to struggle a lot. My mother died when I was sixteen. When my father came to know that I had started earning on my own, he would literally chase me up for money, the bastard!'

'How utterly shameless!'

'Oh, he would set me running across the fields, the rogue. I would run gasping for breath, run on stumbling over stagnant pools of water, over human and animal excreta. I've even slipped and fallen over the excreta, soiling my clothes, feeling disgusted beyond despair.'

I was appalled by what I heard.

'Then the three of us took refuge in an uncle's house. He was my mother's brother. He sucked my blood like a vampire, took away even the little money I earned in exchange for maintenance. As soon as I returned from work, my aunt would break my bones and extract hard work out of me.'

'Then how did you find the time for writing?' I asked. 'There was an old, large bed that I shared with my sister and brother,' she described. 'It was put in a room that was just big enough to hold the bed and nothing else. So one has to jump straight on to the bed even before entering the room! It was so cramped that there was no place even to keep one foot on the floor. At 8.30 sharp in the night, my uncle would shout, "Put off the light, put it off! We can't afford the electricity bill." But he would continue to do his work in the adjoining room with the lights on. Do you know how I wrote under those circumstances?' she asked.

'How?'

'I'd keep the door of our room ajar, just a fraction. Then lying on my belly on the bed, I'd write on a piece of paper over a pad with the help of the light streaming through the slit in the door. A column of light would shoot in like an arrow and that would help me complete my writing,' she said.

'Now I know the secret behind all the awards you have got,' I said.

Maria laughed.

'Whatever I've gone through, I still remain the daughter of the soil I belong to,' she declared. 'We were poor children and yet we were happy playing simple games. *Soonga* is a native game played with *seegai*, that is sea shells. A wooden framework with small niches or pits at regular intervals was used for the game. You shake the sea shells, put them in the pits and play,' she said, sipping at her whisky.

The way she described it, I was reminded of a Tamil game called *pallangkuzhi*[1] played on a smooth wooden framework with two rows of pits on both sides. I used to play a lot of *pallangkuzhi* with the dried seeds of tamarind. I would play with other small girls, sitting in the sunny backyard of my grandfather's house in Mysore. But around me there were warm people, my gentle grandfather, grandmother, my parents and relations.

I sat back on the sofa and closed my eyes. There are so many kinds of cultures, so many kinds of upbringing, conditioning and social values. Behind my closed eyes, I saw fresh green pastures. Wide stretches of rice fields. The sun descending like a cool ball of fire with a charismatic beauty. And a small, poor girl with a flat face and nose who gets all lost in the loveliness of the scene. A mother who has the heart to beat this little girl. A narrow shaft of light, sharp as a blade, flowing through the slit of a door held ajar. The light shooting like an arrow to germinate words on a page. A girl who grew up on the language of Tagalog. A female writer called 'Maria' who bloomed on the pains of growing up, who grew on the wretchedness and misery of poverty. Amazing! I opened my eyes. Maria sat looking at me. Swirls of smoke from the cigarette enveloped her.

'All right, let's go to sleep now. Good night, Maria.' I got up to leave.

'Good night Lakshmi. Don't stay awake for too long. Have a good sleep,' she said.

'Okay.'

I moved towards my room when I felt her hand on my shoulder.

'Is that all?' she asked.

'What Maria?'

'Is that all for a good night?'

I just stood staring at her.

Suddenly, she hugged me tight and kissed me on both the cheeks.

'Hey, Maria, Maria!'

[1] *Pallangkuzhi*: A foldable wooden board that has two rows with seven hollow pits on both sides. Usually, two people play the game with sea shells or the seeds of tamarind.

She chuckled merrily at my shock and I went back to my room.

What a strange woman ...

'Magical realism! Magical realism! For heaven's sake ... all the writers seem to have gone crazy even after Gabriel Garcia Marquez has already shown and proved his skill to stretch the potential of this genre. Now isn't *that* enough for everybody? Why should the rest of us continue following the style of Marquez like a herd of dumb sheep? There are about a hundred spineless followers of *100 Years of Solitude* and they've no originality whatsoever, in their thoughts. Christ!'

That was Guido Rodriguez Akala from Paraguay who was ranting about a school of writing in which he thought his country had got badly stuck. I looked at him with surprise. Is this the same Guido who is usually very quiet and modest and who was never given much to talking?

'Honestly Lakshmi, I'm just put off by all this blind following, this second grade, deceptive output in the name of writing. This is an era of science, of reason. Instead of coming up with the courage of straightforward writing, instead of being clear, everyone is merely imitating the string of adjectives of one major writer and cloaking their own mediocrity within this sham!' exploded Guido.

How I wish that at least a couple of Indians could whip up this kind of moral indignation against imitations. Now every new writer wants to earn the dubious compliment that he/she 'writes in a style that recalls Salman Rushdie'. But Guido had a literary ideology that was so independent. Guido and I got down from the Inter-dorm bus and reached Mayflower Hall. We parted, heading towards our respective apartments.

I changed my clothes and went to the kitchen. Maria was sitting at the dining table, eating something.

'Hi Maria, came home early?' I asked.

Maria did not reply.

'What's the matter, Maria? Why are you so silent?'

Abruptly, she pushed away her plate. She raised her eyes and shouted at me, 'First of all, you tell me why you behaved like that.'

'Ssh! Don't shout. Why, what did I do?' I asked, very perplexed.

'You know very well.'

'Know what, Maria?'

'Why did you bolt your doors from inside?' she demanded.

'Oh, is that all?' I said and sat on a chair opposite hers, fighting back the laughter that rose from within.

'I bolted the door! Good god, what a small thing and you misunderstand me for that. Maria, we chat around for a long time in the kitchen, don't we? I just wanted to finish my work quietly, so I shut the door. Why, I suppose everybody here in Mayflower shuts his/her door. After all, a person needs some privacy, it's only normal,' I reasoned.

'Ah, that's quite enough. You don't have to explain. The reason for your bolting the door is entirely different. You just want to avoid me. You don't like me, or my friendship, that's why,' she said.

'Maria ... '

'Oh shut up! Do you think I can't understand? When I want to hug you affectionately, or kiss you, why you just recoil. You don't like it,' she went on.

Again, I had trouble controlling the laughter that bubbled up from within me.

'Listen to me, Maria. This is just a matter of cultural difference, that's all. You've been brought up in a particular way and my social ambience is different from yours. I'm just not used to all this,' I explained.

'Oh, ho, ho. How very innocent! But when it comes to the men in our program, then things are quite okay aren't they? You're so free with them, and you like it when they approach you. Just look at the guile,' she pushed her point.

'Take care, Maria, watch your word! We're all participants in the program and in that sense, we're all equal here. We're here as writers, first and foremost, so why distinguish men from the women?' I countered.

'Hey, who do you think you're fooling?' she shot back.

'Now that's quite enough!' I said and got up to go.

Suddenly, Maria began to sob. She sobbed so uncontrollably that I was taken aback. Pressing a handkerchief to her nose, she wept, choking over her words, 'All I wished for was friendship with an Indian woman, but you're so cold.'

'Oh no, I'm not cold at all. You can call me reserved by nature. I'll plead guilty to that flaw any day,' I protested.

'I don't know, but you're really icy,' she said, weeping like a small girl.

Is this woman really thirty-eight years old? A writer who got government awards? I patted her and said reassuringly, 'All right Maria, let's do one thing. You see, I can't get even half an hour to myself in India, while you're a free bird in Philippines. So let's come to an agreement. During the day, I'll finish all the work I've undertaken within the quiet of my room. Then let's chat in the evenings and eat dinner together. I won't bolt the door in the evenings, right?'

She smiled brightly, like a little girl. She nodded her head vigorously. I sighed in relief and returned to my section of the apartment. It was very quiet inside my bedroom and the hushed stillness was oppressive. I hated myself for this habit of being orderly, for the way I had got hooked on to the stern command of my father: 'Discipline! Discipline at all cost!' was the whip he cracked, always. Why do I operate like a machine? Father's strict call for 'discipline' follows me till now and it has robbed me of human warmth. Poor girl, Maria. Why can't I relax my routine just a little, for the sake of others? Why can't I ever learn to give in ... ?

I glanced at my reflection in the mirror. I intensely disliked the figure that looked back at me. I stuck my tongue out at the reflection.

We had some shopping to do at J. C. Penney. Shopping over, Maria and I returned to our apartment, cooked and ate together. She cooked something elaborately, all the while singing happily some songs in Tagalog. Suddenly, she stopped and said, 'Can I ask you something?'

'Go ahead.'

'In truth, you're standoffish with me because I eat non-veg food, am I right?' she asked.

'Nonsense! In Delhi, most of my friends are non-veg. If someone prefers to eat meat, why should I object? Don't be silly, Maria.'

'Lakshmi, I really mean it. You only have to tell me in one word and I'll give up all meat and fish for your sake, I promise!'

Good heavens, what a queer complication. Should I dismiss it with a laugh or simply tear at my hair and run out of the room? I wasn't sure. Why have I got stuck with her like this, why?

Aloud, I said, 'Don't be absurd, Maria. It's not necessary to do anything like that. I like you as you are, in fact I like you very much. You're a wonderful person.'

'Really?'

'But of course!'

'Then are you prepared to do anything for me?' she asked.

'My god Maria, why do you talk like a school girl?'

'No, tell me first,' she insisted.

'All right, what do you want me to do for you?'

'First of all, you should stop socialising with the male writers in our program,' she said firmly.

'What! Now look here Maria. Why do you go on endlessly like this, always dividing people into men and women, men and women? And at this age. You're educated and a writer to boot, yet you talk in an immature way,' I said, quite irritated by all that was happening.

'Maturity, with a capital 'M'! Tell me, some of the men who talk to you, *are they* mature?' she asked, her face flushed with anger.

'Certainly! They just mind their own business and quietly go about their work. So what's your complaint? Coming to think of it, we've a nice, dignified lot of men in this program. Some of them are so civilised too, and here you are ... '

'Oh, it's so hot in this kitchen,' said Maria and abruptly disappeared into her section of the apartment. She returned within minutes, wearing something flimsy and diaphanous through which one could see her bra and panties.

'You were talking about their being dignified?' she took my point to continue the argument. 'Don't I know their inner motives? The way they look at you, for instance, and the secret fantasies they nurse about you?'

I looked at her, half-naked, raving like that about all the men indiscriminately. Suddenly, fear gripped me. Is this woman crazed or just drunk?

'Maria, don't talk dirty. I just don't like it. You talk to the men too but have I ever said one negative word about you or them?' I retorted.

'My case is entirely different. Sometimes when I move with the men, I begin to wonder if they're aware of me at all, as a woman? But when they look at you ... Lakshmi, I'm telling you for your own good,' she said, lowering her voice. She sat down at the table and stroked my hand.

I was burning with anger and annoyance. Have I come here miles away from home, leaving my family and my children behind only to be mixed up with this crazy woman? Why should I be trapped in this little apartment with her? I fought back a wave of self-pity that engulfed me.

'All right, who do you mean in particular, when you talked about the men?' I asked her wearingly, not really interested in her answer.

'You know very well who all I mean, yet all the same, listen. There's Peter, then Albert, whey even Jose, the man who is much younger than you, and then ... '

I cut her rambling. 'Stop it! You're really sick Maria. Come on, you're a grown up woman. Can't you see anyone at all with normal eyes? What's your problem anyway? All the men you mentioned are our fellow-participants, they are our colleagues in this program for a temporary length of time. Almost all of them behave decently, then why do you let your mind run wild? Why do you doubt them unnecessarily? Do you think I'm a little girl?'

'Dignity, decency, what have you ... You can say whatever you want but the minute you step out in your salwar-suit or a saree for that matter, all these guys seem to experience a rush of youth returning to them. Do you know how they talk about you amongst themselves? You won't like it. One day, Jose was ... no, you won't like it. I'm warning you because of my affection for you. Lakshmi, on this subject you know nothing. Nothing at all. You just happen to be the mother of two children, that's about all. Otherwise, you're such a novice, a gullible novice! Take care, this is the era of AIDS!' she finished breathlessly.

I felt my blood coursing through me. My hand itched to give her a tight slap.

'Maria!'

Was that my voice? It resounded loudly in my ears. My throat thickened. I rushed out of the room and slammed the door shut. Shall I bolt it from inside? No, let it be open this time. If that woman finds it locked, she may get even more hysterical than she is now.

I slumped on the bed, exhausted. I tossed around but sleep eluded me. Man-woman, man-woman! There's no end to it. In the fast pace of the era of science, can't people get anything else to talk about? Aren't they tired of their own stereotypical, conventional standards, and the limits they set for themselves? When will the human mind break free of this mindset, when will it learn to look at human relationships dispassionately, with equanimity? A skewed outlook about chance encounters, about friendship, about relationship.... It was tedious to even think any more.

I must have dropped off asleep at some point. But the first thing I could sense next was the smell. It was a perfume that was so overpoweringly strong I woke up. Oh, there's something obstructing my feet!

'Who's there? Oh god, it's a thief! A thief!' I shouted in panic.

'Ssh! Lakshmi, it's only me. Don't be scared.'

'Who, who is it?' I shouted again in the darkness. I switched on the light.

'Oh god Maria, it's you! What're you doing *here* at this time of the night? What's the matter?' I asked.

'Ssh! don't get so agitated,' she said. 'I just peeped in. Wanted to see how you look when you sleep. I sat for sometime at your feet, just looking at you. You look like a baby, Lakshmi. How can you have a face like a child at this age, it's amazing!' she said.

I got up from the bed and stood in front of her.

'Maria, just what are you blabbering? First of all, explain! Why on earth are you here, in my bedroom? What eccentric habits you have. Now return to your apartment! My god, is this the reason why you pleaded with me not to bolt my door from inside?'

Maria also stood up, her head tilted to a side.

'Yes!' she said defiantly. 'Yes! At least now do you understand, you child? You dumb kid, stupid kid!'

Her smile was hideous. It was more like a grimace. Those narrow eyes like slits, the flat face, the squat figure ... I was overcome by an obscure loathing.

'Get out!' I screamed.

'Out! This minute,' I screamed again.

The following morning I didn't step inside the kitchen. I decided to forego my morning cup of coffee. Let me have coffee in the IWP (International Writing Program) office, I thought and got ready to go. Without my morning coffee, I soon developed a splitting headache. I got into the bus on an empty stomach and as it sped on towards the university, I felt deeply disturbed. When I reached the IWP office, a surprise awaited me. As soon as the Secretary saw me, she said, 'Ah, Lakshmi, good you came on your own. We rang up your room several times. The Director and Program Assistant have something important to discuss with you.'

I went over to the Director's office, knocked on the door lightly and went in. She was sitting with her Program Assistant and both of them came to the point straightaway.

'Lakshmi, we're all very worried for you. You must change your apartment instantly. #201 is vacant. We'll allot you that apartment,' said the Director.

'But why? I mean, how did you know about what happened? Eh ... who told you?' I asked, beside myself with surprise.

'Calm yourself, Lakshmi We've known for some time now.'

'Known what? Oh god, what's happening here? You say you know ... but what exactly do you know?' I asked in utter confusion.

'I'm sorry Lakshmi. We should've taken action immediately, that is, as soon as we came to know of this,' she said.

'Take action? What action? Please tell me clearly,' I said.

'Lakshmi, that woman who shares the apartment with you, Salina Aguinaldo? It seems she is a lesbian.'

'Good god, what!' was all I could say.

'You mean you couldn't find out?'

'No, no. Who told you all?'

'We had our suspicions for some time now. Besides, many of the male writers in the program reported to us about her queer behaviour. They too had the same suspicion and it only confirmed ours. In fact, your male colleagues are also worried for you. Like us, they felt that it is best the two of you separate and that you move out of that apartment,' said the Director.

I sat speechless on the chair. Things had run on to such an irrevocable end! I've been sharing an apartment with her and yet I didn't have a clue?

'Please move over to Apartment #201 this very evening. Otherwise things can get dangerous,' she said.

'Dangerous? What kind of danger?' I asked, very troubled.

'You won't understand all that, Lakshmi. You're an Indian woman and you come from a very stable society.'

'I agree that our culture is rather conservative in temper, which is why it's considered very normal for women to make friends with other women, and likewise men to be friends with men,' I said. 'There *is* a natural segregation of sexes, I admit. So I thought Maria, I mean Salina, who is another Asian like me, naturally wanted to be friends with me. Why do you want to take an extreme stand and brand her with a label like that? She only strikes me as someone who is very strange and eccentric, someone who is also very scared of being alone,' I explained.

The Director and the Assistant exchanged glances. The Assistant asked me, 'Then Lakshmi, do we take it that you don't wish to change your apartment?'

'Oh no please!' I nearly begged. 'I can rest my mind only if I change the apartment. Salina is a very peculiar woman. She doesn't let me work in peace. At last I'll be free of her. Thank you! Thank you all very much indeed!' I said, heart heaving in my mouth.

'How graciously you've offered to help me, and without wasting any time! You're very kind. I'm very grateful to all of you,' I said.

They smiled in answer and patted me gently. And then they got busy making arrangements for shifting me to another apartment.

#201. Within this space, I regained my sense of peace after what seemed to be a very long time. I bolted the doors from inside and went about my work in the sequestered tranquility of my apartment.

After Maria and I separated, the men in our program were more open in their remarks. They often referred to her explicitly as a 'lesbian' and laughed amongst themselves, as if they were vastly amused by it. One of them was very direct in his eagerness to talk behind her back but I discouraged him witheringly. Because I felt very, very sorry for Maria. It was depressing the way she was suddenly left absolutely isolated. She was severely alone. Poor girl, she had tried to make friendship with me in her own way, and that is perhaps the only way she knew. She is a person who easily loses her balance, loses her poise too. For such a minor lapse, should they crucify her so harshly and brand her as a 'lesbian'?

I tried to talk to Maria one day. She looked very hurt and turned away as if to say, 'It is you who brought about all that has happened!' And yet, even after we separated and stopped talking to each other, I noticed how readily she rushed to help me whenever she felt I needed help. For instance, when we went on an extensive schedule of travelling South, East and West of US, there were many occasions when my organisers would make a slip regarding my special vegetarian meal-orders on board, during our frequent flights. I would then go hungry. Even if the rest of my colleagues happened to notice this mistake, they would merely murmur and make polite noises: 'Oh Lakshmi, you didn't get your vegetarian order? Too bad!' Having said that, they would just move on to enjoy their chicken or mutton placidly. It was only Maria who would somehow sniff the news of my not getting my meal-order from wherever she was on the flight. She would immediately rush to my side and offer a few things from her tray of lunch or dinner. 'Here, take the fruits, green salad, take my ice cream and cake, I don't want them,' she would insist. I would look at the kind soul and feel like kicking myself.

A poetry reading session was scheduled for the evening. One of our participants read a poem in Spanish and another read out the English translation of the same poem. When I heard the English rendering, I was shocked by the explicit way in which it described a gay relationship between two men. In elaborate, blow-by-blow detail, the poem expounded how two gays made love to each other. The presentation lacked subtlety and finesse. It was just awful. Slowly, I stole a glance at Maria sitting in a corner at the far end of the room. She was calmly taking in the details of the poem and was listening with much interest. Okay. It is a poem about gays. Okay. Peter can write about whatever he likes and read whatever he likes. After all, it is a poet's prerogative and this is America. It won't turn a hair at anything. But what surprised me was the way the same Peter bad-mouthed Maria the other day and spoke about 'other women like Maria' so contemptuously! For a man who had argued with so much heat that 'lesbianism' was some kind of a despicable mental disease, the same man was exulting in this poem on a gay relationship. Like he is celebrating this man-to-man love relationship, surrounded by his cronies who generously clapped and cheered him after he finished his reading. How sectarian! He was totally brazen too, about his bias. Furtively, I looked at Maria again. Good god! She too seemed to enjoy the poem and heartily applauded along with the rest of the men.

Let them go to hell, the whole lot of them, I thought. A nostalgic wish to return to India soon, gripped me overpoweringly. I wished to retreat into the sheltered comfort of the social set up I knew and take refuge in the simple earthiness of our people, in the healthy ordinariness of everyday life. I'll feel restored by its median sanity. I felt very homesick as I walked back to Mayflower Hall.

'Hi Lakshmi.'

I turned around.

It was Peter, walking behind me.

'Where are you off to, walking alone like this?' he asked as he briskly caught up with me.

'But I'm not really alone,' I replied. 'See this river Iowa, winding along lazily with me? And then the rows and rows of lush trees on either side of me, with their leaves in lovely fall-colours?'

'You do like solitude, don't you?' said Peter. 'Even when you shared an apartment with Salina, you tried so hard to keep a distance from her. And I know how tough that must've been,' he said, with a wink. 'And now, after separating from her, you prefer to keep your distance from some of us.'

I stood for a second and looked at him.

'Peter, can I ask you something? I hope you won't misunderstand me,' I said.

'Of course not. What is it?' he asked.

'You read a poem just now ... '

'Hmm. Liked it?'

'You've written in such detail about a gay relationship, as if you approve of it?'

'What about it?'

I hesitated.

'Come on Lakshmi, you can surely tell me.'

'Peter, then why were you so derogatory about Maria—I'm sorry, I meant Salina—the other day? First of all, you wouldn't give her the smallest benefit of doubt, if she is really lesbian or not. Secondly, let's take her to be one, for the sake of an argument. You were so disdainful about it, and yet you now seem to celebrate a gay relationship,' I said.

'So that's it! My god, ever since this movement called "feminism" has caught on, there are so many changes. A woman takes up the cause of supporting another woman so earnestly!' he laughed, but soon his face turned serious.

'Lakshmi, you must know one thing, at least on a cerebral level. What's the use of wilfully fighting against nature? A person is born as a girl by a divine act of grace. That she belongs to man is also by the decree of nature. To give you a small example, take the case of the lamb, for instance. Jesus Christ looked upon it as a sanctified symbol of sacrifice, as an animal that deserved that honour. Of course, it's only an animal,' he hurried to say, looking at me.

'Oh no Lakshmi, please, please don't mistake me!' he burst out. 'I don't imply that a woman is born to be sacrificed. Never! Which savage brute would ever say that? What I meant to say is, a woman is an exciting fusion of the physical, mental and spiritual. She is a harmonious quickening of creation. She is ordained to make a man happy, to give him a sense of fulfillment. So how can a woman enter into a relationship with another woman, it's absurd! But a frustrated possibility, nevertheless. Lesbianism is born of failure, and is doomed to end up in failure,' he said, his last words tapering off to a murmur.

We walked alongside the river. By the same logic then, I could have easily asked him, 'If lesbianism is a perversion, so is a gay relationship. They why do you celebrate the second?' It was at the tip of my tongue but I was too lazy to ask. And the river Iowa was sidling along languorously, moving slowly beside the pathway on which we walked. Some birds that I could not identify by names were flying home, making sounds that I could not decipher. The leaves of the maple tree were luxuriously changing colour every day, dripping rich colours. There were so many different colours on the same tree. Why, even a single leaf showed different colours mingling in an interesting confusion.

Novella

Another Hour, Another Hue*

I

'How do you want your salary? Would you like us to prepare a cheque or should we credit it directly to your account in the bank here, at the university? Some people prefer the second option,' said the Accountant.

'Please credit my salary directly into my account,' said Jaya Balachandar.

'Very well, Madam. Have you opened an account here?' he asked.

'No, not yet.'

He laughed. 'Then please do so immediately,' he suggested.

'I'll do that right away. Thanks very much,' said Jaya and walked towards the English department. She needed someone to introduce her to the bank, to open an account. She went over to the faculty lounge. Bhaskar was the first person she saw. She requested him to introduce her to the bank.

'But of course!' he agreed readily. 'Let's do it today. Now. Do you have a class in the next hour?' he asked.

'No, I don't.'

'Neither do I and the hour next to that is the lunch break. So let's finish the work right now.'

'Thanks.'

Jaya opened an account in the university bank. Then along with Bhaskar she went to the Coffee Home for some snacks and coffee.

* Translated from the original Tamil "Pozhurdhoru Vannam" by the author, included in the collection *Inru Maalai, Ennudan*, Narmada Pathippagam, Chennai, 1999 and *Kaaveri Kathaigal*, Mithra Arts, Chennai, 2007.

'What next? Oh, how do you like this place Dr Balachandar?' asked Bhaskar.

'Jaya. Do call me Jaya. It'll take some time for me to know if I really like this place. But I'm happy enough. At last my husband got transferred to a big metro like this after stints in small towns and air force stations. It feels like I've returned to civilisation after having been buried under the soil for a long time,' said Jaya.

'Returned to civilisation? Ha!' Bhaskar laughed. 'You'll soon discover how civilised people are over here.'

'What do you mean?'

'Just wait and see for yourself.'

'Have you been with this university for a long time?' asked Jaya.

'I don't have a choice really. I specialise in linguistics. For the likes of me, there are only a few places where we can earn our bread. For people like you in literature, you can work well, anywhere I guess!' he said.

'Only I haven't had that kind of luck. The frequent job transfers of my husband disrupted my career. All that shunting around from place to place has ruined me professionally,' said Jaya.

'Oh it doesn't matter. Now you've joined our department and you're most welcome. People talked about your paper publications and your book much before you arrived. Our Professor Verma was full of appreciation for you.'

'Ah well ... what else does one do to fill time in small towns except write papers? I didn't have a soul to talk to in places like Jorhat and Jalahalli. Even the book I published is largely based on my PhD dissertation, so it's no big deal,' said Jaya.

'It's two o'clock. Shall we go?'

They got up and made their way towards the Faculty Lounge.

'Have you met everybody in our department?' asked Bhaskar.

'Almost everybody.'

'Met Dr Sudharani Joshi?'

'Not yet.'

'She's on leave and will be joining next week, I think. Do meet her. She's a nice lady.'

II

'What's your area of interest Dr Joshi?' asked Jaya.

'Please call me Sudha.'

'Sudha,' smiled Jaya.

'You mean, what am I working on now?' smiled Sudharani. 'I'm continuing with my research on narrative in the novel. In hermeneutics, the narrative modes of fiction have thrown up a lot of exciting findings that link creativity with philosophy. That would be a fertile ground for study, I thought. So I'm kind of digging in the same area, that is fiction. What about you?'

'I work on poetry,' said Jaya. 'I've worked on Marianne Moore, Emily Dickinson and 'H.D.' and now I've moved over to the works of Adrienne Rich, Sylvia Plath, Judith Wright and Anne Sexton. I'm interested in the directions they take and their language use. Tell me, do you plan to write a critical book on the narrative modes in fiction?'

'Why do you address me again in the plural? Because I happen to be you're senior? In other words, because I'm older than you?'

'Sorry.'

Older? Who would say she was older? Sudharani Joshi seemed to be generously endowed with a cool, unfading youth. She was from the hills of Almora in Uttar Pradesh and her appearance was typical of people from that region. She had a glowing, moist ivory skin and a fresh looking face. She generally dressed with a simple elegance that looked attractive. But she worked hard, untiringly. If anyone happened to wonder aloud, 'How can you be so active at this age?' she had a ready answer for that. 'Want to know the secret? Simple. You should've a lot of problems, huge problems in your personal life. Then where would you get even the time to sit down for a while?'

Jaya came to know that Sudharani's husband Mahesh was without a job. He suffered from some chronic unspecified 'illness'. Hypertension and diabetes were terms often used to legitimise his condition. That was enough for him to withdraw from life totally.

Sudha had to hold the reins of the house. Preeti, her daughter in college, helped her generously. Then there was Sanjay, Preeti's younger brother.

Whenever Jaya asked her to take some rest, Sudharani would protest, 'Oh no, I can't and won't. If I sit still in a place for even half an hour it'll overpower me.'

'What will, Sudha?'

'Oh I don't know what to call it. It's something like loneliness. I feel that I'm standing absolutely alone and that Mahesh, my husband, is standing in front of me, frozen, absolutely still, staring at me stonily, but with a hint of amusement. That's perhaps why I'm moving on from one work to another,' she said. She asked Jaya, 'What about you? What do you do when you return home? You probably have your hands full too, what with two children to look after.'

'Oh yes. And yet, for how long can you sustain your conversation with children?' said Jaya.

'You're right. You know what Jaya? I think part of our loneliness comes from the choice of our discipline, that is literature.'

'Yes. For people like us who teach English and American literature, the choice of our profession in itself distances us from our own social context. Makes us rather remote.'

'It's a somewhat in-between state. We get so influenced by the West that it hinders us from identifying ourselves totally with our own culture. Perhaps that's one reason why we're more prone to loneliness than others are. But you've Balachandar. At least the moments you spend with him may ward off some of the loneliness, don't they?'

'I'm afraid Bala is a rather typical Air Force officer. In his office he is always surrounded by a sense of order. Everything functions in a disciplined manner, each in its proper allotted place. He seeks the same thing at home and can be peaceful only if everyone is in their proper place, the wife, the children, the servant, all in their respective roles.'

'What about the moments he spends with you?'

'Even with me Bala talks about the same things—who is due for the next promotion in office, who is going for a sortie or who is going where for the next posting.... Then he would compare the Air Force with the Army and the Navy to evaluate the advantages, the differences and so on.'

'Then the two of you never talk about literature, or educational matters, or history and things on those lines?'

'No, never. He has no interest in these things.'

'Really?'

'Yes Sudha. We have only two things of common interest to us.'

'And they are ... ?'

'Our babies and bank balance.'

Sudha laughed heartily.

'When you're given a scene like that, why then did you resign your job every time your husband moved on a job transfer? You said the other day that you accompanied him everywhere, even to the remotest small towns to keep house for him, and that you gave up your job every time to do so? I thought you did all that because the two of you are inseparable and that you enjoyed a wonderful togetherness. I thought your husband was such an excellent companion to you that you sacrificed your career and followed him everywhere.'

'Oh no Sudha. Between Bala and me there is ... well, nothing. Nothing at all,' said Jaya and lapsed into silence for some time.

'Really?' asked Sudharani, in a low voice. 'In that case why didn't you choose to settle down with a good university in a decent city and take care of your job? You've suffered so many reverses in your career, Jaya. If you had decided to remain stable in one place and worked your way, your service record would've looked better. You'd have worked with a more professional attitude and avoided all this mess, you see?'

'It has been a mess all right. Hell. But I couldn't decide to stay alone in a place and work. I simply wouldn't be allowed to for it's totally against the tradition of my family. "How can a married woman leave her husband and work in another place? If she does, can the husband accept her again in his family?" This was the rigid convention that ruled his family, even my family. It restricts the movement of educated girls within our family. So no one approved of my flouting this convention, not even my own parents.'

'Dr Joshi.'

They turned around to see who called. A young girl stood at the door.

'Come, come in Akhila,' said Sudharani. 'How are you? Have you re-joined college? Is your baby doing fine?' she enquired.

'He's fine Madam, thank you. I came to see Professor Verma. At last the Principal of our college agreed to grant me study leave on loss of pay for two years. Now I can take up the Fellowship by the UGC[1] to do my PhD. I came here to give this news to Professor Verma. I also wanted to see you and thank you,' said Akhila.

'Thank me? For what?' smiled Sudharani.

[1] UGC: University Grants Commission

'Oh come on Madam! I was able to go this far in drafting my proposal for research only with your help and support. Even though you're not formally my supervisor, you gave me valuable guidelines and helped me. I'll never forget it ever,' said Akhila.

'And I won't help you anymore.'

'What!' Akhila was shocked by Sudharani's reply.

'From now on, she'll help you. Meet my colleague Dr Jaya Balachandar. She joined our department recently. She is an expert in the area of poetry,' said Sudharani, introducing Jaya to Akhila.

'*Namaste* Madam,' smiled Akhila, folding her hands.

'*Namaste*.'

'Jaya, this is Mrs Akhila Sharma. She is a lecturer in Loretto College. She has now registered for PhD with our Chairman Dr Verma and is working on her research.'

'I'm happy to meet you,' said Jaya. 'I'll certainly help you, only ... I wonder if our Chairman Dr Verma may object to that,' said Jaya.

'You should go about it discreetly. Verma is always very busy. After all, he is the head of our department, you see?' said Sudharani.

'Yes Madam,' said Akhila. 'I want to know more about the contemporary scene in poetry. The major trends, directions reflected in poetry. Please help me Madam whenever you've the time to spare.'

'But of course,' assured Jaya.

'I still feel it was unnecessary to take a long leave from your college to work for your PhD on a UGC fellowship,' commented Sudharani.

'What can I do Dr Joshi? My baby is barely three months old. I look after him in addition to my daily grind in college, so where is the time or energy for research? Also, I need to visit a few research centres for my work. The college won't grant me leave frequently, which is why I thought of taking leave at a stretch and complete at least the groundwork for my research. The fellowship also includes a grant for travel expenses to visit research centres and to buy books,' explained Akhila.

'What does Professor Verma say?'

'He had asked me to go to Shimla and had offered to recommend my travel application. I'll try to go to Shimla at the end of the month.'

'For how long?'

'About four weeks.'

'What about your baby?'

'It'll be difficult because I still nurse him. So I'm taking him along with his maid. I was told I'd be given a comfortable room with all amenities. Being a hill resort, Shimla will be a nice, cool change for my baby. That reminds me. It's his feeding time. Let me go now,' she said, folding her hands again in a *namaste* before she left the room.

'Lovely girl.'

'Yes indeed,' agreed Sudharani. 'The more so after childbirth, with fresh, new blood coursing through her body. She glows all over, doesn't she? And she is an earnest researcher and teacher too,' said Sudharani.

'I've a class in the second hour, I better go,' said Jaya, getting up.

'Don't forget the meeting tomorrow,' Sudharani reminded her. 'We've to plan for our research projects and also discuss about the seminar that is being organised by our department.'

'I know. I shan't forget,' said Jaya, rushing out of the room.

III

'It's an international conference, so the main theme should be particularly impressive,' declared Professor Verma. 'We need to do some deep thinking about the main as well as the sub-themes. I'd like to delegate this work to Dr Balachandar. Is that okay with you?' he asked, looking at Jaya.

'Okay Sir,' said Jaya.

'Dr Bhaskar will help us look after the finances of the seminar. He'll maintain accounts about everything, how much we got, how much we utilised and so on. All right?' asked Dr Verma.

'All right Sir,' said Bhaskar.

'Then there is the selection of distinguished delegates, the selection of a chief guest, the choice of an eminent person for delivering the keynote address. In addition to this, we need to select participants for the sub-themes. Can you help me decide about all these details, Dr Joshi?' he asked.

'Certainly,' said Sudharani.

'Sir, I've just one request to make,' said Mala Nayak. 'Why don't *you* give the keynote address?'

'Oh no! That wouldn't be proper at all,' protested Professor Verma. Everybody sat in silence.

'Why not Sir?' insisted Mala Nayak. 'The event would take off with a head start. We'll all be so proud.'

'Let's see,' said Verma smiling at Mala. The meeting dispersed on that note.

'You got an interim break this time, thanks to your friend Jaya,' said Bhaskar to Sudharani. 'Otherwise, every time there is a seminar, you had the onerous duty of giving a shape to the theme and sub-themes of a seminar.'

'Is that so?' asked Jaya. 'Were you doing it all the time? Then please do it this time too, Sudha. I'll help you whenever you need me. I've no experience in this.'

'No. Let's do just as we've been asked to by Professor Verma,' said Sudha. 'A change will be good for the department.' She pulled out the car keys from her handbag and left for home.

Jaya felt very disturbed. Let me talk directly to the professor tomorrow and withdraw my name from this responsibility, she thought, heading for home.

'Why? Don't you have enough confidence in yourself to do this work?' asked Professor Anil Verma.

'It's not like that Sir,' said Jaya. 'What I meant to say is that ... Dr Joshi is my senior. Besides, she has been organising seminars for years now. That's why ... '

'Dr Balachandar, if we keep on talking like this how can others ever get a chance to learn anything?' said Verma.

'Why, one can learn a lot even by observing Dr Joshi. After all, I'm new in the department. Surely, there'll be many more seminars in the future?'

'It's very clear that you don't like to do this work,' said Verma.

'Oh no Sir! I'll do any work that you ask me to do. It's my duty too.'

'Good! Then select an excellent theme for the seminar, something large and wide-ranging in scope. It should give us enough mileage for three days and the sub-themes should fan out in a way that sustains everybody's interest. Usually, things begin to slacken and droop right on the second day itself and everyone gets bored.'

'I'll try to do my best Sir.'

'Why only try? Prove yourself to us. You know Dr Balachandar, having some experience isn't enough in itself. One needs enthusiasm, a freshness of approach, all of which can only come with youth. Do you follow me?' said Verma.

'Uh ... in that case Sir, I'll have to be excused from this work because I'm also getting old.'

'Oh come on, Dr Balachandar. Who do you think you're fooling? Whatever you may say, at least you're very much younger than Dr Joshi, don't you agree?'

'Sir ... '

'This department needs young blood. All right now, let that be. I'm going out for about a week or ten days. Have an Academic Council meeting, then a viva. Please have a plan ready for discussion before I return. We'll then call for another meeting.'

'Very well Sir.'

Jaya came out of the room seething with anger. She crossed over the long corridor and started walking down the steps. 'The department needs young blood.' Indeed! Then surely the first person who should leave is the man Verma himself, for he is nearly fifty-five. May be he can't see that he has himself aged. But if a woman crosses forty, she instantly becomes some kind of an eyesore for him. Come morning, when he reports for work, he wants to see women who're young and fresh as tender cucumber, whether they happen to be on the faculty or they're students. What a weakness!

Students were milling around the place. Some of them greeted Jaya. At some distance, a few students were playing on the tennis court. In the adjoining field she could see a brisk game of soccer. What a large campus, with vast expanses of land. Jaya thought of some of the good students in her class. Being a central university, the salary was relatively better than the state funded ones, and there were some additional perks. After languishing for such a very long time in small towns, I'm in a place like this, thought Jaya. The college in small town Jorhat where she worked for some time was more like a village school. She used to curse it under her breath for the one year she dragged herself to work. And when Balachandar was transferred to Silchar, she couldn't get a chance to teach even in a school. 'All appointments are reserved only for the Assamese. Why, when we refuse jobs even to the Bengalis who can speak Assamese fluently, how can *you*, a South Indian, expect a job here? You don't have a shadow of a chance ... ,' she was told.

She had studied so diligently all through. Each time Balachandar was happy that he was transferred on a promotion, inversely she slipped down, as it were. Down ... down ... I go, somewhere, she reflected, very depressed. Sudharani's question the other day had hit her on the head. '*In that case, why didn't you choose to settle down with a good university in a decent city and take care of your job?*' Jaya had no answer for that.

Jaya reached the road and hailed a three-wheeler. It went wobbling all the way home. God, let me stay on in this big city, let me hold on to my job, for once, just this once, she prayed. I'm on probation now. I hope to get confirmed in my position in due course. I want to settle down with this job. Want to continue working peacefully. But Professor Verma? He may well wreck my peace.

IV

Jaya could not afford to luxuriate in poetry, much as it was her chosen area. She had to teach contemporary hermeneutics to two large classes which meant catching up a lot on new work. She had drawn up a plan for the course and was generally immersed in books that dealt with new literary movements. Along with this she taught Literary History, a paper she shared with five others including Professor Verma. Only Bhaskar and Mala Nayak, who taught linguistics, had less classes to handle.

Jaya would often share the recent changes and movements from the seventies onwards to the present times with Sudharani. Conversations with her were always full of verve and zest. But Jaya noticed that of late Sudha did not respond to anything. She remained cool and aloof. What could be the reason, wondered Jaya. The problem of tending to a sick husband at home? Is she simply exhausted playing both husband and wife in her life? But she looks fresh as ever. And strong. Do all the people hailing from Almora have the same kind of outstanding good looks and cool freshness? In addition to beauty, she has remarkable intellectual energy. She also had a good rapport with her students. Jaya had heard it from the ones who studied fiction under Sudharani. 'Dr Joshi is the only teacher who takes an interest in our growth,' they said. They hold her in high regard, just the way I do, thought Jaya. Why has Sudha slipped away from me, far away from me? Whatever has happened?

In the faculty lounge, Sudharani was quietly going through some essays. Mala Nayak could be seen hurriedly flipping over the pages of a book for her next class. She got up to leave as soon as the bell rang for the next hour. A few others sat around, sipping tea.

'Sudha, are you very busy?' asked Jaya.

'Yes. I've a pile of work to finish,' she replied without raising her head.

'Shall I order for some tea for us?'

'Hmm.'

'Something to eat with it perhaps?'

'No thanks.'

'Please Sudha, don't neglect your health like this. Let me ask for cutlets, or may be *bonda*[2].'

'I don't want anything.'

'Sudha, please, can't you have a bite? For my sake?'

Sudha lifted her head to look at Jaya for a moment, a faint smile hovering over her lips. For a moment, it lit up her whole face. 'Okay. You can order for a *bonda* for me. What'll you have?' asked Sudharani.

'I'll have a *bonda* too. Hey, Chottu!' she called out for the canteen boy.

Sudha got busy again with the evaluation of the essays. She looks like she has been sculpted, thought Jaya, looking at her colleague, all lost in work. What a cool, serene allure. And terrific brains. Why did a woman like her get a useless husband like Mahesh, a numskull who does not realise his extraordinary luck in getting a wife like Sudha? What a fate. Why think of only Mahesh. What about our chairman Verma? Talks like a crude oaf. He is himself ageing but talks about Sudha as someone past her prime. What about *him*? Ah, now I get it! It's very clear to me. Verma has been really mean to Sudha by giving me the main work of the seminar that is usually managed by her. It's irregular, to say the least. Perhaps that's why she is standoffish.

[2] *Bonda*: A salty, fried snack made with potatoes and flour of bengalgram.

They were served *bonda* and tea. Sudha ate in silence.

'Shall I pour another cup of tea?' asked Jaya.

'No thanks. You go ahead.'

'What's the matter Sudha? You look depressed. Can't you tell me, even me?'

'What's there to say? I just feel a bit tired, that's all.'

'Take some rest then.'

'I wanted to. I thought I'd take leave for two days. But Professor Verma has thrust all his work on me and taken off! He is out again. And I'll have to do more work as usual, as the Acting Head.'

'What? Has he gone out again?'

'There's nothing new about that, is there? He is almost always out. He manipulates and grabs his chance to be an Examiner here, or to take a Viva there, or an interview. Footloose guy, loafing around from place to place once he charts his own "travel" plans. Finally it's me, the beast of burden, who has to manage all his work in his absence.'

'Atrocious!'

'Indeed it is. I heard that the students have a secret name for Verma. "The Absentee Professor!"' said Sudha. Jaya laughed.

'I also heard that they've a name for me as well,' declared Sudha.

'What is it?'

'The Permanently Officiating Head!' said Sudha, laughing with Jaya.

Thank god she laughs at last, thought Jaya, emboldened by her lightened mood.

'Tell me honestly Sudha, are you angry with me?'

'Angry? What on earth for?'

'Just tell me.'

'What's all this Jaya, suddenly?'

'Professor Verma shouldn't have given me the job of evolving the theme of the seminar. I can never hope to do it as well as you've been doing all these years. I neither have your depth nor your competence. Sudha, please free me from this responsibility. Take it back from me,' pleaded Jaya.

Sudha laughed aloud. 'So *this* is the problem which has been troubling you all the while. Why do you take it so seriously, Jaya? If you need any help with this work, we're all there to help you. Bhaskar, Mala, me and then that man, what's his name, the one who joined recently? Deshpande! All of us will give you a hand. Why don't you take it up as a challenge and prove it to yourself first that you can do it? Why're you diffident?'

'I'm not diffident. That man Verma, he says ... er ... about you ... '

'Look here Jaya, everybody in our department should get a chance to develop, to grow.'

Jaya felt very small. Shrunk in size. She felt embarrassed about the whole thing. Someone knocked on the door twice.

'May I come in?'

They turned to look. It was Akhila Sharma.

'So you're back. So soon!' said Sudharani, surprised. Akhila said *namaste* to both of them.

'I thought you went to Shimla for four weeks. Have you come home for a short holiday?' enquired Sudharani.

'No Madam. I cut it short and came away. My child isn't doing well.'

'Oh the poor little thing. What happened? You took his maid with you.'

'He had something like convulsion. There are no big hospitals or proper doctors in Shimla.'

'But your work got interrupted,' said Jaya.

'You're right Madam. When my child Raju is in this condition, how can I leave him? Besides, I still nurse him you see.'

All of them sat in silence for some time.

'Doesn't matter. Continue with your research here. You can go out again after your child's condition improves,' said Jaya, soothingly.

'I really don't know what I'm going to do,' said Akhila, looking disturbed. They felt sorry for her.

'Let me get along Madam. I came to the library here,' said Akhila and went out of the room.

'Poor girl,' remarked Sudharani. 'How she struggles to work for her PhD with a small baby to look after.'

'Didn't we all struggle the same way, those of us who married?' said Jaya. 'We literally carried a baby in one arm and wrote our PhD dissertation with the other. And ... '

'What's happening? Some domestic problems again?' Mala Nayak cut in, interrupting Jaya as she came into the room.

'You're wise. You didn't get married,' said Sudharani.

'You should add, "not yet",' Mala corrected her.

'But of course! I meant not yet,' said Sudharani, getting up to leave.

V

'So, how's the preparation for the seminar? Where do things stand?' asked Professor Verma.

'I've a couple of names on mind,' said Sudharani. 'I'll show the list to you. We need some new faces for the sub-themes. I've also made a list of names of people who've made a mark in the last ten years and who've published papers extensively. We can finalise the list after both of us take a look at it and discuss it.'

'Good! Who should we invite as the chief guest? Did you think about it?'

'Hmm. I've noted a couple of names for that.'

'Alright. By the way, I completely forgot! How're my classes going on, Dr Joshi?'

'They're all in order. I took classes for the two sections of Literary History,' explained Sudharani.

'Thank you very much. Please forgive me, Dr Joshi. Whenever I go out of town I'm sort of forced to load you with extra work. See the price you pay for your seniority?' he smiled.

Sudharani kept quiet.

'What news about the theme of the seminar?'

'I don't know, Dr Verma. I think Dr Balachandar must've made a plan for it.'

'Hmm ... ? It was I who put her in charge of that work. Since both of you are close friends I thought you might know how far she has progressed with the work. Perhaps she talked to you about it?'

'No Dr Verma.'

'I see. In that case, why don't you help her? She is not a seasoned person. She is quite raw, in a way. You, on the contrary, have excellent experience.'

'I don't wish to interfere with her work before she talks to me about it,' said Sudharani.

'No, no. You can't call this "interference", surely? As a senior, you've every right to find out how far she has progressed. I gave her this work only to get her more involved in the activities of our department, since she is new around here. I wanted to encourage her. But if you ask me honestly, I've confidence only in you. I trust your maturity, your wisdom and the way you earned your maturity on the job. After all, I organised all those big seminars and international events only with the confidence that I've your help.'

Sudharani did not react.

'I want to tell you something. In strict confidence. Please keep it to yourself, Dr Joshi. You know, there are some people in our department who have an illusion that they are very "young". An illusion that grips them almost like a sickness, I might add. It inhibits their growth, slows down the natural pace of their development. Only you stand out with such a unique sophistication that attracts anybody, honestly!'

'Professor Verma ... '

'Please believe me, Dr Joshi. Er ... may I call you Sudha?'

'As you wish.'

'Come on, how can I call you by your name if you don't like it? I've been waiting for your permission all these years.'

'You're talking about it as if it's a big issue. All right, let me go now,' said Sudharani.

'Okay. One other thing.'

'Yes Sir?'

'Please keep an eye on Dr Balachandar. See how she goes about her work, how she behaves with the students, if she reports to her classes on time and so on. I would like you to observe all that discreetly. This is my personal request. She is new and like I said, still raw. I don't get the time to supervise anybody,' said Verma.

Sudharani went out of the room without a word.

'You sent for me, Sir?'

'Yes. Please take a seat Dr Bhaskar. You must've already heard that our department needs an Associate Professor in linguistics. We've released an advertisement for the post. But as far as we're concerned the post is exclusively for you. Only, keep the matter in strict confidence. Please apply through proper channels, through the university application form and address it to our Registrar. Most probably, we may have an interview within two months from now,' said Verma.

'Thank you very much Sir. I'll definitely apply. I'll get an application form right away. But Mala Nayak, and the new person Deshpande, they too specialise in linguistics, don't they?'

'No, no Dr Bhaskar. Mala Nayak offered only two papers in linguistics for her Masters. She has just completed her M.Phil. Her case is very lightweight. You're the only one with a sound background and scholarship in linguistics. You've published quite a few articles and papers,' said Verma.

'Oh, nothing to write home about, Sir.'

'You must prepare very well for the interview. We'll be getting applications from good external candidates from all over the country. Express yourself with confidence in the interview. I want you to get this post.'

'Thank you very much Sir. I'll try to do my best. Er ... I was telling you about this new person who has joined. Deshpande. He too specialises in linguistics and ... '

'Dr Bhaskar, why do you worry about that? Just as I told you, this post is only for you. Deshpande is too new. And has less work experience than you.'

'I'm indeed very grateful for your support Sir. And Sir, you've also advertised for the post of an Associate Professor in Literature, haven't you? I happened to see it.'

'Yes. Even there we've only one vacancy. For that again, it'll be nice if someone from our department gets it, instead of an outsider,' said Verma.

'Oh yes Sir. You're unlikely to get anyone from outside as worthy for the position as our own Dr Joshi, I'm sure,' said Bhaskar.

'You seem to be quite a fan of Dr Joshi. Let's see what happens. I too wish that she should get it, but it's not entirely in my hands, you see. Ah, Dr Bhaskar, can you do me a small favour?'

'Yes Sir?'

'Could you please ask Dr Balachandar to come and see me?'

'Certainly Sir.'

VI

'Please come in Dr Balachandar. Have a seat.'

'Thank you Sir.'

'Ah ... how's work? Do you like this university?' asked Verma.

'I like it very much Sir. I'm lucky I got a job here,' said Jaya.

'I went through your proposal for the theme of the seminar and the details for the sub-themes during the rest of the days,' said Verma.

'Was it all right? It was just an attempt, that's about all. It's my first attempt too. There could be many flaws in it,' said Jaya.

'Did you say flaws? It's an excellent plan. You've gathered some very subtle points. Fine work!'

'Thank you Sir, thanks very much.'

'See my point now? I was right in my hunch, wasn't I? We do need young blood. Only then work gets started on a brisk pace. And the event will take on a lustre.'

'Sir, you can't refer to me as "young blood" any more. I've completed thirty-five,' objected Jaya.

'So what? That's still very much younger than forty-four, isn't it?'

'What's the big difference, Professor Verma?' said Jaya, her face suddenly flushed. She felt hot. Why does this man go on and on about age as if ageing for women is some kind of a horrendous disease? As if women who age ought to be 'punished' in some way? Wouldn't he slander me the same way a few years from now? It's but natural to grow old. Nobody can stop it. Why, one can take *him* as an example of ageing. He is going to be fifty-five. Then how can he talk about the ageing of women who are far younger than him?

'Tomorrow or some time next week, we'll discuss your plan for the seminar and take a decision,' said Verma.

'Okay Sir.'

'By the way, I've something important to tell you.'

'Yes Sir?'

'Our department needs an Associate Professor in Literature. We've advertised in the papers. Did you see it?'

'I did.'

'You should also send in your application to our Registrar.'

'Who, me?'

'Yes. Why not?'

'It was stated that there was only one vacancy. Surely that must be for Dr Sudharani Joshi? After all, she is the seniormost amongst us, besides being the best and the brightest,' said Jaya.

'Now Dr Balachandar, you're making the same mistake again. We need young people like you for the post.'

Oh god, there he goes on and on! As if the only eligibility for a job is youth. The way he talks, as if all other things such as intellectual capability, academic grooming, competence, energy or scholarship are all quite secondary! What's wrong with him?

'Sir, I don't have enough experience. This is the very first time I've moved up from teaching in a college to a university,' said Jaya.

'I'm very moved by your modesty. But you should take care that the same modesty doesn't clip your wings or cripple you eventually. How does it matter if your experience is less in terms of the length of time spent in teaching? You have a deep interest and involvement in your work and that's quite enough.'

'Sir, compared to other academicians, particularly to Dr Joshi, you can say I'm on a rather basic level. I worked in small towns and ... '

'Really Dr Balachandar, your simplicity, your straightforwardness, all this moves me very much. I request you to apply for the post of an Associate Professor and I'm doing so in my capacity as the professor and head of this department. You have a good chance for this position. It wouldn't be nice if I say anything more about this matter.'

'All right Sir, I'll do as you wish,' said Jaya, getting up. She had to hold back her seething resentment. She wanted to quieten her perplexity before going home. She went to the faculty lounge. Bhaskar was chatting with a few others.

VII

'To tell you the truth, this advertisement was given with only you in mind. The post of an Associate Professor is reserved exclusively for you. But according to the rules and regulations of the university, you're required to send in your application to our Registrar in the application form. We've to go by this convention. I request you to please do so at your earliest convenience,' said Professor Verma.

'Uh ... ,' Sudharani listened with indifference.

'I know very well how you feel about the whole thing. For some one of your calibre and competence, we should've offered you the post a good four years back. But everything seems to move in a slow and sluggish way in this university. We had to wait for the approval of the Syndicate, this, that and the other. It took such a long time,' explained Verma.

The swine! What a glib liar. The interview did take place four years ago. And I did very well in the interview. But he went to any length, plotting and scheming against me to make me lose the post. Then he became the professor and that gave him additional power to destroy others. He freely unleashed that power on me. On the face of it, he is a smooth talker. Behind my back, he stabs and draws blood ...

Four years back ... the professor who was in the Selection Committee told me in confidence: 'you know, Verma deliberately wants a big gap between himself and the rest of the faculty members in English. If you become an Associate Professor, you would be moving closer to him in status, wouldn't you? Then you too may eventually become a professor and that's what bothers him a lot. Actually, he feels very insecure about your maturity and the way you can be attractively articulate. Articulation and expressiveness are, after all, of utmost importance in our profession. Dr Joshi, your personality is your own enemy. Verma wants to impose a lower professional status on you so that you will forever be at a distance from him, as another lecturer.'

At a 'distance'! What kind of distance. Only official? When it comes to socialising with me, he tries to get so shamefully close, the cad.

'I've been thinking of applying for the post of Associate Professor in other universities,' said Sudharani.

'What! You mean in another city?' exclaimed Verma as if he was very shocked.

'Do I have a choice there? My husband is unemployed. The responsibility of running the house is entirely on me. I've been working here for so many years and yet there's no promotion in sight for me.'

'Dr Joshi, I'm really extremely sorry for what happened during the last few years,' said Verma. Sudharani was surprised to see him like this, his voice moist and muffled, as if he was softened by all that had happened. EvenVerma's conscience can function, can it, enough to make him feel sorry?

'Dr Joshi, you're such a seasoned teacher with a wide range in your scholarship. Everybody respects you. I've been pressurising the syndicate for so many years to hurry up and give their approval for this post and to let us release the advertisement. But things crawl on a snail pace in this university. I'm telling you again, our department badly needs people like you. Whatever others may say, we need you,' said Verma.

'What do you mean, "whatever others may say"?' asked Sudharani.

'Oh nothing, nothing at all. Who cares for all the gossip that one gets to hear?'

'What happened Professor? Tell me clearly.'

'Some people talk about you in a very unfair manner. They say you're getting old and so on ... '

'If that's what they said, then they're right about me. I *am* getting old, there's no doubt about that,' said Sudharani.

'Oh come on. Here I am, angry to see people act so petty about you and you're ... '

'What exactly did they say, Professor? Please don't hide it from me.'

'No, you see, if it was anyone else I wouldn't have bothered about it so much. But to think that your own colleague ... '

'My colleague? Who is it? Mala Nayak?'

'No, no. Someone who moves with you like a close friend.'

Sudharani suddenly felt hot in the head, as if all her blood had rushed up to her head. She felt breathless too but she controlled herself as she asked, 'May I know what he or she said?'

'By all means. Why should there be any secrets between us? She said you've slackened your grip over work because you're getting old, that you're losing interest and losing your power of articulation. That you fumble and trip over your lectures while taking a class or when you correct exam papers. I never ever expected to hear such allegations from someone as junior to you as Dr Balachandar, for I always thought both of you were close, loyal friends,' he said, his voice very low.

'Impossible! Jaya will never talk like that,' protested Sudharani.

'I thought so too. I simply couldn't believe my ears. I've never heard her talk so nastily before. Just see the difference that comes over people, the minute they decide to compete with others professionally, for promotion?'

'What! Is Jaya applying for this post? This is news!' exclaimed Sudharani.

'She is. I tried my best to dissuade her, but she is obstinate. She insisted on applying.'

'So what Dr Verma? Anyone who is eligible for the post can apply. Jaya hasn't done a big mistake by sending in her application,' said Sudharani.

'You're far too noble. Even when you know that she talked about you like this. Okay forget it. Nothing can happen. As far as we're concerned—that is, the vice-chancellor, the Academic Council and we are concerned, this post for an Associate Professor is exclusively for you. I'm telling you in strict confidence. I even gave a hint to Dr Balachandar but she is so greedy that she didn't even ... '

Sudharani got up to go.

'Uh ... there's one more thing Dr Joshi. I'll be out of town again for another ten or fifteen days. As usual, I go with the hope that you'll be looking after the department very well. I know I don't even have to ask you, but it's my personal request. Get all the work done by that Lazybones Mishra, my P.A. Don't sanction him any leave if he asks for it.'

Sudharani did not respond.

'Dr Joshi? You look very disturbed. We've worked together for so many years. Which is why I took the liberty of telling you the truth frankly. Please forgive me. But don't worry at all. Nobody but you can become the Associate Professor for Literature, that's for sure.'

Sudharani came out of the room.

'Good evening Madam,' smiled Akhila Sharma, who was standing outside.

'How are you Akhila? Haven't seen you in a long time.'

'I'm fine Madam. I'm going to Kolkata this month, to work in the National Library. They say it's a huge library that houses the rarest of rare books,' said Akhila, her eyes shining eagerly.

'Yes. It's a very fine place. I've also been there a couple of times. One can immerse oneself in studies forgetting everything because the atmosphere is so conducive for study. All around the library you have the fresh green expanse of Belvedere Estate, it's very nice,' said Sudharani.

'After I finish my work in Kolkata, I plan to go to the research center in Hyderabad and then return home,' said Akhila.

'I see. You'll return after completing your work in Hyderabad, will you?'

'Yes Madam. I'll have to hurry up with my work. If I don't use my UGC Travel Grant before the academic year is over, then it'll lapse and I may lose it. That's why I'm going at a stretch.'

'Go ahead. Are you taking your child with you again?'

'No Madam. Now Rajiv has grown up a little. My parents-in-law have come over and they'll look after him. Excuse me Madam, have you seen Dr Balachandar anywhere? I wanted to ask her something but couldn't find her in the faculty lounge. Does she have a class around this time?' asked Akhila.

'Why do you ask *me*? I don't carry her schedule with me!'

Akhila was aghast at the answer.

VIII

As soon as Sudharani reached home, Preeti, her daughter asked her, 'Ma, you promised to come home early today. It's getting very late. Come, have your tea and then let's rush. We should be there by six.'

'Okay. Where's Sanjay?' asked Sudharani.

'He is having a shower. He's also coming with us,' said Preeti.

Preeti set about briskly. They had to leave for the party celebrating the engagement ceremony of their friend's daughter. Sudharani went in. She found her husband Mahesh sitting in corner, reading a magazine.

'Aren't you coming?' she asked him.

'Where?' he asked, looking blank.

'No!' Preeti whispered into her ears. 'Let father stay back at home.'

Sudharani went to the bathroom and had a good wash. She scrubbed and washed her face, hands, arms and feet, patted herself dry and came out. She gulped down her tea hurriedly and changed her saree. All the while, Mahesh did not ask her even once about where she was going. He continued to sit stonily in a corner. Suddenly, a wave of fatigue washed over her. It spread over her shoulders and arms. She was tired by the very thought of driving the car. But I must go, she thought. I must get into a crowd, at least for the sake of Preeti. Otherwise, how am I going to find a boy for her, how am I going to get her married if I don't meet people? I'll have to get her married soon. Mahesh's condition is worsening by the day.

Sudharani got dressed. She put on the first necklace that she could lay her hands on.

'Preeti.'

'Yes Ma.'

'Come here. Try these earrings on. How about this bracelet?'

Preeti just stood there and looked at her mother in silence.

'Ma ... '

'Why, you don't like them? Then select something on your own and hurry! You were the one to hustle me and now you're delaying us. Come on, how you were jumping about your friend's engagement.'

'I feel like performing another engagement for you, Ma.'

'What're you blabbering? Now come here and ... '

'Honestly Ma, you look so lovely in this saree and in these jewels. Who would say that you're my mother? Everybody thinks that you're my sister,' said Preeti.

'Okay, okay, get started. Sanjay!'

'I'm ready Ma!' he replied from somewhere. Sudharani left instructions with her domestic help: 'Make hot *chappatis*[3] for the master and serve him dinner. Ask him if he wants you to make anything else and do accordingly.'

The three of them left for the party.

Sudharani distanced herself from the feast throughout the ceremony. Puja, the bride-to-be, glowed in her new dress and special accessories. Preeti sat close to her. Around them a bunch of lively girls, all friends of Puja, were singing and having a whale of a time. Puja's parents looked happy and content. They had landed a good son-in-law.

'Where's Mahesh? You didn't bring him along?' enquired the hosts, more out of propriety. Actually, no one was surprised by the absence of Mahesh. The hosts introduced Sudharani to some new friends.

[3] *Chappatis*: Unleavened bread made with wheat.

'Is Preeti your daughter? Really? You don't look like you've such a grown-up daughter. What's the secret of your youthful appearance?' asked a woman. It did not register in Sudharani. Her mind circled around Jaya constantly. *After a very long time I thought I had found a fine colleague and a good friend. Does she really talk behind my back like that? Or is Professor Verma up to some wily trick?* She took her glass of fruit juice and crossed over to the balcony of the house. *Even if I console myself that Verma is telling an outrageous lie, the fact remains that both he and Jaya, assuming she said all that are right. I am getting old. That's a fact.*

The sky was deepening in colour. Sounds of conversation floated inside the room. It was very quiet outside, the oppressive quietness of twilight. A quietness that was inexplicably disquieting. *I'm like this hour*, she thought. *I've also set, with the sun. And now darkness is descending on me.*

After the party, Sudharani speeded towards home in the car with Preeti and Sanjay. Her hands and feet moved on the wheels mechanically, as if they were driving on their own. On reaching home she asked Mahesh, 'Have you eaten?'

'I have. Who did you see in the party?' asked Mahesh and did not wait for the reply. He sauntered over to another room. Sudharani went to her room and bolted the door from inside. She took off her clothes, the saree, the blouse, and the skirt worn below the saree. Something pulled her towards the dressing table. She found herself standing in front of the mirror. She switched on the light.

At a first glance her figure looked as if it was well preserved. It looked intact. But her mind did not accept this observation. It coaxed her eyes and compelled them to note a few other details. Her bosom had sagged, although a wee little bit. But it had, nevertheless. Those breasts did not have the proud, heaving fullness that they had once, when she was young. Her eyes did not fail to notice the thickening of flesh around her waist. The traces of darkness around her eyes were faint. Very faint in fact. They were more like a shadow. She saw thin wrinkles flanking her lips. She watched her reflection in the mirror with detachment, as if she was looking at some other woman. She took in every part of herself and evaluated it coolly. She looked at the face reflected in the mirror dispassionately, without any expression. The moment split into two. This image shimmering in the mirror, who is she? How far do I know her? There were signs of ageing that had surfaced here and there. She never had an impulse to hide or camouflage them. On the contrary, something had always urged her on to usher old age. Some indefinable force often urged her on. 'Come on, come on quick', she said to the idea of old age. The inner voice invited old age. And yet, age seemed to crawl upon her very, very slowly, stealing in with the softness of a twilight. It was time to lose youth. To lose the flourishing lushness of youth. After this, there will be the onset of old age. Irreversible. For it'll set in on unambiguous terms. And then there will be no going back.

Perhaps that may bring with it a sense of peace, she wondered. Because there will not be even a residual trace of youth to unsettle anybody. Or unsettle me. Will I find peace at last, in my fifties?

The face in the mirror threw back the question at her. As she gazed at the image in the mirror, the eyes of her mind saw another figure beyond her own. It had small, beady eyes. Sunken eyes framed by thick spectacles. Roving eyes that always peered through the glasses with a sly vigilance. The flesh sagged on both sides of his face. His lips, darkened by the stain of nicotine with constant smoking, had also lost their shape. And whenever they opened in a smile, they showed a set of yellowish-brown teeth. There were dark, swollen pouches under the eyes. Telltale eyes that gave away the fact that he was given to heavy drinking, that in fact he drank every day of his life.

This man who sat on a chair behind a table, who drew an unshakeable sense of security and power by sitting on that professor's chair, and who always talked about the age of women, how old was he? Fifty-five on the records. But he looked sixty. And if you ever ask, he will have the same old explanation given by most people of his generation in north India. 'During the partition of the country, we fled with our family leaving our house behind us. We survived by hiding ourselves. The enemy set fire to our houses and all our records and documents were destroyed.' A standard explanation that helped many a man slide out of an allegation about his age. Verma seems to stand on top of a superior height that is beyond the human span of life and from there he seems to dispense judgement. In his universe, is age supposed to have a feminine gender? Does a woman get punished in that universe, if she gets old? And now, has Jaya allied herself with him? But why? In order to get appointed as an Associate Professor? How does she know in the first place, that Verma has been harassing me in the department vengefully? I never told her the story of my fight with Verma. I don't remember telling her at all ...

It was all so different some years ago. Sudharani was full of spirit when she joined the faculty. She was absorbed in her work, her students and her studies. She had striking looks then, with that lustrous complexion so special to the people from the hills of Almora. She was noticeably attractive.

'You're still so lovely, Dr Joshi,' said Verma.

'What do you mean by "still"? Why the emphasis on "still"?' asked Sudharani.

'I mean even at this age,' explained Verma.

Sudharani laughed aloud.

'Why, haven't you ever noticed that some people—only a few of course—can look quite ordinary in their youth but take on an unusual radiance in their middle age?' asked Sudharani.

'Hmm ... ?'

Instantly, Sudharani regretted her words. 'Oh god, how can I expect *him* to understand anything like that?' she thought, getting up to go.

'Please have a seat. Tell me, why do you harden so much when it comes to me? Can't you accept another person in your life, even as a friend? When you know that your husband is actually no husband at all?'

Of all the things! First of all he can't even qualify as a good, decent colleague. How can he graduate into a 'friend'? Now he jumps the gun and goes so far as to suggest that he can even 'replace' a husband.

'What do you say Dr Joshi? Don't you have a small place, for a friend?'

The cheek!

Of course one can make a place for someone in life. If I create that space, my life would be larger than it is now. But I'll never do that for you, understand? Never. The fool!

'Come on Dr Joshi, after all, we've already been friends, haven't we?'

Perhaps this man has no respect for the word 'friend'. What to speak of being friends, we've been less than acquaintances. So many bitter things have happened between us. How does he expect friendship after all that, wondered Sudharani as she went out of the room.

The events uncurled. Sudharani was new in the department. She looked upon Dr Verma, then the Associate Professor, as a senior colleague. She started off with an implicit trust in him, talked to him freely as a colleague, sharing interesting books or research findings, experiences in other forums and so on. It took her a few years to realise what Verma was up to. With consummate cunning, he had passed on whatever he had culled from her talk or her studies to his students and young PhD scholars as his own! Sudharani got to know about it only when some of the students talked to her in the small departmental seminars, totally innocent of the crafty plots and schemes. That had exploded in a big fight between her and Verma one day.

'I never expected you to do something like this,' said Sudharani.

'Why? What am I supposed to have done?' asked Verma.

'What more do you want to do?' she hissed. 'I trusted you as a colleague and shared everything with you. How can you steal my research findings, my ideas, right down to my own sentences as if they're all your own? You've absolutely no scruples.'

'Did you say steal? Do you have a monopoly over literature? It belongs to everybody. Everybody has a claim over it.'

'Of course it belongs to everybody, who says it doesn't? But there are proprieties and principles. Would it be fair if I take away some portions of your articles and use them as my own?'

'By all means go ahead and use them. I've no objection whatever,' said Verma. In a flash Sudharani realised that she was trapped in a cage of her own making. He was right. He could say with this supreme confidence that he would allow his articles to be plagiarised. Because what could one steal from him? Nothing! Nothing at all. The man was a wasteland. Was a lazybones too. Has been teaching for years without coming up with anything new or original. He was essentially a hedonistic cannibal who hunted around for ideas and swallowed the spoils of others in one gulp with a belch. The shameless sloth!

'See my point? Does it hit home now?' asked Verma and continued. 'Why do you claim exclusive rights over literature? That won't do! The great poet Shakespeare gave peerless plays to the world just by garnering in historical data from the Holinshed chronicles. He processed them, shaped them into plays. Was Shakespeare a thief, tell me?'

Even in that awkward moment, Sudharani felt an uncontrollable urge to laugh aloud. Why, this man is brazen enough to compare himself with Shakespeare! She tried hard to quell the laughter bubbling within her.

'What can I say Dr Verma, after you've told me that you're another Shakespeare?' said Sudharani and this time, in spite of her best efforts, she broke into a smile which spread over her face without her permission.

'I know very well that I'm not a Shakespeare. You don't have to rub it in so sarcastically. You'll feel sorry for this. Soon!' he warned and went off in a huff.

Was she sorry? It would be more precise to say that she was made to feel sorry. Verma ran from pillar to post manipulating his application by fawning on people who mattered. He kissed the dust of their feet to wrench recommendations and finally got his way. He became a professor. And after that, he unleashed his revenge on Sudharani in a systematic way, making an elaborate blueprint to torture her in million ways. The department advertised for the post of an Associate Professor. Sudharani applied for it. Verma sat on the Selection Committee and let loose his newly acquired power to destroy. He proved to the Committee that Sudharani had many 'negative points', that there were serious inadequacies in her scholarship, her style of work, that she lacked a sound academic background and so on. Sudharani, who had earned the respect of her students and colleagues alike, was humiliated and rejected for the post by Verma.

She tried for a change of job in other universities outside the city. Her applications needed a formal 'Forwarding' signature from Verma to make it go 'through proper channels' in academic parlance. Verma refused to forward her applications. One day she asked him directly: 'Why do you stop me from going out of this place? It's meaningless. After all you can't tolerate me and your intolerance gets worse by the day,' she said.

'I didn't ask you to leave the job. It's you who slighted me,' said Verma.

'What do you mean?'

'What else? All that I asked for is your friendship. You can even say that I almost begged for it. It wouldn't be an exaggeration. After all, you're lonely. You've a husband who has withdrawn from life for all practical purposes. I sought to wipe out that loneliness and you rejected me as if I'm unworthy of you,' fumed Verma.

'Dr Verma, you let your thoughts run wild and then get confused by them. The only question that I asked you the other day was a straight one. And that was, if we're to be friends at all, doesn't friendship need or presume a mutual trust, integrity or even some attachment? I only said that we don't have such a thing going between us, that's all. Our taste, our attitudes and lifestyle do not match, do they? How can friendship be possible, in that case? And for that, you now take revenge on me.'

'I didn't take any revenge. That's not revenge. I just expressed my ardour, that's all. At least now do you understand my passion? It's not too late. We can still be friends again like we were before, if you agree.'

Friends like we were before? But we were never friends at any point in time. What an inappropriate proposal for friendship. Perhaps he considers it unnecessary to get my consent or wish for this agreement. She pulled back her thoughts and swallowed them. I've suffered enough, she thought. He has ruined my career, the swine!

During the next few years Sudharani distanced herself from Verma and became very remote. She did her work without getting involved in anything else.

The events that had faded off in a cloud of smoke and vanished. Grief, tedium, disappointment, shock or disgust—she was past the whole gamut of these feelings and sensations as she stood for a moment, looking at herself in the mirror with detachment. Sudharani stood, looking at another Sudharani in the mirror.

IX

'Come on, hurry both of you. Drink up the milk. Then have a bath. It's getting late,' Jaya hustled her children.

'What's the matter, why are you in such a tearing hurry?' asked Balachandar.

'I have a class in the first hour. And another in the next,' explained Jaya.

'I know. But that's your usual schedule on Wednesdays. Then why are you ... '

'Oh, you've no idea,' interrupted Jaya. 'It's not just the classes. I've some work in the library too.' She gathered a heap of laundry and gave it to her maid.

'*Isshh*! I suppose all of you can spend a lifetime reading in a library,' said Balachandar, unhurriedly working up a foamy lather as he shaved in front of the mirror.

The school bus will take her children to Bal Bharathi Air Force Station School at 7 a.m. Jaya stuffed their lunch boxes with food and asked her maid to escort them to the bus stop. Then she had a bath and got dressed. She ate a morsel of something and got ready to leave. Balachandar also got dressed in his Air Force uniform, had his breakfast and was about to leave in his Bajaj scooter.

'Jaya, can I drop you off at the bus stop?' he asked.

'No. I'll grab a three-wheeler and go straight to the university,' she replied.

'Okay then.'

The three-wheeler jolted itself into motion. There was still one hour to go for her class. Even if she got fifteen minutes in the faculty lounge, she could use the time to browse through some of the papers in her folder that was in the staff room locker. There was a sea of information to absorb but where is the time for all that? Hell! It's the same beat—classes, answer papers of examinations, then house work and the children's home work, classes again.... On top of it, there is this new unwritten convention which has caught on for good or bad. It is expected that you make what's euphemistically called a 'comparative study' of anything, anybody. Compare each writer with his fellow literary wayfarers and make a comparative study of their works. What a pain. I'm submitting to all these pressures, taking off in various directions as I hunt for source materials. As if that isn't enough, I now have to study and prepare for this wretched interview.

The three-wheeler stopped abruptly. The driver got down.

'What happened? Why did you stop?' asked Jaya.

'Something is wrong with the spark plug, Madam. I'll fix it in two minutes,' he said, sliding his seat down. From inside, he took out two instruments and got busy in repairing the thing. Jaya sat, waiting. Other vehicles sped up and down the road briskly. Everyone is going about his/her work, hurtling on. I too seem to hare around a lot. To sink into deep research beyond this daily rut is very tough for the likes of me. There's not enough time, not enough strength either. Hell, why did I get trapped into this idea of an interview? It came like a bolt from the blue. I had no intention of applying for this post because I know only too well that I'll never get it. Why then should I suffer the humiliation of a rejection? It's unnecessary. This man, Porfessor Verma. He is so overbearing. We've to go by his diktat. If he hadn't compelled me to apply I would be going about my work as usual, peacefully. I wouldn't be slogging away like this. Hang the interview, what a waste of time.

'Madam, I'm sorry,' said the driver of the three-wheeler.

'What happened?' asked Jaya.

'I don't think I can fix this. It's better to get another three-wheeler for you,' he said.

Oh dear! Jaya paid him the fare and walked on the road slowly. There were no free three-wheelers to take her. It was impossible to board a bus as all buses were overflowing with commuters at that hour. This had to happen today, of all days when I wanted to reach early and catch up on some reading. At least let me be on time for my class. She saw an unoccupied cab. Shall I flag it down? Gracious, it'll cost me the earth. Jaya looked at her watch and called out 'Taxi!'

She reached the university in ten minutes. There were still five minutes to go for her class. 'What can I study now,' she thought, as she sat on a chair and waited. There were three others in the faculty lounge. They were all from different departments. They sat chatting.

She recalled now Professor Verma was furious when she told him for the second time that she did not wish to apply. He was enraged, as if her refusal to apply was, in some way, an insult to him! The whole episode really frightened me.

'What do you mean by this, Dr Balachandar? Here I am, the chairman and head of this department. Even so, I put that aside and patiently explain everything to you in detail in your own interest. For your own good. I offered advice so that you can move up in your career. But you're being obstinate again in refusing to apply. Is this a nice thing to do?' he had said.

'Oh no Sir. I'm very sorry! Please don't misunderstand me. I'm very grateful for your advice and I'm much obliged too, believe me. But there's a small detail. Perhaps you've forgotten about it. Sir, I haven't completed my period of probation yet, so how can I ... ?'

'Probation? A ... h? Oh yes. Good you reminded me. Now look here Dr Balachandar, if you want to complete this period of your probation properly, that is, without any problems and if you want to be confirmed in your present post as a lecturer, then do as I ask you to. Send in your application.'

'Alright Sir, I'll do as you say. I'll apply for this post.'

She had shaken all over with fright as she came out of his room, angry with herself for having blurted out about her probation. What a perplexing situation. I'm between the devil and the deep sea. If I obey his orders and apply for this post, it would be a most foolish act because I'll surely get rejected in the interview. And if I don't apply, the professor would be so angry that it might have an adverse effect on my probation and my confirmation. Why the hell is he bothered whether I apply or not? Does he have an axe to grind in this? What could it be? Finally it's me who is going to suffer from humiliation and unnecessary strain and stress.

On the one hand I'm losing sleep, studying for this needless interview and on the other, I'm still waiting for a chance to explain it all to Sudha. I must explain to her clearly that I'm not responsible for this embarrassing situation that has risen between us. *She has to know* that I have been trapped into this. But for some reason she has become very impatient with me. She just cuts me short whenever I talk to her. In these two months she has pointedly avoided me. Is she angry? What about? Nothing happened between us that I can remember, nothing at all.

Jaya got up for her class and went out of the lounge. She could see Akhila Sharma at some distance, walking through the corridor towards the stair. But it was time for her class.

The next two hours just flew. After her second class, Jaya rushed eagerly to the faculty lounge in the hope of talking to Sudharani. She found Mala Nayak instead, sitting by herself.

'Come, let's have some tea,' she offered.

'Do you have a class in the afternoon?' asked Jaya.

'Yes. I've a class in the fourth hour and then it'll be time to go home and relax. I'll go out and may be see a movie in the evening,' said Mala.

'Lucky girl.'

'Why, you can see a movie too. Care to join me?'

'No, I can't.'

'Why not? Oho, I forgot for a moment. There's only a week to go for your interview. You must be busy preparing, I guess. So, how's it going?'

'An ... interview ... I suppose it's your wild guess that I've applied,' said Jaya.

'Not a guess. *I know* that you've applied. You can't hide our departmental news from me. Professor Verma himself told me,' said Mala with a laugh.

'Really? Did he also compel you to apply for the other post, of an Associate Professor in linguistics?' asked Jaya.

'Compel me? No, not at all! It has been decided beforehand that the post is for Dr Bhaskar. I'm still a half-baked person in this field. Professor Verma told me that with a seasoned contender like Dr Bhaskar, I don't have a shadow of a chance for the post. I liked his straightforwardness. I really appreciate it. I don't like to nurse hopes in a fool's paradise, only to get confused and disappointed in the end,' said Mala, with a mischievous smile.

Jaya went red in the face. 'Even I didn't want to apply for the same reason,' she said.

'Oh come on! Your case is very different,' she laughed.

'What do you mean by that?'

'Well, all I can say is that you're very bold. That's all,' said Mala.

'I'm bold? Just what are you driving at?'

'Of course you're bold. Otherwise, would you try to defeat Sudharani Joshi, of all the people? She is not only your senior with an impeccable track record, she has the additional status of always being our Acting Head,' said Mala.

'Oh no! You're totally wrong about me. I certainly don't wish to defeat Sudharani. It's impossible too.'

'Everybody knows that. Why did you apply at all in that case, if I may ask?'

'Because I was compelled to. It was a compulsion that I couldn't fight against.'

'Now don't give me those tall stories. Professor Verma himself told me how you covet the post of an Associate Professor. He remarked with much regret that it's probably the brashness of youth which makes you misguided enough to try winning against Dr Joshi,' said Mala.

'My goodness, this is atrocious! It really is. Is that what he said? Outrageous liar! He is lying through his teeth. I would never compete against Sudharani. I've great regard and affection for her and I consider myself lucky that I found a friend like her.'

'Indeed. You speak so ornamentally. If that's how you really feel, then why did you ... '

'Mala, listen to me. Please. I didn't wish for this post even in my wildest dreams. It was Professor Verma who twisted my arms to apply. He bullied me and threatened me in so many ways and forced me to apply. He warned that if I don't, it may even seriously affect my period of probation and the confirmation.'

Mala laughed aloud. 'A nice cock-and-bull story, if ever there was one. Jaya, I don't agree with your allegations about Professor Verma. He is very frank by nature, and straightforward. For instance, he had no hesitation whatever in telling me that the post in linguistics was not for me and that I shouldn't even bother to apply. How can you accuse him?' she said, getting up.

'Mala, please believe me. You're very much mistaken. Actually ... '

'You can conclude as you wish, but I've got to go now. Bye,' she said, walking away. She suddenly stopped and came back to Jaya. 'Oh, I forgot to wish you. All the best for the interview!' she chuckled.

'Nonsense! Go on if you don't want to believe me. I'll explain the whole thing to Sudharani. In fact I came here searching for her,' said Jaya.

'Sudharani hasn't come today,' said Mala. 'She is on leave. It seems she is ill.'

'Oh, what happened? She ... '

Mala laughed aloud. 'Are you really concerned about her? Surprising. Okay. I must rush.'

Jaya could not stand the place any more. She came out of the lounge. The corridor stretched out long in front of her. She crossed the passage, feeling very tired. She climbed down the stair and reached the large square on the grounds. Ah, there is Akhila, coming out of the library. But she is walking away as if she hasn't seen me. What's the matter with her? Why is everyone behaving so strangely today?

'Akhila!' she called out.

Akhila stood for a moment. Then she walked towards Jaya and said, 'Good afternoon Madam.'

'Good afternoon. Where are you off to?'

'I came to the library.'

'Dr Joshi said you've gone to Kolkata.'

'I went to Kolkata. And from there to Hyderabad, to the American Studies Research Center. But I returned earlier than I planned to,' said Akhila.

'You said you were planning to make some notes for your research and also do an extensive bibliography. I'm sure most of the books would've been for reference only in Hyderabad. Even if you had stayed for four months, it wouldn't have been enough,' said Jaya.

'That's very true Madam. Still, I just came away leaving everything in the middle.'

'Really? But why?'

Akhila kept quiet.

'Akhila, is your child keeping well?'

'He is well enough. But I ... over there ... oh Madam, don't ask me anything, please!' she said and burst into tears.

'Akhila, what's the matter? What happened?'

Akhila sobbed uncontrollably. Then she just walked away briskly.

'Akhila, listen.'

Jaya thought of following her but noticed that she had already disappeared through the second gate of the university.

What could be the matter? Does her husband object to her working for a PhD? Did he summarily order her to come back? Or has she herself fallen ill this time? But she looked fine.

Jaya got into a three-wheeler and went home.

X

'Amma, we're going next door to see a movie on the video. We've finished our home work,' said Siddharth to Jaya.

'Ah, Amma I forgot to tell you,' said her daughter Shalini. 'Appa called to say that he'll be late today.'

The children left for their video session. Jaya sat down beside the telephone, all lost in thought. Then she dialled Sudharani's number.

'Hello?'

'Is that Sanjay?'

'Yes. *Namaste* Auntie.'

'*Namaste*. How are you, my child? Can I speak to your mother?'

'Sure Auntie. I'll call her.'

Jaya waited.

'Hello.'

It was Sanjay again. 'Uh ... Auntie, er ... I'm sorry but my mother is not at home. It seems she'll be coming back late,' he added.

Has Sudharani given these instructions to her son? Jaya hung up. She rose and got busy with making dinner for the family. But she felt restless. She could not concentrate on anything. She reached for the phone again and dialled Sudharani's number.

'Yes?'

She recognised the voice.

'Sudha, please don't keep the phone down, I beg of you. Don't hang up,' said Jaya, agitated and nervous.

'What do you want?'

'I want to have a frank talk with you, at least once. But in private. Please don't say no,' said Jaya.

'I don't think that's necessary.'

'Sudha, do listen to me, please! Before you reject me altogether, please give me one chance to explain. At least for old times' sake. Let's meet somewhere and talk. Only then you'll come to know what actually happened. You'll understand, surely you will, for you're wise,' said Jaya.

'So what if I'm wise? That can't quite stop me from becoming an old woman, can it?' asked Sudharani.

'What did you say? I'm sorry but I didn't get it,' said Jaya.

'No? Don't you recognise your own words?'

'Good God, things are really getting weird around here. Before they get worse, the two of us must meet and talk face to face. We simply must. I've a strong hunch. I can find out if I'm right in my hunch only if we meet. It'll be good for both of us, believe me. After this meeting you can do what you want with me, Sudha,' Jaya entreated, quite breathless by the exercise.

There was complete silence on the other end of the line.

'Sudha, shall I drop in at your place?'

'No, no. You know how it'll be at my place. Mahesh will keep hovering around us and he will stare at us blankly. How about meeting in our department?' asked Sudharani.

'Oh no, of all the places! It's such a gossipy den. We can never talk in private.'

Sudharani seemed to have lapsed into silence once again.

'Sudha! Are you there? Have you kept the phone down? Hello, hello.'

'Hush Jaya, I'm just thinking about where we could meet.'

Thank God.

'Jaya, have you seen the Guest House beside the Coffee Home? Shall we meet there at the lounge? Around four?'

'Okay. See you then.'

They sat on the cane chairs in the verandah of the Guest House.

'By all means, anyone who is eligible can apply for the post of an Associate Professor. So you have every right to apply and there's nothing wrong *per se* in that. But my question is, why should you talk about me like that to Professor Verma? Behind my back too?' asked Sudharani.

'Gracious! Do you really believe that I could've talked like that?' said Jaya.

'I don't wish to believe.'

'Then why do you suspect me? Sudha, you really ought to know what actually happened. It was Professor Verma who forced me to apply for this post. Rather he bullied and threatened me into it. What's worse, he warned me that if I don't apply he would see to it that my period of probation and the eventual confirmation would be affected, as revenge. I got scared. I've already suffered terrible reverses in my career, thanks to Bala's frequent job transfers. After all the tangled mess in my career, I thought I got my first real chance to work in a decent university. To think that even here feel threatened that I may be uprooted by the wily Verma.... The way it's going, I think he'll not even confirm me in my present position,' said Jaya, gasping for breath.

'Of course he'll confirm you. After all, you'll have to get the post of an Associate Professor you see.'

'Oho Sudha,' she said, reaching for her hands and holding them. 'You still don't understand the situation. Let's leave aside that fact for a moment that Verma brutally forced me to apply. Do you know how obnoxiously he talked about you? Do you know how viciously he slandered you? Ran you down? I was outraged!'

'What!' exclaimed Sudha. She leaned back on the sofa, closed her eyes and lapsed into silence. Jaya looked at her and wondered how she could exude a certain sculpted charm even in a stressful moment like this.

'Sudha,' she called out, softly.

Sudha slowly opened her eyes, only to close them again.

'Tell me Jaya, tell me everything from the beginning. What did Verma say about me? I'm sure it would be a long-drawn-out story. That's why I'd like to listen with my eyes closed. Tell me.'

'The cad! He talked about you as if you're already an old hag. I was too angry for words. The man who is past fifty-five, how does he have the nerve to talk about you who are years younger than him? He went on and on about age, as if it was the main, overriding point. He said we need young blood for the department, that only young people have the drive for work. I'm also getting old I argued, and reminded him that I'm thirty-five. But he reverted to talking about you. He alleged that because you're ageing, you're losing the power of concentration, of articulation, that you falter in your work. He went on blabbering like that,' said Jaya.

Sudha opened her eyes and laughed. 'The poor wretch. Do you note his poverty of vocabulary? All that you quoted just now as Verma's words, he put the same words *in your mouth* the other day, when I sat in his office. Word for word!'

'What're you saying? I don't get it,' said Jaya, puzzled.

'Just now you told me in detail how Professor Verma slandered me, didn't you?'

'Yes ...'

'Verma said that it was *you* who said all those things, down to every single word you quoted,' said Sudharani.

'My God!' Sudharani cried out. 'How can a man go so far as to pile lies on lies?'

Akhila, who was strolling out of the Coffee Home with another girl, turned in their direction. She said something to the girl and started walking towards the Guest House. She opened the gate and let herself in.

'What's the matter, Madam? What happened?' she asked.

'Why, nothing at all,' said Sudharani.

'I thought I heard one of you say "My god!" So I got scared. I wondered what happened,' said Akhila.

Sudharani and Jaya exchanged glances but sat without saying anything. Akhila looked at them and felt that she had probably intruded.

'Okay madam, let me go now,' she said, turning away to leave the place when Jaya suddenly roused herself to speak: 'Wait, Akhila, please come here. Tell me, how are you and how's everybody at home?'

'Fine Madam.'

'What do you mean by "fine"? Then why did you sob like that the other day when I saw you? What happened, dear girl?' enquired Jaya.

'I may have been the cause for it,' said Sudharani.

'You!' said Jaya, utterly shocked.

'Tell us Akhila, didn't you actually sob out of anger, that I wouldn't sign your papers?' asked Sudharani. Akhila stood, her head bent down.

'Akhila?'

The girl shook her head but remained silent.

'Dr Balachandar says that you wept a lot. Is it because of me?' asked Sudharani.

'No, no!' said Akhila and burst into tears.

'I say what's happening here? I can't make anything of it,' said Jaya

'Have a seat Akhila, come here and sit with us. Just calm down a little,' said

Then she explained the whole thing to Jaya:

'You know, Akhila came to see me in my office room the other day after she returned from Hyderabad. She said there was some exigency for which she had to rush home without completing her work. I thought that the trips she had made to the two cities, in Kolkata and Hyderabad, had fully used up her Travel Grant. But there was still some money left from the grant. She wrote an application requesting that the residue from the Travel Grant be carried over to the next academic year for another research trip outside the city. She asked me to sign my approval for this application. She pleaded that she fell ill which is why she said she had to return without completing her work.'

'I see. But Akhila, you said you were doing fine when I met you the other day?' asked Jaya.

Akhila did not respond.

'See the technical complication, Jaya?' said Sudharani. 'If you don't use up the Travel Grant for that year, then it lapses. It can't be carried over to the next year. And Akhila herself had talked about it once. How can I do something against the rule? It would be very wrong.'

'Yes indeed,' agreed Jaya.

'Please try to understand my point, Akhila,' said Sudharani. 'I've to tread even more cautiously as an Acting Head. If I do something wrong, Professor Verma will blow me up when he returns. I'm sure he will. He would yell, "How can you take a decision about this without consulting me? What right do you have to do so?" he would ask.'

'You're very right,' said Jaya to Sudharani. 'Akhila, please appreciate her predicament. It's Dr Joshi who'll finally get it in the neck. After Professor Verma returns ask him if he can suggest a way out of this for you. After all, he is your Supervisor for your PhD, so he'll have a natural interest in your case. We'll see. Let him come.'

'How will he return now, Madam? He is going to stay on in Hyderabad for some more time,' said Akhila.

'In Hyderabad? How did he get there? He said he was going first to Assam, to Guwahati University and then to the university in Tirupathi?' said Sudharani, surprised by the news.

'That's what I thought too. He told me that he was going to Assam, then to Tirupathi,' said Jaya.

'No Madam, he first went to Kolkata and from there straight to Hyderabad,' said Akhila.

'Really? Very strange. He says one thing and does something very different. So, you met him in both the places?' asked Sudharani.

'Yes I did.'

'Then you could've asked him about this point regarding your Travel Grant?'

'Oh ... how ... how can I ask *him* of all the people? How could I? When it's because of him that I ran back both the times without completing my work,' said Akhila. She was gasping.

'What do you mean?'

'Madam, I don't know how to tell both of you. But the fact is, Professor Verma is the cause for my running back without completing my work,' she said and covered her face with her hands. She started sobbing.

'Goodness! Whatever happened? Akhila? Do tell us, please,' said Sudharani.

'Madam, do you know that each time I go out of town, Professor Verma also turns up in the same place? I get trapped alone with him, in another city. And he ... he ... misbehaves with me.'

'What!'

'Yes! Every time. Remember when I went to Shimla before this? He came there too.'

'Hmm ... when you went to Shimla ... ?' Sudharani tried to recall the time. 'Ah! I remember now. He told me he was going to Chandigarh.'

'I don't know, but he was there in Shimla on the second day of my arrival. He behaved most disgracefully. I was very embarrassed for there were so many people around us,' said Akhila, tears rolling down her cheeks. Sudharani and Jaya sat, speechless with shock.

'So, *this* is the reason why you run back every time?' said Sudharani.

'Yes. What else can I do? I was so shocked, you can imagine how I felt. I'm a married woman with a small baby. Everybody gave us strange looks. Professor Verma didn't look bothered by it all but what about me? What'll my people think of me—my husband, mother-in-law, father-in-law and others? He doesn't seem to be concerned about any of these things.'

'How very deplorable!' said Jaya. 'Because of him, the money allotted for the Travel Grant is getting wasted.'

'Just look at that Madam. Do you know how he talks? "You're very intelligent, and you're yet young. Just team up with me and I'll give you a good position, make you somebody some day. All these extraneous factors such as husband, relations and so on, they're all meaningless," he says. "If you follow my advice, you can complete your PhD. You'll have a good future too," he told me. It was all very gross and crude.'

'What kind of man is he? All those trips he takes off to—Mumbai, Assam, wherever—giving me a donkey-load of work to do in his absence.... To think that it's all a device to frighten and seduce young girls. Shame!'

'When I objected to his behaviour he scolded me. "How can you be so arrogant when I, a professor and chairman of a department takes an interest in you? Who do you think you are?" He rants on like that. "I can ruin your career, don't underestimate my strength, I warn you," he threatened. "You can't transfer your PhD program without my permission, think of that. I'll see to it that no one else takes you. You don't know how far I can take revenge," he roared,' said Akhila, overcome by exhaustion. Her tears had dried up and she sat staring blankly ahead as all three of them sat in silence.

'You're very young, so he thinks he can easily seduce you,' said Sudharani to Akhila. 'The same way, when he looks at Dr Balachandar, he feels our department now has some young blood. On the same lines, when he looks at me, he thinks "here's a woman who is ageing by the minute". See how agitated he gets by this thing called age?' said Sudharani.

'What are you saying Madam,' asked Akhila.

'One thing which binds the three of us is that sensitive something which has a skin and bone relationship with our femininity. And that is "age". See how deeply and in how many ways it disturbs and excites a man like him?' said Sudharani.

'Youth is a cruel thing Madam. A woman should get old quickly. Only then can she live with some dignity,' said Akhila.

'One can't be too sure of that either,' said Jaya. Sudharani laughed. Akhila looked from one to the other, not comprehending what they implied.

'All right, do one thing. Come and see me tomorrow at four,' said Sudharani.

'Very well Madam.'

XI

'So, what news? Anything special?' asked Professor Verma, in his usual, routine tone. 'I'm very tired,' he added. 'Whenever I go out of town on work, I end up working three times harder than I do here. I have to, I guess,' he said, wearily.

'Yes, it's really difficult,' said Sudharani. 'Even so, surely it must be refreshing in some ways to get out of the routine work that piles on here?'

'True. Only when I go out I get a chance to feel refreshed,' said Verma. Someone rapped on the door twice. Jaya walked in.

'Excuse me, I hope I'm not intruding on you?' she asked. 'Both of you seem to be deep in conversation,' she said.

'No, not at all. Please come, Dr Balachandar. Have a seat,' welcomed Verma. 'So, how're you? I haven't seen you for two days. Whenever I return to the department, I immediately get bogged down with work,' he remarked.

'You haven't seen Jaya for two days. Why, even I haven't seen her for the last three days. You must be very busy,' said Sudharani, turning to Jaya.

'Hmm ... there was work to do,' said Jaya.

'Well naturally! There *will* be work to do,' remarked Sudharani archly. 'After all, you must be very preoccupied preparing for the interview.'

'Dr Joshi, let me tell you one thing. If you've the motivation and the drive to earn this post, you too can prepare very well for the interview. Who's stopping you?' asked Jaya saucily.

'Well, I never ... ! What do you mean by *if* I've the motivation and the drive? Do you know for how many years I've served this department?' hissed Sudharani. 'Do you have any idea? Besides, I've taken on the additional responsibility as an 'Officiating Head'. And you talk to a senior like that, without even a shred of respect?'

'Ah ... huh ... Dr Joshi ... Dr Balachandar ... please, just a minute. Why do you ... ,' Dr Verma began to stammer nervously.

'So what if you happen to be a senior? Big deal!' said Jaya, ignoring Verma's intervention. 'I didn't want to put it like this, but ... our department needs young blood, do you know that?' she said, raising her voice a bit.

'Please, oh please ... I request both of you to kindly calm yourselves,' began Verma but was interrupted by Sudharani.

'Just leave it to me Professor Verma. I can handle it,' said Sudharani, turning her fury on Jaya. 'Young blood indeed! What a sweet illusion. Remember Jaya that you're thirty-five!'

'So what? That's still considerably younger than forty-four, isn't it? Am I not right, Sir?' Jaya asked Verma, trying to pull him into the talk.

'My God! What's come over you both?' asked Verma. His face went pale.

'You tell me Sir. See how this obsessive illusion about "youth" seems to take hold of some people like a disease. For instance, Jaya can't tolerate the fact that I'm a senior with all the work experience and scholarship that goes with it. So she is resorting to slandering me, spreading nasty rumours that I'm ageing, and therefore losing my power of articulation and so on,' said Sudharani.

'What! I never said anything like that,' protested Jaya.

'See for yourself Dr Verma. She refuses to acknowledge her own words. You're my only witness,' said Sudharani.

Verma got up from his chair. 'Excuse me,' he said. 'I'll have to go out. Have some work to do.'

'Oh no! Please stay on Sir. Your presence is such a protection for me,' pleaded Jaya.

'No, I really can't. I must go,' he said. They heard a knock on the door.

'May I come in?'

'Who is it?' asked Verma.

'It's me Sir,' said Akhila, hesitating near the door.

'Oh, it's you. Ah ... you see ... we're a little busy right now. This is a meeting. Why don't you come after some time?' said Professor Verma.

'After some time?' echoed Akhila, lingering on, looking uncertain. 'I just needed your signature Sir, on this application and on the statement of my expenditure. Please, could you give me just two minutes? I'll have to submit it to the Accounts, you see?' she requested.

'I don't have any time now. See me later,' said Verma brusquely.

'All right Sir, I'm sorry I disturbed you,' said Akhila, turning to go.

'Just look at her, innocent as a lamb!' said Sudharani. 'Come here Akhila, I want to tell Professor Verma in your presence about the way you wanted me to flout rules.'

'Oh Madam!' entreated Akhila, looking very scared now. She withdrew from them and tried to go out of the room.

'I say come in. Come and sit here,' commanded Sudharani. 'Dr Verma, you should know about this. Akhila frequently goes out wandering around to Shimla, Kolkata, Hyderabad or wherever in the name of research work, using the Travel Grant given by the UGC. She takes off on these merry jaunts but returns almost within a week sometimes, without completing her work. Tell me, how can she progress in her research work? I'm getting worried for you. She may jeopardise your name and reputation as a supervisor.'

'Correct! You're absolutely right,' said Professor Verma. 'It's not nice at all Akhila, the way you work by fits and starts, without any steady commitment, and the way you always return without even completing your work.'

'Not only that. Do you know what she wants now?' said Sudharani.

'Tell me.'

'The money that's given in the Travel Grant for a year, if unused, would lapse for that year, wouldn't it?' asked Sudharani.

'Correct,' said Verma.

'Akhila wants this residual amount to be carried over to the next year. So she asked me to recommend her application to the UGC,' said Sudharani.

'No! That's highly irregular. Impossible,' said Verma.

'That's what I explained to her,' said Sudharani.

'Akhila, how did you ever expect Dr Joshi to give her signed approval for all the irregular shortcuts that you want to take?' said Verma angrily. 'She is very honest and straight. After all, don't forget that she trained with me!'

'Sir, please hear me out for at least a minute,' begged Akhila, her voice very low and hesitant.

'Listen Akhila,' Sudharani retorted. 'I'm telling you for your own good. Don't return from a trip halfway like that, without completing your work. First of all, you should learn to make Professor Verma happy.'

'Ah ... Madam ... ,' Akhila turned to Jaya. 'Dr Balachandar, at least you could listen to what I've to say?' she asked.

'No Akhila,' said Jaya, her voice firm. 'You're yet a young girl. How can you reject a distinguished person like Professor Verma and run away like this? It's foolish. The very fact that you're doing your PhD here is by his gracious consent. Conduct your self according to his wishes. And don't ever underestimate his power. Can you imagine how far he can go in taking revenge on you?'

Verma got up again from his seat.

'I've some urgent work. I really must go now,' he said, pushing back his chair to leave the room.

'Please Dr Verma, please wait. It's only with your support I can hope to clarify some of the rules and regulations. And I want to have a word with Jaya too,' said Sudharani.

'What about?' asked Jaya.

'You were preaching to Akhila just now. Practise what you preach! If you want to successfully complete your period of probation and get confirmed in your job, then you jolly well have to act according to the wishes and desires of Professor Verma. Understand?' said Sudharani.

'What about you, in that case?' retorted Jaya. 'You look as if you've drunk from the elixir of youth, so your appearance strikes quite a contrary note to your erudition and maturity. No wonder Professor Verma feels profoundly disturbed and perturbed by the contradiction. You should understand his agony with some compassion.'

'I ... I ... Let me go now. I've some very urgent work,' stuttered Dr Verma. He rushed past them, and went out. The three women looked at his retreating figure for a moment and then burst out laughing. They laughed, shaking all over. Silver bells of laughter, carefree and light, vibrated in the room. The sounds of laughter carried no discernible signs of age.